ENLISTING
MADISON
AVENUE

The Marketing Approach to Earning Popular Support in Theaters of Operation

TODD C. HELMUS | CHRISTOPHER PAUL | RUSSELL W. GLENN

Prepared for the United States Joint Forces Command

Approved for public release, distribution unlimited

RAND NATIONAL DEFENSE RESEARCH INSTITUTE

The research described in this report was prepared for the United States Joint Forces Command. The research was conducted in the RAND National Defense Research Institute, a federally funded research and development center sponsored by the Office of the Secretary of Defense, the Joint Staff, the Unified Combatant Commands, the Department of the Navy, the Marine Corps, the defense agencies, and the defense Intelligence Community under Contract W74V8H-06-C-0002.

Library of Congress Cataloging-in-Publication Data is available for this publication.

ISBN 978-0-8330-4156-2

Published 2007 by the RAND Corporation
1776 Main Street, P.O. Box 2138, Santa Monica, CA 90407-2138
1200 South Hayes Street, Arlington, VA 22202-5050
4570 Fifth Avenue, Suite 600, Pittsburgh, PA 15213-2665
RAND URL: http://www.rand.org/
To order RAND documents or to obtain additional information, contact
Distribution Services: Telephone: (310) 451-7002;
Fax: (310) 451-6915; Email: order@rand.org

Preface

Counterinsurgency (COIN) and other stability operations are prominent in the contemporary operating environment and are likely to remain so in the future. These operations demand a keen focus on shaping indigenous audiences through the synchronization of both word and deed. U.S. force actions can set the conditions for credibility and help foster positive attitudes among an indigenous population, enabling effective and persuasive communication. Alternatively, they can undermine opportunities for success. The authors of this monograph review the challenges the U.S. faces in this regard, drawing on lessons from commercial marketing practices that may assist the U.S. military in its shaping endeavors. Study recommendations also include those influenced by the insights of U.S. military personnel based on their past operational experiences.

This monograph will be of interest to U.S. and allied military commanders, officers, and senior noncommissioned officers (NCOs) charged with conducting maneuver, civil affairs, and communication efforts in support of U.S. COIN and other stability operations. This monograph will also be of interest to senior civilian personnel in the U.S. Department of Defense (DoD) and others interested in the shaping of international opinion with respect to U.S. policies.

The contents of this monograph rely heavily on interview comments made by members of the U.S. military and the commercial marketing industry. When an interviewee or point of contact is quoted or otherwise associated with spoken or written remarks, it is with the individual's explicit permission to be recognized for these contributions.

This research was sponsored by the U.S. Joint Forces Command, Joint Urban Operations Office, and conducted within the International Security and Defense Policy Center of the RAND National Defense Research Institute, a federally funded research and development center sponsored by the Office of the Secretary of Defense, the Joint Staff, the Unified Combatant Commands, the Department of the Navy, the Marine Corps, the defense agencies, and the defense Intelligence Community.

Opinions, conclusions, and recommendations expressed or implied here are solely those of the authors and do not represent the views of DoD or U.S. Joint Forces Command.

For more information on RAND's International Security and Defense Policy Center, contact the Director, James Dobbins. He can be reached by email at James_Dobbins@rand.org; by phone at 703-413-1100, extension 5134; or by mail at the RAND Corporation, 1200 South Hayes Street, Arlington, Virginia 22202-5050. More information about RAND is available at www.rand.org.

Contents

Figures

Tables

Summary

Shaping, in traditional U.S. military parlance, refers to battlefield activities designed to constrain adversary force options or increase friendly force options. It is exemplified in the U.S. landing at the Port of Inch'on, which caused the redeployment of North Korean forces threatening the city of Pusan and dramatically altered the course of the Korean War. Recent analysis of field requirements and joint urban doctrine has expanded the concept of shaping to include influencing resident populations in military operational theaters. These populations constitute a significant component of stability operations, particularly through their decision to support friendly force objectives or those of the adversary.

Virtually every action, message, and decision of a force shapes the opinions of an indigenous population: how coalition personnel treat civilians during cordon-and-search operations, the accuracy or inaccuracy of aerial bombardment, and the treatment of detainees. Unity of message is key in this regard. The panoply of U.S. force actions must be synchronized across the operational battlespace to the greatest extent possible so as not to conflict with statements made in communications at every level, from the President to the soldier, sailor, marine, or airman in the theater of operations. Given the inherent difficulty in unifying coalition messages across disparate organizations, within and across governments, and over time, shaping efforts must be designed, war-gamed, and conducted as a campaign. The goal of such a shaping campaign is to foster positive attitudes among the populace toward U.S. and allied forces. These attitudes, while not the goal in and of themselves, help decrease anticoalition behaviors and motivate the population to act in ways that facilitate friendly force operational objectives and the attainment of desired end states.

This study considered how the United States and its coalition partners can shape indigenous attitudes and behavior during stability operations via the character of those operations and the behavior of coalition armed forces and those responsible for communication. While successes have been achieved in this regard, U.S. forces stand to benefit from the application of select, proven commercial marketing techniques. As such, we consider successes and missteps from the marketing and advertising industries and how lessons from those events might assist U.S. military men and women. We also present recommendations based on observations and insights from previous operational endeavors, including ongoing operations in Iraq and Afghanistan. All recommendations are predicated on a discussion of the challenges posed in developing effective shaping efforts.

What Makes Shaping So Difficult?

Chapter Two addresses the many challenges inherent in the conduct of an effective shaping campaign. Many challenges confront policymakers and the U.S. military in their efforts to shape indigenous populations during stability operations, including COIN undertakings such as those ongoing in Iraq and Afghanistan. Anti-American attitudes are on the rise. U.S. foreign policy, including its support for Israel, influences the character of this distaste among some populations. U.S. forces on overseas deployments that require interaction with individuals who are so negatively inclined face an immediate obstacle to successful shaping. An adversary who is equally eager to shape public opinion further challenges U.S. military operations. Adversaries' shaping tools include intimidation, publicity for anti-U.S. attacks, disinformation, and the provision of basic humanitarian assistance in an effort to undermine U.S. assistance efforts, to name but a few. The nature of contemporary news reporting further complicates U.S. efforts. The 24-hour news cycle creates a rush to report without verification. Retractions, when made, are often weak and low profile; real bias and adversary disinformation regularly appear in the news. The military often gets a rough ride in the press when these factors are coupled with the perception of a domestic press corps acting as the people's watchdog over the government and the military. Finally, in today's global media environment, messages are spread to audiences broader than originally intended, with potentially negative consequences. Culturally based perceptions can compound these negative effects as audiences perceive messages and actions in ways not intended.

There are additional challenges to shaping that are specific to the U.S. military. First, the traditional kinetic focus of U.S. military operations often jeopardizes communication-based shaping efforts. U.S. forces are trained primarily for kinetic operations and inflicting casualties on an enemy, not for shaping noncombatant attitudes. Both force structure and mind-set can be incompatible with shaping goals. For example, collateral damage can increase popular support for U.S. adversaries. The perception of U.S. cordon-and-search operations as heavy-handed further alienates Iraqi and Afghan populations, as do violations of cultural mores. Similarly important are the relationships formed between U.S. service personnel and their indigenous counterparts. These relationships are frequently disrupted by unit rotations.

Information fratricide, or the failure to synchronize and deconflict messages, puts a great burden on U.S. shaping initiatives. Synchronization is a particular problem for public affairs (PA), civil affairs (CA), and information operations (IO) and its psychological operations (PSYOP) component. Contributing factors include overlapping PSYOP and IO portfolios, limited PSYOP access to commanders, and negative PA and CA perceptions of PSYOP. PA, PSYOP, and IO also suffer from limitations in funding and personnel. Training underemphasizes the impact these functions can have on operations and their potentially vital role. Prohibitions against even inadvertent PSYOP targeting of U.S. civilians further confound U.S. shaping efforts. Other challenges beset PSYOP efforts in the theater: It is exceedingly difficult to identify target audiences in complex and dangerous operating environments, and there is often a lack of access to segments of a population critical to conducting message pretesting.

Identification of appropriate measures of effectiveness (MOE) is a difficult task, as is delineating the specific causes and effects associated with U.S. communication campaigns. Surveys constitute a critical component of existing MOE, though some question their accuracy in complex and dangerous security environments.

Shaping activities have very extensive intelligence requirements related to target-audience analysis. The existing intelligence apparatus has been slow to fulfill these requirements.

U.S. personnel will make mistakes (e.g., rules-of-engagement [ROE] violations or prisoner abuse) that pose significant obstacles to U.S. shaping operations. U.S. responses to these mistakes can either mitigate the extent of damage or exacerbate the negative situation.

The communication assets available to assist shaping need to be allocated to that function by force commanders. This can create several challenges, such as commanders lacking sufficient information or interest to effectively use communication assets under their control, commanders failing to recognize that shaping can be very time-consuming, and commanders failing to accept accountability and responsibility for shaping.

Applying Marketing Principles to Shaping

Business marketing practices provide a useful framework for improving U.S. military efforts to shape indigenous audience attitudes and behaviors. This framework and its application to U.S. military contingencies are reviewed in Chapter Three. First, the U.S. military should adopt the business strategy of segmentation and targeting whereby it would partition the indigenous population into selected groups based on their level of anticipated support for coalition presence and objectives. Positioning is another marketing tool of potential value, one used to create an intended identity for each product that is meaningful, salient, and motivating to the consumer marketplace. Such a process may assist U.S. efforts to craft end states for indigenous audiences.

Branding concepts potentially also hold great value for the U.S. military. Brands are the associations that people make with a product name. They are formed through each and every interaction people have with a product line and those who stand behind it. Properly managed brands have a unique and clear identity and are defined by an explicit set of associations. Virtually every organization and product has a brand identity or reputation. The U.S. military is no different. Like commercial firms that must update unattractive brand identities, so too should the United States consider updating its military's brand identity to suit current and future operational environments.

Businesses that are referred to as *branded houses* offer a line of products under a single brand identity (e.g., Apple[1] computers, digital music players, and software). These businesses seek brand identities that are clear and nonconflicting. A business' brand is hurt when it overreaches and offers poorly synchronized products, as was the case when BIC,[2] the maker of disposable pens, attempted to launch a line of BIC-branded perfumes. Strategies that help businesses craft their line of products can help the U.S. military ensure that operations do not conflict with shaping-campaign goals. To this end, the military should thoroughly explain the necessity for kinetic operations, place the burden for such operations (and their negative consequences) on the adversary, rebuild damaged infrastructure, and monitor the impact such operations have on civilian attitudes toward the U.S. force. They should similarly monitor the impact of U.S. government policies and statements that contradict shaping-campaign themes.

Interactions between U.S. service personnel and civilians drive popular perceptions of the U.S. force. Business practices that help align customer service representative actions with the intended brand identity can benefit the U.S. military. These include training for U.S. force–civilian interactions, addressing civilian complaints quickly, conducting an inventory of all U.S. military–civilian points of interaction, and carefully selecting and training U.S. personnel charged with negotiating with key indigenous points of contact.

Customer satisfaction refers to the level of contentment consumers experience after using a product or service. Popular satisfaction

---

[1]   Apple® is a registered trademark of Apple Inc.

[2]   BIC® is a registered trademark of Societe BIC.

with U.S. force presence can similarly determine allegiances. There are three overarching principles related to customer satisfaction. First, the management of expectations plays a prominent role in customer satisfaction; unfulfilled promises leave dissatisfied customers. The U.S. military should be wary of making promises to civilian populations at the strategic (e.g., improved standard of living upon U.S. force arrival in the theater), operational, and tactical (e.g., promising a CA visit) levels unless shaping messages assist in managing related expectations (e.g., improved standards of living will not be noticeable for some time, and improvement depends on specified public support) and those promises will be met. Second, the most successful business endeavors are those premised on meeting customer needs and desires. The U.S. military should seek to tailor CA and reconstruction activities around projects that meet civilian priorities. Third, businesses frequently monitor customer satisfaction via surveys in an effort to improve operations and products. They also utilize customer advisory boards and complaint lines. Coalition forces can use these techniques to gauge populace attitudes and opinions about U.S. force actions and determine modifications that can increase popular support.

Businesses use influencers and word of mouth to credibly convey their messages. The U.S. military can use business word-of-mouth tactics in several ways. For example, it can cultivate partner-based relationships with important influencers in the indigenous area of operation (AO), then reinforce their procoalition appeals with further information and access to coalition commanders. It could further harness the influencing power of indigenous government employees and security forces by having them keep blogs about their experiences with coalition forces and the indigenous government. Third, it could consider the benefits of enhancing Internet access to indigenous populations.

Social marketing is the application of well-grounded commercial marketing techniques to influence noncommercial behavioral change (e.g., quitting smoking and giving blood) in a target audience. Social marketing practices provide a template for U.S. military efforts to motivate specific behaviors in the indigenous population.

Shaping Solutions Based on Recent Operational Experiences

Chapter Four presents additional recommendations for improving U.S. shaping efforts based on recent operational experiences. First among these, U.S. forces should continue anticipatory shaping activities that influence the attitudes and behaviors of indigenous populations in areas in which the United States is not presently involved (training indigenous security forces, engaging in CA activities, cultivating relationships with indigenous influencers, collecting cultural intelligence, and providing humanitarian assistance). These efforts should include fostering enduring relationships with previously U.S.-trained foreign military personnel. Similarly, humanitarian and other forms of international assistance should continue even long after the initial disaster has subsided. Such anticipatory shaping requires U.S. forces to plan and conduct shaping operations in advance of possible deployments in addition to activities conducted during and after such missions.

Beyond anticipatory shaping, the United States should better leverage CA/civil-military operations (CMO) activities in operational theaters. This includes ensuring effective publicity of U.S. initiatives while concurrently taking advantage of indigenous word-of-mouth networks. Leaders should balance short-term CMO projects and demonstrations of good will with long-term support of ultimate end states. Shaping campaigns should also incorporate CMO with a high probability of encouraging civilian behaviors that abet COIN success.

Careful management when using force must be a part of such initiatives. It is essential to minimize the number of civilian casualties and other collateral damage while simultaneously demonstrating U.S. commitment to security by vigorously pursuing adversaries who deal retribution on those who support friendly force efforts. Persuasion can be influenced by both the carrot and the stick.

U.S. forces should be careful to preserve their credibility among indigenous audiences. This requires careful consideration of deceptive communication and the credibility threat it poses. Because real and perceived deceptions have, in the past, undermined civilian views of PSYOP and IO activities, a reorganization of these entities into shaping components that are completely free of deception and components that are allowed to deceive merits consideration.

U.S. government and DoD organizations should also integrate and coordinate their shaping messages across operating environments. Current plans call for a U.S. Department of State (DoS)–based coordination cell to synchronize strategic communication at the interagency level. Similar coordination entities, potentially comprised of PA, PSYOP/IO, and maneuver force personnel, should be a part of combatant command, joint task force (JTF), and other headquarters, as appropriate, depending on the mission. These coordination cells would assist in ensuring that messages are properly nested and nonconflicting throughout the chain of command, down to the soldier on the street.

Training exercises should regularly integrate maneuver and PSYOP/CA units, focusing on shaping concerns as an elemental part of operations for all organizations. A review of legal barriers that put U.S. shaping initiatives at a competitive disadvantage is in order (and should include looking at the implications of the Smith-Mundt Act,[3] which limits the use of the World Wide Web for shaping activities).

There is a call for supporting intelligence analysis that seeks to gain a thorough understanding of prospective indigenous audiences. This focus may require modifications to intelligence doctrine; tactics, techniques, and procedures (TTP); and related training. Expansion of reachback capabilities that would facilitate field contacts with regional experts could be a component of this intelligence capability enhancement.

The United States should actively foster relationships between U.S. force personnel and their indigenous counterparts in theaters of operation. Longer rotations may be desirable, with critical personnel staying for longer periods (perhaps on accompanied tours during which families are housed in regional countries with acceptable security environments). The negative impact of unit and personnel rotations on indigenous relationships can be further mitigated by increasing overlap during reliefs in place and giving the handoff of local relationships high priority. It might be possible to further reduce the negative impact of

---

[3]   22 USC 1461-1a, Ban on Domestic Activities by the United States Information Agency.

rotations through maintenance of contact among replaced U.S. personnel, their replacements, and local citizens via email or other means of communication.

The United States should improve the way it responds to actions that have potentially negative shaping effects. Given the likelihood of such events being made public, potential responses should include government disclosure, thereby enhancing U.S. credibility by admitting mistakes as early and completely as is feasible and accompanying these admissions with explanations regarding likely follow-on actions to address the problem. The U.S. military, and PA personnel in particular, should prepare in advance for predictable mistakes, such as inadvertent collateral damage and ROE violations. War-gaming should likewise include conducting worst-case scenario analyses for kinetic operations and developing shaping contingency plans for selected outcomes.

Adversaries fabricate stories and events that paint the United States and its armed forces in a negative light. U.S. kinetic operations, especially those that inflict civilian casualties, can provide the backdrop for adversaries' shaping efforts. Both PA and PSYOP personnel should be involved in planning and war-gaming kinetic and other relevant operations; they can help spot adversaries' shaping opportunities and assist in planning effective mitigation strategies. The United States should counter potentially damaging false allegations with fact and transparency, enlisting the help of allies and indigenous partners who may more credibly correct misrepresentations.

The United States should continue to promote close relations between its armed forces and the media, assisting reporters in their efforts to cover military operations. Improvements in U.S. efforts to reach out to indigenous media and assist in cultivating legitimate journalistic techniques are called for.

This review of challenges to shaping and related recommendations based on commercial marketing practices and recent operational experiences provides a stepping stone to improving U.S. shaping operations. It is hoped that the recommendations contained herein will contribute to improved international perceptions of U.S. forces and, thereby, to increased support of U.S. efforts in the field.

Acknowledgments

Many a friend and colleague contributed to the crafting of this monograph. Robert Jenks, Scott Petroski, and LTC Jack Amberg (U.S. Army) hosted visits and arranged interviews with 4th PSYOP Group, Joint Information Operations Center, and PA personnel, respectively. On the commercial side, Ned Clausen went to extraordinary measures to arrange contact with leaders in the marketing industry. J. D. Power III and Chris Denove cheerfully opened the intellectual doors of J. D. Power and Associates. COL Dave Maxwell (U.S. Army), Col. Michael Walker, (U.S. Marine Corps, retired), LTC Kevin Doyle (U.S. Army, retired), and Scott Feldmayer and Dirk Blum of the Lincoln Group generously provided the authors their assistance and candid insights. Gayle Stephenson and Maria Falvo prepared this document with great skill and otherwise lent an invaluable hand to all facets of the research process. This monograph would be but an idea without their assistance. Megan McKernan crafted an extremely helpful review paper on U.S. public diplomacy efforts. Gordon Lee provided an extensive critique and deserves much credit for transforming a rough draft into a finished product. Major Simon Bergman (British Army, retired) and Kim Cragin provided expert review and carefully considered critiques. Lauren Skrabala, the adept editor of this document, shot the cover's Madison Avenue streetscape photograph during her vacation. Finally, scores of individuals lent invaluable time to the authors for formal interviews. It is their insightful comments that make the substance of this monograph. To each and every one of these professionals, the authors extend their most sincere debt of gratitude.

Abbreviations

ACM	anticoalition militia
AO	area of operation
BSC	best-case scenario
CA	civil affairs
CERP	Commander Emergency Relief Program
CIMIC	civil-military cooperation
CMO	civil-military operations
CNO	computer network operations
COCOM	combatant command
COIN	counterinsurgency
DoD	U.S. Department of Defense
DoS	U.S. Department of State
DSPD	defense support to public diplomacy
EW	electronic warfare
FID	foreign internal defense
GO	general officer
GWOT	global war on terrorism

HUMINT	human intelligence
IED	improvised explosive device
IO	information operations
IPB	intelligence preparation of the battlefield
JFC	joint force commander
JTF	joint task force
MEDCAP	medical civic action program
MILDEC	military deception
MND (SE)	Multi-National Division (South East)
MOE	measures of effectiveness
MOS	military occupational specialty
NCO	noncommissioned officer
NGO	nongovernmental organization
OEF	Operation Enduring Freedom
OIF	Operation Iraqi Freedom
OPSEC	operations security
PA	public affairs
PAG	public affairs guidance
PAO	public affairs officer
PLC	product life cycle
PRT	Provincial Reconstruction Team
PSYOP	psychological operations
RAMSI	Regional Assistance Mission to Solomon Islands

RIP	relief in place
ROE	rules of engagement
TOA	transfer of authority
TTP	tactics, techniques, and procedures
USAID	U.S. Agency for International Development
USCENTCOM	U.S. Central Command
USEUCOM	U.S. European Command
USNORTHCOM	U.S. Northern Command
USPACOM	U.S. Pacific Command
USSOUTHCOM	U.S. Southern Command
VOA	Voice of America

CHAPTER ONE

Introduction

> We are not going to win the struggle for men's minds merely by tripling Congressional appropriations for a super loud Voice of America. Rather it will be the planned and effective use of every means of appeal to men and women everywhere. . . . [E]verything we say, everything we do, and everything we fail to say or fail to do, will have its impact in other lands.
>
> —*President Dwight D. Eisenhower*[1]

The Shaping Construct

Since the dawn of warfare, militaries have used fires, maneuver, and even information to shape adversaries' behavior and will to fight. Consider the predicament faced by U.S. and South Korean forces in the summer of 1950. After a surprise invasion, the North Korean military overwhelmed South Korean forces to compel a precipitous retreat. U.S. and South Korean troops were quickly pushed back into the southeast of the peninsula, around the port of Pusan. Prospects for an allied breakout other than via costly frontal assaults looked dim. General Douglas MacArthur therefore conducted an invasion through the port of Inch'on, west of Seoul. This end-around proved a decisive shaping operation, forcing North Korea to redeploy much of its strength from

---

[1] Dwight D. Eisenhower, campaign speech, San Francisco, October 8, 1952, Eisenhower Presidential Archives, records of C. D. Jackson, box 2.

the Pusan perimeter, thus weakening its defenses and allowing a subsequent breakout by allied troops.

In 2002, new joint urban doctrine expanded the concept of shaping beyond the traditional focus on the adversary and the battlespace. Shaping now includes

> all actions that the JFC [joint force commander] takes to seize the initiative and set the conditions for decisive operations to begin. The JFC shapes the battlespace to best suit operational objectives by exerting appropriate influence on adversary forces, friendly forces, the information environment, and particularly the elements of the urban triad [physical terrain, infrastructure, and the population].[2]

This expanded shaping construct, particularly its newfound, if perhaps too subtle, focus on the population, is particularly relevant to today's stability-and-support operational environment. Like Mao Zedong's proverbial pond, the population, if so willing, provides adversaries material and financial support, intelligence, and a source of new recruits and part-time adherents. To ensure victory, U.S. forces must effectively shape the indigenous population.

Doctrinal shaping is a valuable construct, but shaping as a concept has even broader implications. Virtually every action, message, and decision by a force shapes the operational environment: treatment of civilians at vehicle checkpoints, accuracy or inaccuracy (and the results) of bombings, and treatment of detainees are but three examples. U.S. forces, their government, and the governments and forces of other coalition members would ideally present a unified message that is coordinated across the operational battlespace. The messages communicated by political leaders, upper military echelons, and tactical psychological operations (PSYOP) units ultimately face a reality test at ground level. Themes of U.S. good will lose appeal if coalition forces inflict excessive numbers of civilian casualties or if soldiers demonstrate a lack of respect for the basic humanity of those met during opera-

---

[2]   Joint Chiefs of Staff, *Doctrine for Joint Urban Operations*, Joint Publication 3-06, September 16, 2002, p. II-10.

tions. Even when U.S. forces meet the challenge in one locale, less well-trained or otherwise ill-led forces elsewhere can undo the good work. Such actions belie the words spoken by civilian and military leaders and tear at the foundation of credibility. In contrast, actions in keeping with assurances of regard for the rights of the population and synchronized across a theater of operations demonstrate coalition commitment, build trust, and work to align civilians with coalition efforts.

We are not alone in holding this view. LtGen. James N. Mattis and LtCol. (retired) Frank G. Hoffman of the U.S. Marine Corps understand the necessity of aligning actions and words. Knowing the operational realities that confront U.S. forces today and in the future, they expand on Marine Gen. Charles C. Krulak's three-block war concept, in which marines hand out humanitarian supplies in one block and separate warring factions or otherwise maintain stability in an adjacent second block, all while fighting adversaries in a third.[3] In Mattis and Hoffman's view, there is a fourth block, in which U.S. forces may or may not be located but in which they will nonetheless be conducting psychological and information operations that seek to gain popular consent. All four blocks are interconnected. They write,

> Our actions in the three other blocks are important to building up our credibility and establishing relationships with the population and their leadership. Thus, there is an information operations aspect within each block. In each of the traditional three blocks our Marines are both "sensors" that collect intelligence, as well as "transmitters." Everything they do or fail to do sends a message. . . . The information ops component is how we extend our reach and how we can influence populations to reject the misshaped ideology and hatred they are offered by the insurgents. Successful information operations help the civilian population understand and accept the better future we seek to help build *with* them.[4]

---

[3]   Charles C. Krulak, "The Strategic Corporal: Leadership in the Three Block War," *Marines Magazine*, Vol. 28, No. 1, January 1999, pp. 26–33.

[4]   James N. Mattis and Frank G. Hoffman, "Future Warfare and the Rise of Hybrid Wars," *Proceedings* (U.S. Naval Institute), Vol. 132, No. 11, November 2005, pp. 18–19. Emphasis in the original.

Shaping operations seek to create positive indigenous attitudes toward U.S. and coalition forces. They also should act to reduce support for the adversary (even without a shift to a more favorable attitude toward the United States). Attitudes in this respect are learned predispositions that influence how the population behaves. While the goal of shaping is not to make the indigenous population fond of U.S. forces, positive attitudes toward coalition forces should increase indigenous support for operational objectives. Negative views, possibly precipitated by unnecessarily aggressive actions, will likely engender negative behavior, such as withholding intelligence, supporting adversaries, or taking up arms. Similarly, positive views about the coalition may diffuse tensions, make coalition forces more approachable, and reduce violent attacks. These attitudes also impact the extent to which the coalition force can persuade the indigenous population to back operational objectives or accept messages that seek greater public participation in elections or higher response rates to appeals for more indigenous security service recruits.[5] Attitudes function as enabling (or disabling) factors that help the coalition create a safe and secure environment and motivate the population to act in ways that facilitate key operational objectives and end states.[6]

There are many examples of how U.S. actions, in turn, influence the behaviors of the indigenous population. During the stability and reconstruction phase of Operation Iraqi Freedom (OIF), a translator

---

[5]   Richard M. Perloff, *The Dynamics of Persuasion Communication and Attitudes in the 21st Century*, 2nd ed., Mahwah, N.J.: Lawrence Erlbaum Associates, 2003; David G. Myers, *Social Psychology*, 8th ed., New York: McGraw-Hill, 2005; Robert B. Cialdini, *Influence: The Psychology of Persuasion*, New York: William Morrow, 1984; Icek Ajzen and Martin Fishbein, "The Influence of Attitudes on Behavior," in Dolores Albarracin, Blair T. Johnson, and Mark P. Zanna, eds., *The Handbook of Attitudes*, Mahwah, N.J.: Lawrence Erlbaum Associates, 2005, pp. 173–221.

[6]   It should not be assumed, however, that only attitudes related to U.S. and coalition forces matter. An assisting international force is only one of several key players. Even positive views toward this force will be insufficient if the population does not accept coalition force end states or their manifestation in the indigenous government. In addition, positive attitudes held by foreign populations beyond those in U.S. operational environments facilitate broader U.S. foreign policy objectives. While "liking" is not a goal in and of itself, such positive attitudes do facilitate acceptance of U.S. foreign policy.

approached the coalition deputy governor of Amarah with the following message:

> Yesterday, I was on the highway at a checkpoint and they stop a car and they are shouting at the driver, "Stay in your car" in English. He cannot understand what they are saying—he was not [an] educated man—he is opening the door. And I am running to him and saying in Arabic, "Do not get out." But I cannot [reach him] in time and they shoot him. Dead. [. . .] You do not believe me. Listen, I saw this with my eyes. This is why they are losing Iraq.[7]

Major David Rasmussen of the 10th Mountain Division in Afghanistan conveyed a more positive vignette:

> Before Ghazni, we established a firebase near the town of Nangalam. We stayed there for five weeks and people started bringing us weapons and passing us information. We're seeing the same thing starting now in Ghazni. Nobody wanted to talk to you when you're in and out in 72 hours. What I would do, and we're moving toward this, is assign units areas of responsibility. If we think there is an area that is active in ACM [anticoalition militia], the unit's presence scatters [the enemy], but we know they come back. If we're in an area long enough, we're going to make friends. It took some time for [the townspeople] to know that we weren't Russians [who would massacre a whole town where a land mine went off]. . . . We hit a mine yesterday and were going to do a MEDCAP [medical civic action program] there tomorrow. We thought about not having the MEDCAP, as a punitive measure, but then thought that's just what they wanted us to do, so we're going ahead with it. And we're getting more information every day. . . .[8]

---

[7] Quoted in Rory Stewart, *The Prince of the Marshes and Other Occupational Hazards of a Year in Iraq*, Orlando, Fla.: Harcourt, 2006, p. 105.

[8] MAJ David C. Rasmussen, U.S. Army, Battalion Executive Officer, 2-87th Infantry Battalion, 10th Mountain Division, interview with Russell W. Glenn and Todd C. Helmus, Bagram, Afghanistan, February 14, 2004.

This study considered how the United States and its coalition partners can shape indigenous attitudes and behavior during stability operations. While the United States and its coalition allies have achieved some success in this regard, they could logically benefit from the application of proven techniques adopted from the realm of commercial marketing. This study considers successes and missteps from industry in the service of assisting U.S. and coalition servicemen and -women in achieving their objectives. Because commercial marketing approaches cannot provide all the necessary lessons, we further provide recommendations based on observations and insights from previous operational endeavors. The goal is to provide an expanded concept of shaping and offer recommendations on how the United States and its coalition partners might more effectively shape the attitudes and behavior of relevant populations before and during operations.

Research Approach

This monograph is structured as follows:

- Chapter Two presents a systematic review of the challenges inherent in U.S. shaping efforts in an effort to clarify why the United States and its allies have struggled so hard to effectively gain the support of indigenous populations in Iraq, Afghanistan, and in the broader war on terror.
- Chapter Three addresses applicable lessons from the commercial marketing industry. State-of-the-art marketing practices are reviewed, and those practices suitable to shaping civilian populations in theaters of operation are identified and summarized. Following each marketing lesson is a description of its military application. The chapter addresses segmentation, branding, achieving customer satisfaction, influencers, and communication campaigns.[9]

---

[9] Eric V. Larson, Richard E. Darilek, Daniel Gibran, Brian Nichiporak, Amy Richardson, Lowell H. Schwartz, and Cathryn Quantic Thurston, *Foundations of Effective Influence*

- Chapter Four makes observations about topical areas critical to shaping that remain otherwise unaddressed in marketing. These areas include the use of force, the implementation of civil affairs (CA) programs, and the integration of U.S. military communication efforts.
- Chapter Five summarizes and synthesizes the recommendations presented in Chapters Three and Four.

This research is based on a variety of interview and written sources. More than 30 interviews were conducted with active-duty military, retired military, and defense civilian personnel from public affairs (PA), CA, PSYOP, and its information operations (IO) umbrella.[10] We have also drawn liberally from more than 100 interviews conducted in support of previously conducted research on joint urban operations lessons learned. Written resources include formal analyses, briefings, scholarly articles, newspaper articles, and op-ed pieces that debate relevant key issues. The material on marketing approaches draws on in excess of 25 additional interviews with active marketing practitioners in business and academia. A host of marketing and advertising books and corresponding scholarly and trade articles were also reviewed.

The wealth and abundance of material reviewed for this study demanded active vetting on the part of the authors. This vetting was based on logically constrained analytical judgment and expertise acquired through 10 years of experience in matters pertaining to urban operations, including authorship of upward of 1,000 pages of analysis on joint urban operations in Iraq and Afghanistan. We attempted to discriminate between observations and recommendations that were valuable and those that either failed to pass muster or were not fully ger-

---

Operations, unpublished RAND research, April 2006, provide an evaluation of the psychological research applications of U.S. military influence campaigns.

[10] IO consist of five core capabilities: PSYOP, military deception (MILDEC), operations security (OPSEC), electronic warfare (EW), and computer network operations (CNO). Of these, PSYOP (and MILDEC, to a lesser degree) constitute the abundant share of a campaign's IO influence effort. This monograph occasionally makes simultaneous reference to PSYOP and IO. In such cases, the reference to IO is meant to include both the core capabilities and the broader coordinating and integrating functions of IO.

mane to the topic at hand. This approach demands critical and insightful consideration from those who seek to benefit from this analysis. We similarly hope that the defense community will accept our invitation to discuss and critique these ideas in military trade and scholarly journals and briefings. Finally, this monograph is necessarily based on what can be learned from past and ongoing operations and ways of thinking. While it is often and truly said that history serves as a guiding light for the future, history misapplied to future events will fail to prove valuable. Consequently, readers must use a discerning eye in applying concepts to new operational settings and otherwise unanticipated realities, a venture in which the study recommendations seek to help.

CHAPTER TWO

What Makes Shaping So Difficult?

> Perhaps the most compelling argument for paying attention to perception management is that America's adversaries, which do not really have the means to defeat the United States conventionally, have used and will continue to use perception management to weaken American resolve and commitment.
>
> —*Pascale Combelles Siegel*[1]

Having identified in the previous chapter the broad goals that shaping campaigns need to address, the discussion now turns to the challenges of shaping. What makes shaping so difficult? The problems faced by U.S. shapers and shaping efforts are extensive. This monograph does not offer solutions to all of these problems. By outlining the extent of these challenges, we place the suggestions offered in the subsequent chapters in a broader context. This careful elucidation of shaping challenges will help others find solutions beyond those presented here. This chapter discusses the shaping difficulties that policymakers and the U.S. military encounter in two dimensions: those contextual challenges that the military will encounter in general and those specific to the U.S. Department of Defense (DoD).

---

[1] Pascale Combelles Siegel, "Perception Management: IO's Stepchild?" *Low Intensity Conflict and Law Enforcement*, Vol. 13, No. 2, Autumn 2005, pp. 113–134 [p. 122].

General Challenges to Shaping

The U.S. military and other executors of U.S. shaping efforts face at least four broad challenges:

- anti-American sentiment
- adversaries' shaping efforts
- news and news media
- context, including global media, local information
- environment, culture, and technology.

Anti-American Sentiment and Its Challenge to U.S. Policy and Military Operations

Public opinion polls demonstrate increasing worldwide anti-American sentiment (see Figure 2.1). While ensuring that citizens of other nations are fond of the United States is not a policy goal in and of itself, unfavorable baseline attitudes held by the international community decrease the likelihood of support for or tolerance of U.S. operations and policies. At its most extreme, hostility toward the United States in the Muslim world helps terrorists gain recruits and support. At lesser levels of animosity, anti-Americanism impedes U.S. efforts to promote political and social reforms and commercial and cultural relationships in Muslim countries.[2]

Public opinion polls suggest that much of the anti-Americanism observed in the Muslim world today is attributable to U.S. policies rather than to U.S. culture, values, or people. In a 2004 poll, for example, Zogby International found that residents of most Arab countries had positive opinions about "American services and technology," "American freedom and democracy," "American people," "American education," "American products," and the like. But many of those same

---

[2]   Craig Charney and Nicole Yakatan, *A New Beginning: Strategies for a More Fruitful Dialogue with the Muslim World*, Washington, D.C.: Council on Foreign Relations, May 2005, p. iii.

Figure 2.1
Favorable Opinions of the United States Have Decreased in Recent Years

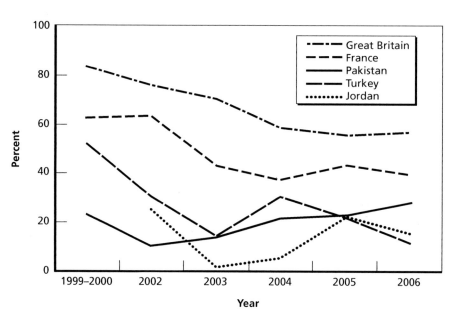

SOURCE: Pew Global Attitudes Project, *America's Image Slips, but Allies Share U.S. Concerns Over Iran, Hamas: No Global Warming Alarm in the U.S., China,* Washington, D.C.: Pew Research Center, June 13, 2006, p. 1.
RAND *MG607-2.1*

respondents held negative opinions about U.S. policies toward the Palestinian conflict and Iraq.[3]

Such policies prove unattractive to international audiences for a variety of reasons. Some are relics of the Cold War and use paradigms that fall flat in the contemporary operating environment. These could include the acceptance of authoritarian regimes for Cold War motives or a model of information dissemination aimed at "huddled masses yearning to be free" that may not accurately characterize the popu-

---

[3] Zogby International, *Impressions of America 2004: How Arabs View America, How Arabs Learn About America,* a six-nation survey commissioned by the Arab American Institute, 2004, p. 1.

lations in the contemporary operating environment.[4] Others encourage social or political reforms, such as universal suffrage, representative government, and freedom of religion. Although such "social engineering" may correspond with deeply held American values, it may not hold the same appeal to populations or cultures in certain areas, rendering shaping difficult if not impossible.

Other policies lack attractiveness because they are inadequately explained or understood. U.S. policy must be clearly articulated. This does not always happen. Policy explanations can ring hollow in situations in which the motivation offered publicly differs from the true, private motivation, or when the offered explanation is not compelling. In an example of the latter case, many international audiences, including those in Iraq, perceived the U.S. rationale for the invasion of Iraq as a war for oil.

If existing U.S. policies are hated, new U.S. policies are likely to be met with suspicion and may already have at least two strikes against them; this would include U.S. military intervention overseas. Popular resentment and distrust pose immediate shaping hurdles to expeditionary U.S. forces.[5] The association of messages and messengers with the United States poses at least three additional challenges to effective shaping:

- *U.S. involvement "taints" messages.* Some shaping messages have better chances of success if broadcast by an apparently neutral third party. Many existing U.S. shaping efforts distance the United States at least one step from the message. For example, the United States does not actively disclose U.S. Agency for International Development (USAID) funding for dozens of Afghan radio stations. USAID explains, "We want to maintain the per-

---

[4]   U.S. Department of Defense Office of the Under Secretary of Defense for Acquisition, Technology, and Logistics, *Report of the Defense Science Board Task Force on Strategic Communication*, Washington, D.C., September 2004, p. 36.

[5]   Even seemingly attractive U.S. policy goals and shaping messages can be perceived as unattractive. This was the reason behind the suspension of the publication *Hi*, the U.S. Department of State's (DoS's) Arab youth magazine at the end of 2005 (Middle East Online, "US Suspends Publication of Arab Youth Magazine," last updated December 23, 2005).

ception (if not the reality) that these radio stations are in fact fully independent."[6]

- *Past and present actions damage U.S. credibility.* U.S. credibility is damaged when the United States fails to do what it says it will do and when actions contradict stated intentions. For example, Pentagon news releases asserted that U.S. forces were "conducting operations side by side with our Iraqi brethren." This was not the case in all areas of operation (AOs), and indigenous civilians aware of this discrepancy likely lost some trust in U.S. force pronouncements.[7]

- *Contradictory messages increase confusion.* U.S. credibility is impaired when two speakers give different accounts or explanations of the same thing or when the same speaker explains something differently to two audiences. After the U.S. invasion of Iraq, DoS talking points highlighted different rationales for the invasion. To a U.S. audience, they would assert, "We're fighting them there so we don't have to fight them here," with the secondary implication that the United States intends to make the world a safer place. This emphasis was reversed for foreign audiences. Unfortunately, a globalized media made separate messages impossible.[8]

Adversaries' Shaping Efforts

The United States is not alone in the information environment. Today's asymmetric adversaries use a variety of approaches to shape attitudes and behaviors of noncombatants and opinions of foreign observers. Adversary kinetic action, along with associated media attention, contributes to a wide range of adversary goals. For example,

---

[6]   Peggy O'Ban, USAID spokesperson, quoted in Jeff Gerth, "Military's Information War Is Vast and Often Secretive," *New York Times*, December 11, 2005, p. 1.

[7]   Joshua Kucera, "Military and the Media—Weaponising the Truth?" *Jane's Defence Weekly*, June 8, 2005a.

[8]   Farah Stockman, "US Image a Tough Sell in Mideast," *Boston Globe*, October 23, 2005, p. A5.

By attacking the police station, Iraqi insurgents hoped to achieve their strategic objectives of influencing Iraqi perceptions about security and safety; contributing to the delay or cancellation of free elections; de-legitimizing an interim Iraqi government; and degrading domestic support for U.S. policy in Iraq.[9]

Many terrorist organizations recognize shaping (under different terms, of course) as a primary operational objective, and they integrate operations with related media requirements as a matter of course. Such integration is a fairly recent development. Hizballah innovatively subjected "virtually all its military action to its propaganda and mass media requirements."[10]

Adversaries employ a wide range of general approaches to shaping, including the following:

- *Intimidating or coercing noncombatants:* Threats, intimidation, and coercion are readily available tools to shape noncombatants' behavior. While they are unlikely to encourage favorable attitudes, such approaches can effectively prevent unfavorable attitudes from being turned into actions (consider insurgent efforts in Iraq to assassinate "collaborators"). Physical threats and intimidation discourage locals from "defecting" in favor of even a well-meaning outsider.

- *Intimidating journalists and controlling their access:* By controlling which journalists are allowed into an area and by influencing what they are allowed to witness (or influencing the subjects on which they feel they safely can report), an adversary shapes the content of the news. In Iraq, journalists face an ongoing barrage of threats of violence, kidnapping threats, and outright attacks.[11] Following

---

[9] Norman Emery and Donald G. Mowles, Jr., "Fighting Terrorism and Insurgency: Shaping the Information Environment," *Military Review*, January–February 2005, pp. 32–38 [p. 32].

[10] Ron Schleifer, "Psychological Operations: A New Variation on an Age Old Art: Hezbollah Versus Israel," *Studies in Conflict and Terrorism*, Vol. 29, No. 1, January 2006, pp. 1–19 [p. 5].

[11] Faraydoon Jalal, "Iraqi Journalists Risking Their Lives," *Kurdish Media*, June 16, 2005.

an attack on Al Arabiya's Baghdad bureau, the group claiming responsibility called the attack a "warning" and protested the station's coverage, "demanding that the station support the 'jihad' against the U.S. occupation and Iraqi government."[12]

- *Filming and distributing records of operations:* Many insurgent or terrorist groups have adopted this tactic. Regarding Hizballah, Ron Schliefer observes,

> Stills, video, and film became so central to the organization's military activities that it might reasonably be claimed that they dictated both its overall strategy and daily operations. Indeed, the organization's motto could be summed up in the words: "If you haven't captured it on film you haven't fought."[13]

The effect of distributing video recordings of operations to friendly media multiplies when the original recipients make them available to a broader range of media outlets.[14]

- *Forging "special" or exclusive relationships with certain media:* Adversaries often tip off reporters from sympathetic media outlets about operations, which allows them to record the events, "scoop" other news agencies, and report operations in a manner favorable to the insurgents. The government of Iraq barred Al Jazeera and Al Arabiya from reporting there for two weeks in September 2005 because they were "tipped to attacks on convoys and filmed the events without warning authorities."[15]

- *Engaging in disinformation:* Adversaries sometimes fabricate events or, more effectively, lay down a fabrication atop a base of

---

[12] Committee to Protect Journalists, "Attacks on the Press 2004: Documented Cases from Middle East and North Africa: Iraq," undated Web page.

[13] Schleifer (2006, p. 6).

[14] Ibrahim Al-Marashi, "Iraq's Hostage Crisis: Kidnappings, Mass Media and the Iraqi Insurgency," *Middle East Review of International Affairs*, Vol. 8, No. 4, December 2004, pp. 1–11 [p. 8].

[15] Bing West, *No True Glory: A Frontline Account of the Battle for Fallujah*, New York: Bantam Books, October 2005, p. 91.

fact. Case in point: On March 12, 2006, attacks in the Sadr City neighborhood of Baghdad killed 48 people (fact). However, radical Iraqi cleric Muqtada al-Sadr accused both terrorists (plausible accusation) and the U.S. military (false accusation) of responsibility for the attacks. "We consider the attack was carried out by groups of Takfir [a derogatory term used to describe terrorists literally meaning 'those who have put themselves outside Islam'] thanks to the cover of American spy aircraft."[16] Today's operating environment facilitates disinformation. In Iraq, adversary forces do not wear uniforms, so, after any engagement, there are casualties in "civilian clothes."[17]

- *Providing basic services:* Doing good works is a classic approach to winning friends and influencing people. Both insurgent and terrorist networks have adopted this strategy. In Iraq, Muqtada al-Sadr boosts his popularity by building schools, improving the welfare of the poor, and providing food and clothing to coreligionist refugees.[18]

- *Supporting youth and childhood education:* Adversaries also integrate shaping messages into school curricula. Some messages are in textbooks and other materials disseminated by those not considered U.S. adversaries. Consider the middle school textbook from Saudi Arabia that teaches that "Jews and Christians were cursed by Allah, who turned them into apes and pigs."[19] Other shaping messages are passed on in educational settings in which adversaries have more direct control, such as the madrassas of the Taliban.

---

[16] "Iraq: Al-Sadr Accuses Al-Qaeda and U.S. of Sunday's Carnage," Adnkronosinternational, March 13, 2006.

[17] LTC Steve Boylan, U.S. Army, Public Affairs Chief, Strategic Communication, Combined Arms Center, telephone interview with Christopher Paul, May 24, 2006.

[18] Salih Al-Qaisi and Oliver Poole, "Sadr Shows How to Win Hearts and Minds," *Daily Telegraph* (London), August 29, 2005, p. 12.

[19] Don Losman, "Hate's Inevitable Harvest: Sources of and Solutions for Middle East Hatred," *Indonesia Watch*, February 2006, p 2.

- *Making cultural, religious, or national appeals:* Adversaries also draw on approaches that are unique to their culture, region, religion, or nation. These are particularly challenging to U.S. shaping efforts, as there is little opportunity to reply in kind. Fatwas—Islamic religious/legal proclamations—are growing in frequency and are often directed in support of adversaries' shaping goals.[20]

Adversaries employ such shaping approaches through a variety of media platforms. This diversity makes countering adversaries' shaping efforts difficult for friendly forces. Each of these media platforms holds its own challenges for U.S. shaping efforts:

- *Internet:* As one interviewee noted, "The enemy is Web-dominant. We have to work on that."[21] Internet posting is inexpensive, easy, and relatively safe for an adversary. Further, the technology has reached a critical mass in accessibility, with high-speed Internet access available worldwide, if not at home, then in many communities through Internet cafes or other publicly available resources. Thus, shaping messages and materials are easy for the adversary to get onto the Web, where its target audiences have relatively easy access to those materials.
- *Adversary-owned television stations:* Adversary groups have set up their own television stations, either locally broadcast or satellite. The station run by Hizballah in Lebanon is the longest-running example:

> [B]eamed by satellite throughout the Middle East and beyond, [it] has continuously broadcast Death to Israel via martyrs' bullets and blood. Death to America is a relatively recent addition to its repertoire, with a commonly used video depicting the Statue of Liberty's head portrayed as

---

[20] These tactics are likely employed to achieve ends that range from recruitment and radicalization to appeasing and pacifying largely uninvolved publics.

[21] LTC Gary Tallman, U.S. Army, Public Affairs Officer, interview with Christopher Paul, Pentagon, Arlington, Va., April 24, 2006.

a skull with hollow eyes, dripping in blood, and holding a knife instead of a torch.[22]

- *Pulpits and fatwas:* Many adversary groups, especially Islamist groups, make extensive use of religious media platforms. Sermons and fatwas justify terror attacks, call people to arms against "infidels," and encourage demonstrations against policies or perceived slights.
- *CDs and DVDs:* Adversary groups distribute shaping messages via CDs or DVDs, providing them to the news media. The use of portable disk media allows messages to be distributed in areas otherwise isolated from traditional media such as radio or TV. CD and DVD sales allow adversaries to recoup some of their costs.
- *Word of mouth:* Adversaries spread shaping messages via rumor, word of mouth, and "the grapevine." A recent international study found that people indicated that they got their most reliable information from acquaintances or others "just like them."[23] Adversaries take advantage of this phenomenon.

News and News Media Issues

We miss *every* news cycle.

—*Anonymous interview*

Long-time media scholar Michael Schudson notes with regard to the U.S. press that "[a] comparison of any leading metropolitan paper of 1995 with one of 1895 demonstrates instantly that today's news is shaped much more by a professional ethic and reflects fewer partisan hopes or fears than a truly political press."[24] Journalistic standards guide much of today's free press. These standards are not codified, but there is a U.S. media way of doing business, and the vast majority

---

[22] Losman (2006).

[23] Edelman, *2006 Edelman Trust Barometer*, New York, 2006.

[24] Michael Schudson, *The Sociology of News*, New York: W. W. Norton, 2003, p. 48.

of U.S. journalists adhere to those standards, or at least to their own interpretations of those standards.[25]

Nevertheless, there are at least seven emerging trends that color today's news and complicate U.S. shaping efforts:

- *Emergence of the 24-hour news cycle:* Historically, news was deadline-driven and had a daily news cycle. It appeared in daily papers or was presented on the evening news. However, with the dawn of continuous 24-hour cable and satellite news networks and continuous live-feed Internet news, the concept of news cycles has changed. Adversaries can time actions to result in leading stories on U.S. television during daytime or evening news hours.[26] The continuous and live nature of television news puts pressure on journalists to report stories first and to fill the news void with content, sometimes to the advantage of U.S. adversaries.

- *Importance of framing:* How a story is structured and the attitude presented regarding an event constitutes the frame of the story. Frames are the perspective of the story.[27] News simplifies the complex, exemplified by the ever-prominent role of "sound bites." Choices about images also contribute to frames. A demonstration involving dozens of protestors seems more poignant with a close shot of a small group of protesters and the outrage clear on their faces. That same protest is visually dismissed with a long-range shot showing the small gathering of protesters contrasted with the large and empty square behind them.

- *Bias:* Accusations of bias are increasingly leveled against "non-Western" media and Arabic media in particular. President George W. Bush complained that Arabic television often gives

---

[25] With these ethical principles in mind, U.S. media outlets do tend to cater to audience's political perspectives to a greater or lesser degree (Dirk Blum, Lincoln Group, written comments provided to the authors, February 1, 2007).

[26] Tim Ryan, "Media's Coverage Has Distorted World's View of Iraqi Reality," *WorldTribune.com*, January 18, 2005.

[27] David L. Paletz, *The Media in American Politics: Contents and Consequences*, New York: Longman, 2002, p. 66.

a false impression of the United States.[28] Iraqi civil leaders have also referred to Al Jazeera as a "channel of terrorism."[29] Given Al Jazeera's dominance in the Arabic language market, such accusations have particular resonance with respect to shaping.[30]

- *Too few reporters:* Financial pressures force many news outlets to make do with fewer reporters than in the past. Having too few reporters on the scene is tantamount to having an insufficient number of credible witnesses, which creates an environment rich for adversary disinformation.
- *Control of journalists' access:* With reporter safety a very real concern, insurgents in Iraq control journalistic access in parts of the country where they have influence. Lack of access impacts the depth of reporting; selective access contributes to biased reporting. As LTC Tim Ryan observes,

> Because terrorists and other thugs wisely target western media members and others for kidnappings or attacks, the westerners stay close to their quarters. This has the effect of holding the media captive in cities and keeps them away from the broader truth that lies outside their view. With the press thus cornered, the terrorists easily feed their unwitting captives a thin gruel of anarchy, one spoonful each day.[31]

- *Perceived double standards:* Interview respondents asserted that the media, particularly the Western media, hold DoD and U.S. forces to an impossible or unreasonable standard while practically giving the adversary a free pass.
- *Propensity for errors and weak retractions:* The 24-hour news cycle pressures journalists to get their stories out first. This pressure dramatically compresses the time available for fact-checking and frequently results in erroneous stories. Active adversary efforts to

---

[28] "Bush: Arabic TV Gives False Impression of US," Reuters, January 5, 2006.

[29] "Al-Jazeera a 'Terror Channel,'" Agence France-Presse, November 24, 2004.

[30] Bing West (2005, pp. 90–91).

[31] Ryan (2005).

disseminate disinformation compound this problem. At the same time, news organizations fail to give retractions space or prominence comparable to the original erroneous story.

Context: Global Media, Local Information Environments, and Culture

Shaping occurs in the context of global media, the local information environment, and culture. These contextual issues influence the execution and success of shaping.

With globalized media, every message has the potential to be seen anywhere. Even locally targeted messages—a single flyer or poster stuck to a wall—can be transposed to another medium (e.g., a camera phone) and retransmitted anywhere. It is consequently impossible to qualify a message's audience with the word "only" (for example, "only Americans" or "only Baghdad residents"). For example, Figure 2.2 depicts a message from a simple leaflet dropped by U.S. forces in Afghanistan that found its way, via an Afghan-crafted rug, to a New York City–based retailer.

This affects U.S. government shaping efforts in two significant ways. First, "Catering principally to the national audience may create inadvertent messages worldwide, as comments 'targeted' at US citizens are seen around the world."[32] For example, presidential rhetoric for the domestic audience regarding the global war on terrorism (GWOT) included phrases such as "crusade against evil," which increased perceptions in the Arab world that the United States intended a war against Islam.[33] Second, it is impossible to prevent information spread abroad from returning for domestic consumption. This is particularly consequential for military PSYOP messages, which are restricted to foreign audiences by 22 USC 1461-1a, better known as the Smith-Mundt Act.[34]

---

[32] Combelles Siegel (2005, p. 131).

[33] Peter Ford, "Europe Cringes at Bush 'Crusade' Against Terrorists," *Christian Science Monitor*, September 19, 2001, p. 12.

[34] This is clearly a military-specific problem and receives more extensive treatment in the section on legal issues in the discussion of military-specific challenges to shaping, later in this chapter.

Figure 2.2
An Afghan Rug Sold in the United States Carries a U.S. Military PSYOP
Message

SOURCE: Kevin Sudeith, courtesy of WarRug.com. Used with permission.
NOTE: Inset depicts a PSYOP pamphlet distributed in Afghanistan.
RAND MG607-2.2

The local information environment is another relevant part of the context. In this monograph, we use the term *information environment* to denote the scheme of media and modes of information exchange within a region or area. What media are in use in an area? How are they used? Which population groups use predominantly which media? Knowing the answers to these sorts of questions is just the beginning of understanding the information environment in a given area.

Information environments vary; there is variation at the regional level ("tabloids" appear in Europe, but not so much in Africa), at the national level (Americans watch CNN or Fox News; Saudis watch Al Jazeera), and within different parts of a country (Los Angeles has 20 FM radio stations; Pittsburgh has 15). Variation operates in the information habits among groups at any of those levels. For example, college students in Los Angeles may listen predominantly to two or three FM radio stations, while working Hispanics choose others. Area sports enthusiasts may prefer AM to FM radio. There may be regional differences in how those media are displayed and what they are used for, even where a particular medium is fairly ubiquitous (newspapers, posters or flyers). Europe, for example, more than the United States, tends to have kiosks on which to post notices.

The information environment in an AO is a crucial part of the context for shaping. Effective shaping of a desired audience occurs only through media used by that target audience. Understanding a given information environment and casting shaping messages in forms that are appropriate to that environment pose significant challenges to shaping.

Culture constitutes another piece of the context in which shaping takes place. We use *culture* as a shorthand way of referring to a group or people's way of life or way of doing things that can vary across contexts or locales and can cause confusion, misunderstanding, or other "losses in translation" when different cultural assumptions come into contact.

Certain things do not translate well, and certain actions (or inactions) in the wrong cultural context can be confusing, funny, or highly offensive. What one should or should not do varies across cultural contexts. Danger lies behind assumptions of similarity. Two examples illustrate forms of cultural norm violation.

Figure 2.3 shows President Bush celebrating at his January 2005 inaugural parade by making the "hook 'em horns" salute, familiar to all who attended the University of Texas. Unfortunately, that particular gesture is not unique to Texas, and it carries different meanings elsewhere in the world. Norwegians seeing the image were shocked to see the President of the United States making the "sign of the devil."[35]

Mediterranean viewers and those in parts of Central and South America were shocked for different reasons: They saw the President indicating that someone's wife was unfaithful (that they were

---

[35] "Bush Salute a Satan Sign? Norwegians Think So," Associated Press, January 21, 2005.

Figure 2.3
President Bush Makes "Hook 'Em Horns"

SOURCE: White House photo by Paul Morse.
RAND *MG607-2.3*

cuckolded and had "grown horns").[36] This is a clear example of the way in which global media can spread a message beyond its target audience.

A second example, depicted in Figure 2.4, involves a message that offended its recipients. This shows a coalition PSYOP leaflet dropped to intimidate insurgents in Iraq. However, this airdropped leaflet did not just reach insurgents; it also reached noncombatants. And, while its message implies that insurgents deserve to be brought to justice, in cultural fact, it gave everyone who picked it up the "evil eye."[37]

Words cause similar cultural confusion. Some serve as cultural shorthand for value-laden concepts that seem clear in translation but lose something essential. *Freedom* and *democracy* are two examples of

---

[36] Jack Douglas, Jr., "Mixed Signals: Bush's Use of UT Hand Sign Causes Confusion Overseas," *Ft. Worth Star-Telegram*, January 22, 2005, p. 1.

[37] Anonymous interview.

Figure 2.4
Coalition PSYOP Leaflet

SOURCE: Task Force 20 leaflet IZG-7525 in Friedman, "Operation Iraqi Freedom," undated.
NOTE: Translation reads, "No matter where you run, no matter where you hide, Coalition Special Operations Forces will find you and bring you to justice" (Herbert A. Friedman, undated).
RAND *MG607-2.4*

English words that imply more than they denote in certain cultural contexts, and perhaps less in others.

> Thus when American public diplomacy talks about bringing democracy to Islamic societies, this is seen as no more than self-serving hypocrisy. Moreover, saying that "freedom is the future of the Middle East" is seen as patronizing, suggesting that Arabs are like the enslaved peoples of the old Communist World—but Muslims do not feel this way: they feel oppressed, but not enslaved.[38]

Jihad is another example of a word with greater depth of meaning to its native users than to those across the cultural divide.

---

[38] U.S. Department of Defense, Office of the Under Secretary of Defense for Acquisition, Technology, and Logistics (2004, p. 40).

Bin Laden has also insidiously convinced us to use terminology that lends legitimacy to his activities. He has hijacked the term "jihad" to such an extent that U.S. and other Western officials regularly use the terms "jihadist" and "terrorist" interchangeably. In doing so, they unwittingly transfer the religious legitimacy inherent in the concept of jihad to murderous acts that are anything but holy.[39]

Shaping efforts that transcend linguistic and cultural divides face the challenges of translation and cultural understanding of certain concepts. Shaping efforts need to be contextually sensitive, and culture can be a minefield.

What Makes Shaping So Difficult for DoD?

American officers train for years on infantry tactics, how to maneuver on an enemy and lead soldiers into battle. But some of the most crucial challenges for American soldiers today may be the human interactions for which they are often less prepared.

—*Julian E. Barnes*[40]

The previous section identified general challenges inherent in conducting shaping activities. This section narrows the focus and explores challenges specific to DoD shaping activities. The discussion considers several factors that make shaping challenging for DoD and its representatives, including

- the traditional "kinetic" focus of military operations
- interactions between U.S. forces and indigenous personnel
- information fratricide
- the reputation of PSYOP
- the lack of shaping resources

[39] John Brennan, "We've Lost Sight of His Vision," *Washington Post*, February 26, 2006, p. B4.

[40] Julian E. Barnes, "When Banter Beats Bullets: In Afghanistan and Iraq, Soldiers Try New Ways to Gain Support," *U.S. News and World Report*, March 7, 2005.

- legal barriers to shaping
- matching message, medium, and audience
- the difficulty of measuring shaping effectiveness
- intelligence requirements for shaping
- dealing with mistakes
- fallout and second-order consequences of expedient choices
- "damned if you do, damned if you don't" situations
- command use of communication assets
- balancing short-, medium-, and long-term goals.

The Traditional "Kinetic" Focus of Military Operations

> In *Insurgency and Terrorism*, O'Neill cautions that failure to grasp
> the gradations of insurgent type and strategy often leads govern-
> ment forces to pursue a one-size-fits-all approach, generally taking
> the militaristic overwhelming-force-and-firepower tack that actu-
> ally prolongs and exacerbates an insurgency.
>
> —*Jason Vest*[41]

U.S. forces may win every combat engagement but fail to garner the support of the noncombatant population. A focus on kinetic opera-tions to the exclusion of shaping activities increases the likelihood of this kind of outcome.

U.S. military doctrine and training has traditionally focused on actions against an adversary and on force projection. Operations in which the operational focus is on noncombatants and with methods of engagement that do not involve "putting steel on a target" are a step—often, too lengthy a step—away from tradition.

At the tactical and operational levels of war, U.S. forces have been trained to fight, not shape. British Brigadier Nigel Aylwin-Foster, in a seminal *Military Review* article, contends that an overemphasis on killing and capturing insurgents, combined with liberalized rules of engagement (ROE) and an overemphasis on force protection, has

---

[41] Jason Vest, "Willful Ignorance: How the Pentagon Sent the Army to Iraq Without a Counterinsurgency Doctrine," *Bulletin of the Atomic Scientists*, Vol. 61, No. 4, July–August 2005, pp. 40–48 [p. 45].

resulted in unacceptably high numbers of civilian casualties. These casualties have necessarily angered the population. Combined with a culture that requires the vengeful righting of perceived wrongs, the casualties have, in part, swelled insurgent ranks and their well of support.[42] Consider the following observations:

> The American approach was markedly different [according to a senior British Army officer]: "When US troops are attacked with mortars in Baghdad, they use mortar-locating radar to find the firing point and then attack the general area with artillery, even though the area they are attacking may be in the middle of a densely populated residential area.

> "They may well kill the terrorists in the barrage but they will also kill and maim innocent civilians. That has been their response on a number of occasions. It is trite, but American troops do shoot first and ask questions later. They are very concerned about taking casualties and have even trained their guns on British troops, which has led to some confrontations between soldiers. . . . The US will have to abandon the sledgehammer-to-crack-a-nut approach—it has failed," he said. "They need to stop viewing every Iraqi, every Arab as the enemy and attempt to win the hearts and minds of the people."[43]

> American commanders acknowledge that military might alone cannot defeat the insurgency; in fact, the frequent use of force often spurs resistance by deepening ill will. "This war cannot be won militarily," said Maj. Gen. John R. S. Batiste, commander of the First Infantry Division, which oversees a swath of the northern Sunni triangle slightly larger than the state of West Virginia. "It really does need a political and economic solution."[44]

---

[42] Nigel Aylwin-Foster, "Changing the Army for Counterinsurgency Operations," *Military Review*, November–December 2005, pp. 2–15.

[43] Sean Rayment, "US Tactics Condemned by British Officers," *Sunday Telegraph* (London), April 11, 2004, p. 6.

[44] Edward Wong and Zaineb Obeid, "In Anger, Ordinary Iraqis Are Joining the Insurgency," *New York Times*, June 28, 2004, p. A9.

Violence, destruction, and death can have a positive shaping effect when they hit their targets without undue collateral loss.[45] Kinetic operations are unavoidable in most conflict situations. The challenge is to minimize the adverse shaping consequences of these actions.

Interactions Between U.S. Forces and Indigenous Personnel Have Shaping Consequences

> We often raided houses late at night, so people awakened to soldiers bursting through their bedroom doors. Women and children wailed, terrified. . . . I imagined what it would feel like if soldiers kicked down my door at midnight, if I could do nothing to protect my family. I would hate those soldiers.
> —*Brian Mockenhaupt*[46]

> You can't win the hearts and minds when you're driving people into a ditch.
> —*LTC Robert J. Duffy, U.S. Army*[47]

The behavior of every soldier, sailor, airman, and marine in a theater of operations shapes the indigenous population. This section discusses the shaping challenges inherent in the "strategic corporal" phenomenon, the danger of differing cultural perspectives in personal interactions, and the importance of personal relationships in shaping.

"Strategic Corporal." Because of the globalization of media, how a single soldier handles a tactical situation in an out-of-the-way location still has the potential to make global headlines and have strategic impact. The strategic corporal phenomenon has shaping implications that go beyond mass media; indigenous individuals with whom troops

---

[45] During ongoing operations in Iraq, U.S. forces used a 2,000-pound bomb on an insurgent stronghold. As a direct result, intelligence tips from locals immediately poured forth.

[46] Brian Mockenhaupt, "I Miss Iraq. I Miss My Gun. I Miss My War," *Esquire*, March 2007, pp. 120–123 [p. 122].

[47] LTC Robert Duffy, U.S. Army, Civil Affairs Officer and Provincial Reconstruction Team Commander during Operation Enduring Freedom, interview with Russell W. Glenn and Todd C. Helmus, Bagram, Afghanistan, February 14, 2004. Robert Duffy has since been promoted to colonel.

interact form favorable or unfavorable impressions from those interactions and spread those impressions by word of mouth throughout surprisingly large networks.

Prior to September 11, 2001, U.S. forces received no significant training for their future interactions with noncombatants. U.S. urban operations, particularly those early in OIF and Operation Enduring Freedom (OEF), proved troublesome. U.S. tactics involving wholesale round-ups and, at times, unnecessary aggressiveness were perceived as heavy-handed. Robert Jenks of the 4th PSYOP Group witnessed these tactics first hand. He was lodged in a traffic jam on Route Irish (the highway running between Baghdad International Airport and the Green Zone–U.S. embassy compound) while U.S. soldiers investigated a possible improvised explosive device (IED). In the midst of this, Ambassador Richard Jones' security detail, fearing for their charge, began yelling and pointing weapons at civilians, who were themselves immobilized by the traffic. To extricate the ambassador, the security detail forced its way through by ramming civilian vehicles.[48]

The recent findings of a first-time ethics survey illustrate the challenges posed by soldier-civilian interactions. Fewer than half the surveyed soldiers and marines deployed in Iraq in 2006 agreed that noncombatants should be treated with "dignity and respect." More than a third of soldiers and marines believed that torture to "gather important information about insurgents" should be allowed. In addition, more than 25 percent reported insulting or cursing noncombatants in their presence, with approximately 10 percent admitting to unnecessarily damaging or destroying Iraqi property. Small-unit leadership may play a key role in this regard. A third of marines and a quarter of soldiers stated that their unit-level noncommissioned officers (NCOs) and officers failed to clearly prohibit the mistreatment of noncombatants.[49]

---

[48] Robert Jenks, Deputy Commanding Officer for Research, Analysis, and Civilian Affairs, 4th Psychological Operations Group, interview with Todd C. Helmus and Christopher Paul, Ft. Bragg, N.C., December 15, 2005.

[49] Office of the Surgeon, Multi National Force–Iraq, and Office of the Surgeon General, U.S. Army Medical Command, *Mental Health Advisory Team (MHAT) IV: Operation Iraqi Freedom 05-07*, November 17, 2006.

Maintaining proper civilian-soldier interactions is an extraordinarily difficult task in dangerous operating environments. However, overzealous efforts to maintain proper force protection make U.S. troops (or other personnel) their "own worst enemy."[50] Preparing personnel to be the first line of successful U.S. shaping efforts remains a critical challenge.

Dangers in Different Cultural Perspectives. Cultural assumptions pose a significant threat to shaping operations. Coalition forces have learned the hard way that many cultural assumptions are repeatedly proven wrong. As coalition helicopters fly over urban areas, the gunners, whose feet hang from the aircraft, have inadvertently offended thousands of Iraqis who gaze above. Similarly, the use of dogs in house-to-house searches and the wearing of dark sunglasses have also angered some in the Iraqi population. Observes Colonel Steven Boltz,

> Using a stick to separate people during a search. They use a stick to guide animals. . . . We use dogs. They are considered very low. To hold somebody down with your boot, that's the lowest of the low. . . . If you separate men from women, it's a mistake. If you didn't have an enemy when you went in, you've got one now.[51]

Dramatic efforts have since been taken to learn Iraqi and Afghan dos and don'ts and to educate troops accordingly. It is a daunting task, given the young soldiers who bear the brunt of learning and implementing the infinite array of cultural decorum. While coalition forces have learned much during their time in the Afghan and Iraqi theaters, future contingencies in other locations, especially those that cannot be easily envisioned, will bring similar challenges.

There are limits to how far such sensitivity should go. It may be necessary for those in helicopters to hang their feet outside the aircraft. Dogs may be essential in conducting search operations. Some clashes of culture are unavoidable, and coalition personnel should not be overly

---

[50] James Rainey, "Aiming for a More Subtle Fighting Force," *Los Angeles Times*, May 9, 2006, p. A1.

[51] COL Steven Boltz, U.S. Army, G-2, V Corps, interview with Russell W. Glenn and Todd C. Helmus, Heidelberg, Germany, February 26, 2004.

defensive. However, efforts to explain the need to conduct operations in the manner undertaken can help mitigate negative effects. These explanations will be even more effective if the person providing the explanation is aware of local cultural norms. Military operations will involve educating both the local population and military personnel. The logical objective is to minimize the number of avoidable misunderstandings, not entirely eliminate them. Common sense must be a guide.

Power of Personal Relationships. Great things have been accomplished through personal relationships formed between U.S. servicepeople and indigenous noncombatants. Even when other shaping efforts have failed or when credibility has been damaged, the sincerity and personal warmth of a U.S. soldier has won over many a reticent sheik or tribal elder. As company commander Daniel Morgan recounts,

> Since we were the first forces into Mosul, Iraq, my soldiers and I had to get out into the streets and meet people. We developed a "list of influence" and began developing relationships.

> On 13 September 2003, one of my platoons was ambushed, wounding three of my soldiers. . . . [A] member of an Iraqi political party called me and said he saw the ambush and knew the attackers. . . . This ambush cost the leg of one of my soldiers and through relationships we caught the culprit.[52]

Several features of military life make shaping through personal connections difficult. First, there is the tendency to seek technological solutions to problems. As Dave Champagne, head of the 4th PSYOP Group Strategic Studies Directorate noted, "They are trying to come up with a computer solution to a human problem."[53] This emphasis results in constrained resources being focused on technological solu-

---

[52] Daniel Morgan, "Going to Fight in Iraq? Lessons from an Infantry Company Commander," *After Action Report, Infantry Company in Iraq*, January 23, 2004, p. 6.

[53] Dave Champagne, Head of Strategic Studies Directorate, 4th Psychological Operations Group, interview with Todd C. Helmus and Christopher Paul, Ft. Bragg, N.C., December 14, 2005.

tions rather than on better shaping preparation for troops who will have direct personal contact with foreign noncombatants.[54]

Second, troop rotations constantly disrupt relationships between U.S. troops and members of the indigenous population. When new troops rotate in, personal relationships that have been cultivated over the course of a year restart from square one. As LTC Gary Martel notes, "It's a new game every time we have a TOA [transfer of authority]."[55] Rotations also result in the loss of institutional knowledge as incoming units must become familiar with cultural decorum, local influencers, population characteristics, and overarching shaping strategies.

Information Fratricide at All Levels

> The White House has launched several recent initiatives designed to promote the coordination of U.S. public diplomacy efforts, and agencies are working to improve public diplomacy operations, but the government does not yet have a national communication strategy.
> —*U.S. Government Accountability Office*[56]

> PA does not want the PSYOP/IO stink on them.
> —*Anonymous interview*

Several barriers confront coordination and deconfliction within DoD, between DoD and the rest of the U.S. government, and between DoD and U.S. coalition partners. According to Army Field Manual 3-13, "*Information fratricide* is the result of employing information operations elements in a way that causes effects in the information environment that impede the conduct of friendly operations or adversely

---

[54] Combelles Siegel (2005, p. 117).

[55] LTC Gary Martel, Joint Information Operations Center, interview with Christopher Paul, Lackland AFB, Tex., February 16, 2006.

[56] U.S. Government Accountability Office, *U.S. Public Diplomacy: Interagency Coordination Efforts Hampered by the Lack of a National Communication Strategy*, Washington, D.C., GAO-05-323, April 2005, p. 2.

affect friendly forces."[57] All too often, information fratricide results in credibility loss, contrary messaging, or other limitations to shaping.

Our analysis and interviews regarding recent operations in Iraq and Afghanistan suggest that information fratricide has manifested in at least three areas:

- lack of coordination or synchronization of strategic communication between DoD and other U.S. government agencies
- lack of coordination or synchronization with coalition partners
- lack of coordination between military "shaping" entities.

Lack of Coordination or Synchronization of Strategic Communication Between DoD and Other U.S. Government Agencies. To avoid information fratricide at the highest levels, shaping activities must be coordinated across the government. This is often not the case for several reasons. First, even if we consider only DoS and DoD, combatant commands' (COCOMs') geographical boundaries do not directly correspond with DoS regions.[58] This poses a coordination obstacle between these two organizations that becomes compounded when other U.S. government entities, such as USAID and the Department of Justice, are also participants.

Further, no single federal executive agency has the authority and personnel to dictate and enforce other agencies' compliance with shaping objectives. DoS has the "lead" in proposed strategic communication-coordinating structures in several instances. However, it is unclear whether DoS has been given sufficient authority to actually coordinate high-level shaping and whether it has the personnel to do so. DoS has a very small workforce in comparison to DoD. Those numbers are smaller yet when only DoS's deployable workforce is taken into account. As LTC George McDonald noted, if you need to have an

---

[57] Headquarters, U.S. Department of the Army, *Information Operations: Doctrine, Tactics, Techniques, and Procedures*, Washington, D.C., Army Field Manual 3-13, November 28, 2003a, p. 1-5. Emphasis in the original.

[58] Martel (2006).

"American face" on your information efforts, "State Department just doesn't have the footprint."[59]

Third, there is a lack of guidance regarding the objectives of strategic communication themes. "A lack of national-level themes to guide message formulation" is a consistent observation in shaping-related lessons-learned studies.[60] Perhaps a structure that clearly gave the National Security Council or DoS the lead in developing shaping themes and the authority to enforce compliance would ameliorate some of the existing problems in this regard. However, unless the President and other officials avoid messages that conflict with existing themes, their words will cause inconsistency and confusion and are likely to compel rapid changes in shaping themes. An anonymous interview respondent called this "policy by transcript" and indicated that it is a serious challenge to efforts to integrate and coordinate shaping activities and messages.

Lack of Coordination or Synchronization with Coalition Partners. In addition to difficulties coordinating with the rest of the U.S. government, DoD faces the challenge of coordinating shaping efforts with U.S. coalition partners. Once again, this problem spans the spectrum, from strategic to tactical. A classic example pertains to variation in ROE across multinational boundaries in Iraq. Multi-National Division (South East) (MND [SE]) employed more restrictive ROE, while those employed by U.S. forces to the north were frequently more liberal. This created friction when U.S. convoy units traversing MND (SE) fired warning shots to disperse crowds gathering by the roads, an activity proscribed by coalition ROE in effect there.[61]

Other problems resulting from failure to coordinate with coalition partners include problems similar to those discussed previously:

---

[59] LTC George McDonald, Joint Information Operations Center, and MAJ George Brown, Joint PSYOP Planner, Joint Information Operations Center, interview with Christopher Paul and Todd C. Helmus, Lackland AFB, Tex., February 17, 2006.

[60] Christopher Lamb, *Review of Psychological Operations Lessons Learned from Recent Operational Experience*, Washington, D.C.: National Defense University Press, September 2005, p. 2.

[61] Lieutenant Colonel J. G. Wilford, "OP TELIC—COIN LESSONS IDENTIFIED," briefing, notes for slide, "OP TELIC—COIN Lessons Identified—Firepower," undated.

possible conflicting messages, "say-do" gaps, and loss of credibility. Imagine the surprise of British forces operating in Iraq when Iraqis approached them with U.S. "leaflets that said, 'The good guys are coming with food, water . . . whatever,' and the commander had never heard about it."[62]

Lack of Coordination Between Military Shaping Entities. Coordinating shaping efforts within DoD is also a challenge. Several organizations have shaping-specific responsibilities: PA, IO (including PSYOP), defense support to public diplomacy (DSPD), and civil-military operations (CMO). Then there is also the shaping influence of all other U.S. force elements.

IO is the umbrella coordinating entity most clearly charged with coordinating shaping. According to joint doctrine, IO has five pillars: EW, CNO, PSYOP, OPSEC, and MILDEC.[63]

PA, CMO, and DSPD are considered *related capabilities* and are charged with "work[ing] in close coordination with the IO planning staff."[64]

As is sometimes the case, things do not work as smoothly in practice as is laid out in doctrine. The following discussion highlights the coordination problems that can arise among these entities.

Doctrinal Issue: IO-PSYOP Overlap. PSYOP and MILDEC are the only IO pillars that involve content development. The other pillars concern *information systems* rather than information content. While this creates a bit of a split personality in IO doctrine, it does not carry over too heavily in IO practice: In ongoing operations in Afghanistan and Iraq, "PSYOP is the biggest tool."[65] During stability-and-support

---

[62] BG Steve Patton, interview with Russell W. Glenn, the Pentagon, Arlington, Va., November 7, 2003.

[63] Joint Chiefs of Staff, *Joint Doctrine for Information Operations*, Joint Publication 3-13, February 13, 2006, p. iii.

[64] Joint Chiefs of Staff (2006, p. x).

[65] LTC Jayson Spade, J-31 Team Chief, Combatant Command Support Team for U.S. Pacific Command, and MAJ John Hill, J-24 Intelligence Support to Special Operations Team Leader, interview with Christopher Paul and Todd C. Helmus, Joint Information Operations Center, Lackland AFB, Tex., February 16, 2006.

operations, four of the five IO pillars are given lower priority. This leads to a situation in which IO efforts are almost exclusively PSYOP. The redundant layers of command can create challenges.

RAND conducted interviews with both PSYOP and other IO personnel as part of the research for this study. We were struck by the startling similarity in the concerns and frustrations expressed by PSYOP and IO representatives. Responses to interview questions were nearly identical. This suggests that, in current operational practice, IO and its PSYOP pillar have highly overlapped portfolios. This creates at least three challenges:

- There is overlapping authority between IO and PSYOP responsibilities (and a potential for consequential animosity).[66]
- There is confusion between respective roles. IO is a staff function and, doctrinally, has strictly a coordinating role. Yet RAND heard anecdotal accounts of IO staffs releasing "IO products" and releasing them without their passing through the rigorous approval process demanded of PSYOP products.[67] Such was the case when one anonymous member of the 4th PSYOP Group encountered an IO cell in Iraq giving product information to an interpreter for vetting. The product went to the newspapers the next day.
- PSYOP's lack of a "seat at the table."[68] With PSYOP subordinate to IO, an IO representative gets direct access to the commander, while PSYOP representatives report to the IO chief. Unless the IO

[66] CDR Ed Burns, U.S. Navy, Joint Information Operations Center, interview with Christopher Paul and Todd C. Helmus, Lackland AFB, Tex., February 16, 2006.

[67] One PSYOP interview respondent, upset with this apparent usurpation, asserted that, according to doctrine, there is no such thing as an "IO product" other than a synchronization matrix for a staff meeting and further remarked that there is no "IO product" that an Iraqi ever sees (anonymous interview). An IO respondent agreed and indicated that he gave his IO team members these instructions: "IO can develop the theme; let the PSYOPers develop the message" (Burns, 2006).

[68] COL Kenneth A. Turner, U.S. Army, Commanding Officer, 4th Psychological Operations Group, interview with Todd C. Helmus and Christopher Paul, Ft. Bragg, N.C., December 14, 2005.

chief is also an expert in PSYOP, this means that relevant shaping expertise is one step removed from the commander. This may contribute to the challenge of integrating shaping activities with other military operations during both the planning and operating phases. Christopher Lamb notes, "A major problem documented in OEF, OIF, and OIF 2 lessons learned is that IO planners did not adequately understand PSYOP and thus failed to appreciate its capabilities sufficiently or employ them appropriately and effectively."[69]

Doctrinal Issue: PA Is Hesitant to Coordinate with Representatives of Other Shaping-Specific Functions. PA organizations are often hesitant to coordinate with IO for a variety of reasons. First, the traditional PA culture holds that PA missions are to "inform, not influence" and to communicate PA messages on behalf of the commander. More contemporarily, several of the public affairs officers (PAOs) we interviewed freely admitted that there is no such thing as *value-free information* and that they do indeed influence, though they were very clear that it was always with 100-percent true information. Current joint doctrine, while requiring PA and IO coordination, prohibits PAOs from "planning or executing" PSYOP:

> PA capabilities are related to IO, but PA is not an IO discipline or PSYOP tool. PA activities contribute to IO by providing truthful, accurate and timely information, using approved DOD PAG [public affairs guidance] to keep the public informed about the military's missions and operations, countering adversary propaganda, deterring adversary actions, and maintain trust and confidence of the US population, and our friends and allies. PA activities affect, and are affected by, PSYOP, and are planned and executed in coordination with PSYOP planning and operations. PA must be aware of the practice of PSYOP, but should have no role in planning or executing these operations.[70]

---

[69] Lamb (2005, p. 15).

[70] Joint Chiefs of Staff, *Doctrine for Public Affairs in Joint Operations*, Joint Publication 3-61, May 9, 2005, p. III-21.

A second reason for PA hesitation to coordinate with IO is the constraint that it use only the truth.[71] IO and PSYOP are not similarly bound.[72]

Third, many PAOs are cautious in establishing closer relationships because they misunderstand PSYOP. A significant number of PAOs we interviewed were under the impression that most of what PSYOP does is based on falsehood, so-called "black" PSYOP, and that PSYOP is exclusively tactical. In fact, the vast majority of PSYOP activities are not based on deception.[73]

PA hesitancy to engage in shaping coordination means that PAOs do not provide input on the possible shaping consequences of planned operations from the perspective of their audiences.[74] Moreover, when PA and IO are not coordinated, the two could release contradictory messages about the same event, undermining the credibility of both sources.

Doctrinal Issue: Coordination with CMO/CA on Shaping Issues. CMO and CA forces aim to deliver goods and services to noncombatants. Since these are actions, and since actions speak louder than words, the potential positive shaping benefit is enormous, yet it often

---

[71] LTC Ryan Yantis, Director, U.S. Army Public Affairs—Midwest, telephone interview with Christopher Paul and Todd C. Helmus, May 15, 2006.

[72] "In theory, the idea of merging PA, IO, and PSYOP appears to make sense; in practice, however, the goals of these three functions are quite different. Public affairs is charged with informing the public with factual, truthful information, while IO and PSYOP seek to influence their audiences to change perceptions or behavior" (Pamela Keeton and Mark McCann, "Information Operations, STRATCOM, and Public Affairs," *Military Review*, November–December 2005, pp. 83–86 [p. 84]).

[73] One respondent was not surprised by the misunderstanding. He examined the PA Defense Information School training curriculum and found that students receive only 30 minutes of IO training, all of it focused on MILDEC, which *is* all about lying (Bob Giesler, Director, Informations Operations and Strategic Studies, Office of the Deputy Under Secretary of Defense, Intelligence and Warfighting Support, interview with Christopher Paul, the Pentagon, Arlington, Va., April 26, 2006).

[74] "[P]ublic affairs officers do not typically provide input about potential media fallout of specific targeting—in no small part because they frequently are not involved in strike planning. They often are far enough out of the loop so as not to have knowledge of specific situations or the context of operations" (Combelles Siegel, 2005, p. 130).

goes unrealized. CA forces are not trained to publicize or leverage their activities for shaping purposes, much less coordinate them with PA or IO representatives.[75] As an anonymous interview respondent noted, "CA guys are great, but they do not 'get' that what they do has to be exploited." Also, many CA personnel are hesitant to work with PSYOP (if not PA) personnel, for many of the same reasons that PA is hesitant. One anonymous CA officer observed, "CA wears the white hat; PSYOP can wear the black hat. We should not switch hit." Another anonymous officer to whom we spoke did not mince words: "PSYOP is the evil tool."

Doctrinal Issue: Informing Line Troops About Shaping Themes. Even though DoD has centralized shaping themes and coordinated shaping professionals, shaping is difficult, given that it involves virtually every soldier, sailor, airman, and marine in a theater of operations. Themes must be effectively disseminated to the troops who are in daily contact with noncombatants in such a way that they can understand and adhere to them.

So far, training with regard to shaping themes has been scant. Here is how one interviewee described it:

> The only message we got was the brief. . . . You got a 30-minute brief [on the shaping campaign theme in February 2004, prior to entering the theater]. . . . We had a division message. There couldn't have been a consistent message across the country if all you do is give a 30-minute video message off the plane and no follow-up after that.[76]

---

[75] "The problem is that we think of CMO as something that [the civil affairs group] does. We are all more comfortable with kinetic operations so that's what we focus on, and then [we] leave the detailed planning for Phase IV operations to the CA guys on the [operational planning team] who often lack the background and expertise to make it work. We do this even though we all say the Phase IV is the most important phase" (unidentified Marine Expeditionary Force Planner, U.S. Marine Corps, "Perspectives on HA/CMO in Iraq," briefing, Security Cooperation Education and Training Center, undated, slide 2).

[76] LtCol. William R. Costantini, U.S. Marine Corps, Commanding Officer, 1st Light Armored Reconnaissance Battalion, 1st Marine Regiment, Operation Iraqi Freedom (February–October 2004), interview with Todd C. Helmus, Naval Postgraduate School, Monterey, Calif., April 4, 2005.

Just giving troops dos and don'ts is insufficient. Soldiers at the tactical level may not understand the overall goals of the shaping campaign and therefore may not understand why specific tactics, techniques, and procedures (TTP) that serve the shaping campaign are necessary.[77] For example, troops may express frustration at rules requiring them to knock before entering a dwelling, believing that it gives potential adversaries time to flee or otherwise prepare. However, if those troops come to understand that apprehending insurgents is subordinate to gaining the support of the local populace, troops will not only be more likely to adhere to knocking rules, but they will also find their own additional ways to earn local support. This challenge applies to all in the chain of command.

Doctrinal Issue: Reactive Rather Than Proactive Information Approach. The final information fratricide challenge stems from DoD's reactive approach. Virtually no military commander would dispute the value of having "initiative" in battle. However, the current system presents several obstacles to proactive shaping. First, it is difficult to get the lead time necessary to conduct proactive shaping because shaping is rarely a high priority. Generating shaping messages takes time, and it takes time for shaping to take effect. Second, because they are out of the planning loop, many with shaping-specific responsibilities do not have the opportunity to propose proactive shaping as part of an operation. They instead end up reacting to the (likely negative) fallout. As one PSYOP representative mentioned, "[T]he command tended to fall back on public affairs–type stuff and only when a crisis would occur, they would go, 'Oh my God! Where are the PSYOP guys?'"[78] Third, many aspects of existing processes are not sufficiently agile to "get out in front" of a breaking crisis or opportunity.

---

[77] Russell W. Glenn, Christopher Paul, Todd C. Helmus, and Paul Steinberg, *"People Make the City," Executive Summary: Joint Urban Operations Observations and Insights from Afghanistan and Iraq,* Santa Monica, Calif.: RAND Corporation, MG-428/2-JFCOM, 2007.

[78] Nicholas Novosel, Balkan Area Analyst, U.S. European Command, Strategic Studies Detachment, 4th Psychological Operations Group, interview with Todd C. Helmus and Christopher Paul, Ft. Bragg, N.C., December 14, 2005.

The Reputation of PSYOP

> Exaggeration, even in its mildest forms, was not approved, the attitude being that, if we were once caught out in a lie, we should find it very difficult to live down that lie and our value would at once diminish.
>
> —*Anonymous*[79]

Currently, many shaping activities are under the auspices of IO and PSYOP. As already noted, the very terms *psychological operations* and *information operations* have a negative connotation, borne, in part, of Vietnam-era activities, that smacks of propaganda, deception, and illicit human influence in ways that are contrary to U.S. values. IO officer LTC Jayson Spade explained, "PSYOP has negative connotations. The problem? It seems to be the notion that we are trying to influence people."[80] This is not a new problem:

> [Certain actions by] the U.S. mission in Iraq have re-ignited fears about government acting to replace independent reporting with wartime propaganda. The same fears have been expressed during past wars as the U.S. government sought to promote a positive view of the nation and its policies.[81]

It is unclear from our research whether this reputation problem causes concern among indigenous audiences. After all, they attribute messages to the U.S. military in general rather than to an operational entity, such as PSYOP. It does, however, cause problems with important U.S. actors whose successful integration with IO is critical to operation success. As suggested previously, PA, CA, and other interagency

---

[79] Anonymous Far Eastern Liaison Officer in 1944, quoted in Allison B. Gilmore, *You Can't Fight Tanks with Bayonets: Psychological Warfare Against the Japanese Army in the Southwest Pacific*, Lincoln, Neb.: University of Nebraska Press, 1998, p. 21.

[80] Spade and Hill (2006).

[81] Lowell Schwartz, "War, Propaganda and Public Opinion," *Baltimore Sun*, December 18, 2005.

partners have evidenced great reluctance to coordinate with PSYOP personnel and activities.

Lack of Resources for Shaping

In today's environment, DoD information resources are underfunded by a factor of 10, according to one observer.[82] Here are some of the most critical shortfall areas:

- *Personnel:* The force structure of PA and PSYOP is much too limited. PSYOP, for example, has only one active-component PSYOP group—the 4th PSYOP Group, out of Fort Bragg, N.C., totaling around 1,300 personnel—and two reserve-component PSYOP groups (the 2nd PSYOP Group and the 7th PSYOP Group, comprising another 2,600 personnel). The only other element is the 193rd Special Operations Wing, with six aircraft and associated crews. According to some senior officers, there are not enough PSYOP personnel to do their assigned missions, let alone conduct joint training exercises with other units so that those units are comfortable working with PSYOP.[83] The PA force structure is even thinner.
- *Training and preparation:* PSYOP is significantly limited by training shortfalls. One anonymous interviewee observed,

  > It is assumed that the officer corps, sergeants, [and privates], know PSYOP, that they are graphic experts, can do target analysis, have cultural knowledge . . . which is ridiculous. The average individual is out of high school, they have some cultural training as part of the MOS [military occupational specialty] and no PSYOP background.

  There are similar training inadequacies in PA. While some PAOs participate in a valuable industry training program, the program's expanse is too limited. PAO interviewees also indicated that the

---

[82] Jeffrey B. Jones, "Strategic Communication: A Mandate for the United States," *Joint Force Quarterly*, No. 39, October 2005, pp. 108–114.

[83] Bloom (2005).

training they received was not always well focused with respect to pending deployments.

- *Equipment:* Shaping operations and communication equipment for the support of shaping have not traditionally been DoD priorities. Budget allocations for communication entities reflects that. If resources are allocated for increased end strength and more extensive training, money will still be needed for new and additional equipment.

- *Translators:* Translators and interpreters are an underresourced capability in maneuver and CA units and in IO and PA. Capable ones provide key cultural insights and can aid in the acquisition and analysis of intelligence, in addition to helping produce and disseminate shaping products. Shaping initiatives often require better translators or interpreters than do other operations. Much face-to-face communication is nonverbal. Able translators are critical to fully understanding the moods, attitudes, and impressions of those present during face-to-face encounters, in addition to determining the meaning of spoken words.

PSYOP Barriers to Shaping

> The PSYOP approval process has merit but it's called *the murder board* for a reason.
>
> —*Anonymous interview*

PSYOP suffers from two additional barriers to successful shaping. First, Public Law 402, the U.S. Information and Educational Exchange Act of 1948 (the Smith-Mundt Act), prohibits DoD from targeting U.S. audiences. With the reach of the Internet and 24-hour news, however, many of the Pentagon's information efforts can wind up in the U.S. media.[84] Currently, PSYOP forces need to obtain the direct permission of the Secretary of Defense before distributing material on

---

[84] Mark Mazzetti, "Planted Articles May Be Violation: A 2003 Pentagon Directive Appears to Bar a Military Program That Pays Iraqi Media to Print Favorable Stories," *Los Angeles Times,* January 27, 2006, p. A3.

the Internet, even in a foreign language.[85] The result, according to one interviewee: "We're hamstrung in a lot of ways."[86]

The PSYOP approval process constitutes a second barrier. A rigorous product development and approval process makes sense. However, product approval needs should be balanced with timeliness. Finding a process that leads to the right balance is the challenge. As Christopher Lamb notes,

> A dilatory PSYOP product approval process is detrimental to the execution of an effective PSYOP campaign. Before operations begin, a delayed process inhibits PSYOP planning and rehearsal time, while slow approval during an actual campaign can render some military and political products useless, since they may be overcome by events.[87]

An anonymous commentator also observed that "so many people make edits and give input that at some point they begin to correct each others' inputs and edits."

Matching Message, Medium, and Audience

> Doctrinally, we are supposed to pre- and post-test, but they do not provide the money to do those things. They do not provide the money or training or expertise.
> —*Robert Jenks, 4th PSYOP Group*[88]

Every member of a given population is different—and different in ways that can affect perceptions of a message. Communications that treat everyone in a large population as a homogenous target audience risk missing the mark or, in the extreme, prove deleterious to shaping objec-

---

[85] COL Jack Summe, J-39, PSYOP Division Chief, interview with Todd C. Helmus, MacDill AFB, Fla., January 19, 2006.

[86] Bloom (2005).

[87] Lamb (2005, p. 14).

[88] Jenks (2005).

tives. However, the military can actively seek to aggregate the populace into like-minded and meaningful audiences.

Yet identifying target audiences is a difficult task in military operational venues. According to one observer,

> PSYOP access to one target audience for assessment and feedback is more constrained than in other persuasive communications disciplines, and it must compensate with extraordinary efforts to understand the target audience.[89]

Especially prior to the commencement of operations, direct access to target audiences can be difficult, though not impossible, to achieve. The intermingling of adversaries and noncombatants and the possibility of an individual's role as friendly, neutral, or enemy changing from day to day compounds the challenges of audience segmentation.[90] Another challenge is anticipating how messages will impact the target and other groups that are part of the "inadvertent" audience. As suggested previously, culture, language, and other features of the receiving audience (whether targeted or not) impact how messages are perceived. Both doctrine and industry best practice suggest that focus groups and other forms of product pretesting are important in message development. However, in this case, product pretesting is hindered on several levels. First, the pace of operations and the corresponding need to quickly move products limit the necessary time pretesting requires. U.S. shaping forces may also lack adequate access to target audiences. In some cases, such access is simply not available; in others, there may be missed opportunities to pretest, as was the case in at least one instance noted by an interviewee speaking of Afghanistan: "They are doing products for Taliban and using civilians to pretest. We had Taliban as prisoners and defectors; they should have used them."[91]

---

[89] Lamb (2005, p. 40).

[90] Jamison Jo Medby and Russell W. Glenn, *Street Smart: Intelligence Preparation of the Battlefield for Urban Operations*, Santa Monica, Calif.: RAND Corporation, MR-1287-A, 2002.

[91] Spade and Hill (2006).

Identifying the appropriate media to convey a message to a given target audience requires care. Different locales have different information environments and different cultural preferences for the form and style of the media they consume. For example, residents of Kabul, Afghanistan, likely vary considerably from their rural counterparts in terms of media consumption habits. Resource availability and reliance on traditional PSYOP TTP can also hinder optimal matching of target, message, and media.

Measures of Effectiveness (MOE)—How Do You Know That What You Are Doing Is Working?

> MOE's tough. MOE's almost impossible.
> —*LT Robert Dunn, U.S. Navy,*
> *Joint Information Operations Center*[92]

MOE for shaping are particularly challenging. The biggest problem is connecting the shaping action or message with some measurable quantity or quality that is not confounded by other possible causes. For example, many Iraqi soldiers surrendered at the outset of OIF. Was this due to the PSYOP leaflets dropped instructing them to do so? Was it instead due to the impact of the coalition's massive military might? Were there other causes? What was the most likely combination of causes that resulted in the desirable end? In this case, the possible causes are highly conflated, even though the objective being measured—surrender—is an observable behavior. It would be even more difficult to assess the multiple possible causes underlying other objectives, such as creating positive public attitudes toward the coalition.

However, direct observation, polling, surveys, interviews, and other methods can be used to gauge the effectiveness of the shaping campaign.[93] Yet challenges remain. These techniques are difficult to get

[92] LT Robert Dunn, U.S. Navy, Joint Information Operations Center, interview with Christopher Paul, Lackland AFB, Tex., February 16, 2006.

[93] Lamb (2005, p. 29).

right and are expensive to implement. Additionally, they are subject to various forms of bias—including response bias (i.e., when the respondent tells the interviewer what he or she wants to hear), selection bias (i.e., when the sample is not chosen in a representative fashion), and self-selection bias (i.e., when only people who want to participate in a poll do so, and the responses of these individuals differ substantially from the hypothetical responses of those who did not participate).

Intelligence Requirements for Shaping

> Dedicated IO intelligence: There is not any.
> —*LTC Jayson Spade, Combatant Command Support Team,*
> *U.S. Pacific Command*[94]

Previous RAND research has shown that shaping activities have very extensive intelligence requirements. Audience segmentation, target-audience analysis, and MOE all require intelligence support. Further, many of these intelligence requirements specifically demand human intelligence (HUMINT), while, traditionally, U.S. forces have focused on technological means of intelligence gathering.[95] This proved to be the case in OIF, in which intelligence support for IO was excellent with regard to technical sources but struggled with human and cultural intelligence.[96]

One observer suggests that part of the problem is that "key IO intelligence requirements are not identified anywhere outside of IO doctrine."[97] To the extent that this is the case, shaping personnel are under an increased burden to make their needs clear to intelligence personnel.

Another factor is that gathering good cultural intelligence and other forms of HUMINT is a difficult and time-consuming task. It

---

[94] Spade and Hill (2006).

[95] Aylwin-Foster (2005).

[96] MAJ John J. Strycula, "Intelligence Support to Information Operations," unpublished briefing, Santa Monica, Calif.: RAND Corporation, undated.

[97] Strycula (undated).

also differs in character from more traditional collection efforts. "Our intelligence is still geared to [maneuver warfare]," one interviewee noted. "Human analysis and human influence is a secondary skill in our sector."[98] Given the need to support counterinsurgency (COIN) requirements, such as understanding the motives, relationships, and likely reactions of key members of the public, there is a need for change in this preparedness for maneuver, PSYOP, and other operations.

Mistakes and Errors

> When we say, "We're investigating something," that's the biggest way to never talk about it again. Intentionally or otherwise, that ends up being stonewalling.
> —*LTC Steve Boylan, U.S. Army Public Affairs*[99]

Shaping is much less challenging when everything goes as planned. Unfortunately, sometimes, U.S. personnel make mistakes or judgment errors, or ordnance goes astray and hits an unintended target. Mistakes can have considerable negative shaping consequences.

In such situations, DoD's shaping responses have habitually been poor. "That's the immediate response capability, and we traditionally have not done that well."[100]

Ongoing operations in Iraq and Afghanistan have included several situations in which U.S. forces have made some kind of substantial error with potentially negative shaping consequences. The burning of Taliban corpses; the reputed mass murder in Haditha, Iraq; and the abuse of prisoners at Abu Ghraib are examples of mistakes with adverse shaping consequences.[101]

---

[98] Bloom (2005).

[99] Boylan (2006).

[100] COL George Rhynedance, Director, Army Public Affairs Center, telephone interview with Christopher Paul, May 23, 2006.

[101] Tom Allard, "Film Rolls as Troops Burn Dead," *Sydney Morning Herald*, October 19, 2005.

Fallout and Second-Order Consequences of Expedient Choices

> As he courts the Sunnis, Col. [Chris] Hickey [a U.S. cavalry
> squadron commander] knows he must take care not to lose the
> Shiites. One of his biggest worries is that horrific attacks like this
> week's suicide bombings—which make three in seven days tar-
> geting Shiites or Iraqi Security Forces—will spur the Shiites to
> take revenge.
>
> *—Greg Jaffe*[102]

Implicit in the recognition that every action has shaping consequences
is the challenge of thinking through the possible consequences. Expedient choices often have negative shaping consequences. Sometimes,
these are obvious: Using threat of force to disperse a crowd will not
make members of that crowd any better disposed toward U.S. forces.
More subtly, failure to disperse the crowd by certain means may
embolden it to further action, thereby leaving an impression of U.S.
inability to control the situation.

This is a situation that is often generically called *the dilemma of
force.*[103] Using force can injure the very noncombatants U.S. forces want
to protect (and shape), but failure to use force in some circumstances
may allow adversary forces to escape or prevail, leading to lack of
belief in friendly force capabilities to overcome the foe. Threat of force
results in the same kinds of credibility issues faced by other shaping
efforts. If threat of force is no longer credible, a valuable shaping tool
is lost.

Sometimes, the consequences of expedient choices are less obvious: Choosing to work with a specific tribe may appear as inappropriate favoritism in the tangled web of political, religious, and tribal dis-

---

[102] Greg Jaffe, "Widening the Gulf: For U.S. Military, a Key Iraq Mission Is Averting Civil
War; a Small Victory in Tal Afar, as Sunnis, Shiites Form Reconciliation Committee; Col.
Hickey's Ramadan Feast," *Wall Street Journal*, October 14, 2005, p. A1.

[103] A dilemma of force confronts coalition forces in Iraq. By many accounts, excessive force
will not resolve the conflict. Others argue that avoidance of force will only embolden the
insurgents (Glenn et al., 2007).

putes in an area.[104] Similarly, while existing indigenous militias might be attractive partners in the short term, their favored status may grant them undue legitimacy in the eyes of locals and—depending on the motivations of the militia leaders—later inhibit political reform.[105]

Damned If You Do, Damned If You Don't: Events with Both Potentially Positive and Negative Shaping Consequences

Another shaping challenge is choosing the lesser of two evils, or managing shaping efforts that have both positive and negative consequences: "damned if you do, damned if you don't."

First, there is the dilemma of force, mentioned previously. Another example is the use of adversary body counts. Body counts earned a bad name in Vietnam, as they were neither a reliable measure nor an appropriate metric with which to gauge success. In Afghanistan and Iraq, U.S. forces initially resisted estimates of enemy killed or wounded. However, detailed information has always been made available about U.S. force fatalities. Said one correspondent,

> The problem we ran into by not reporting enemy killed/captured/ wounded was [that] our press was reporting our casualties very accurately, which gave the impression we were losing, since there [were] no enemy figures to counterbalance.[106]

---

[104]Joshua Kucera, "Djibouti: US Foothold in Africa—African Foothold," *Jane's Defence Weekly*, October 26, 2005b.

[105]The possible second-order consequences of U.S. actions, even well-reasoned ones, can be quite severe. One observer suggests that U.S. policy in Iraq places the United States precariously in the divide between Sunni and Shia Muslims:

> [M]any Sunni Muslims are convinced that the Bush administration is subverting their faith by favouring the Shia cause in Iraq and hence promoting Iranian influence. In the slums of eastern Amman, for example, people hardly knew what Shia Islam was until recently. Now the word has spread that neighbouring Iraq is about to get a Shia-dominated government—and, moreover, that it is all America's fault. ("Political Islam, Forty Shades of Green," *Economist*, February 4, 2006, p. 23)

[106]COL (retired) Glen Collins, "WP: Enemy Body Counts Revived," email to Russell W. Glenn, October 25, 2005.

Command Use of Communication Assets

> [Sometimes, we] have to produce a product without adequate target-audience analysis. That is problematic and is very hard to fix. When a general tells us they want something, you say, "Yes, sir!" and give them the product.
>
> *—Anonymous interview*

> Public affairs is a function of command. I have a first, last, and always obligation to protect the soldiers, but I work for my commander.
>
> *—LTC Ryan Yantis, U.S. Army Public Affairs*[107]

Like all military assets, control over the drafting and dissemination of PSYOP and other messages is a command responsibility. Unfortunately, there are some commanders—or staff officers acting on behalf of their commanders—who do not fully appreciate the subtleties involved in developing and distributing such materials. There are several possible consequences in such situations:

- Interviewed PA, PSYOP, and other IO personnel lamented the missteps made when individuals untrained in the nuances of creating messages took the responsibility upon themselves. Part of the problem is the default assumption that developing such communications is easy. Said one anonymous interviewee,

  > In the 18th Airborne, it is the artillery guy. He's a hell of an artillery officer. He's making great decisions. Are they great officers? Absolutely . . . but they make beginner mistakes [with communications] and lack background, credibility or confidence to argue for what is required.

- There are unnecessary delays in the review of shaping products forwarded for approval.

---

[107] Yantis (2006).

- Accountability and going to the most appropriate source for information are problems. One of our interview respondents recalled an incident involving the relationship between the U.S. Army as a force provider and the COCOMs as those employing the forces in the theater. He recounted a situation in which something within the COCOMs' operational context went poorly, but questions went to Army PA, which knew far less about the incident.[108]

Balancing Short-, Medium-, and Long-Term Goals

The final challenge facing U.S. forces with regard to shaping is the need to balance short-, medium-, and long-term goals. A major challenge of short- versus longer-term objectives involves shaping issues that differ from one phase of operations to the next. Consider a sampling of four phases of an operation: a preoperational phase ("phase 0"); a combat phase ("phase 1"); a postcombat support, stability, and reconstruction phase ("phase 4"); and a final transition to indigenous authority ("end phase").[109] The most significant challenge is to shape toward the end phase from phase 0 forward, but each phase contains its own shaping challenges beyond keeping the ultimate policy goal in mind.

In phase 0, access to the theater of operations may be the primary, though not an insurmountable, challenge. Shaping capabilities generally lack sufficient predeployment access to target audiences for either analysis or message transmission. Since phase 0 is furthest from the end state, the end state may not be well articulated, or the path to the end state may not be clear, which makes shaping toward that path challenging.

The dilemma of force is most challenging during phase 1. General Krulak's three-block war inherently introduces a difficult operational environment, one in which inadvertent noncombatant casualties are a likelihood.[110] Shaping efforts in phase 1 struggle to balance

---

[108] Yantis (2006).

[109] Of course, a different number of phases with different names can be envisioned; these four are cited for illustrative purposes only.

[110] Krulak (1999).

short-term tactical objectives with longer-term postcombat goals. For example, during the investment of Um Qasar during the first phase of OIF, marines encountered regular Iraqi Army and fedayeen units. They responded with tank and missile fire to destroy buildings of tactical value to the enemy. Lieutenant Colonel F. H. R. Howes of the Royal Marines commented on the aftermath, noting, "When I moved through the town with my ops officer, there was an incredibly tense feeling about it. . . . The people were extraordinarily scared of the Americans."[111]

At the beginning of phase 4, there is the potential for an even greater shaping challenge: the "gap" in authority between the regime replaced by the U.S. operation and the new order that phase 4 will introduce. Bridging that gap is a considerable challenge, one that was not fully successful during OIF.[112] It is in phase 4 that shaping shortcomings in phases 0 and 1 become apparent. The possible presence of an insurgency or of intragroup conflict is an additional shaping challenge, one that makes the dilemma of force more acute and, perhaps, changes the balance point for use of force.

Transitioning to the end phase also has unique challenges. Several interview respondents had been in Iraq during the formal "transfer of sovereignty" and noted that it raised a number of issues. One PAO lamented the near blackout of the media associated with the "put an Iraqi face on it" campaign. "Information flow stopped dead, and that created a large vacuum. No one trained or otherwise prepared the Iraqis to take over their own PA," essentially leaving the shaping "battlefield" to adversaries.[113] Another officer lamented the actual loss of authority and consequent loss of control over shaping initiatives:

> We couldn't unilaterally patrol in built-up areas; battalion commanders' ability to detain people was severely restricted. I didn't

---

[111] Lieutenant Colonel F. H. R. Howes, Commander, 42nd Commando Royal Marines during Operation Telic, interview with Russell W. Glenn and Todd C. Helmus, Upavon, UK, December 12, 2003.

[112] Glenn et al. (2007).

[113] Boylan (2006).

control resources like paying salaries. That is how I ensured that every placement got paid, and now I couldn't and it got subject to corruption.[114]

Moving to the end phase requires careful management of non-combatant expectations, expectations of U.S. forces in theater, and others in the region. Failure can seriously undermine support for the new government and coalition.

---

[114] Costantini (2005).

CHAPTER THREE

Applying Marketing Principles to Shaping

The country that owns Madison Avenue ought to win this one easily.

—*Col. John C. Coleman, USMC*[1]

If you are going to defeat an insurgency, the people have got to want to eradicate the violence from their society. You have to go into the street and treat the people as your customers, because they are [the customers] in defeating an insurgency. With the ordinary people, you cannot burst into their houses and slam them up against the wall, because that is not how you treat your customers.

—*Anonymous interview*

It is an oft-cited lament that a nation with the vast skills and resources of the U.S. commercial marketing sector should not have such difficulty in effectively influencing the populations that reside in U.S. operational theaters. Despite considerable differences between military operational venues and the commercial marketplace, a common thread exists, one that allows the weaving of insights from one into new shaping approaches and opportunities in the other.

It is true that the realm of U.S. military stability operations is worlds apart from the comparatively safe and genial environment of

---

[1] Col. John C. Coleman, Chief of Staff, First Marine Expeditionary Force during OIF, interview with Russell W. Glenn, Camp Pendleton, Calif., December 17, 2003.

U.S. business promotion activities.[2] However, there are key similarities between commercial marketing practices and the military's efforts to shape noncombatants. At the most basic level, both efforts have as their objectives a change in behavior. Businesses ultimately seek to move customers to purchase products or services. The military seeks to cultivate popular support (or, at a minimum, to deny that support to adversaries) and motivate compliance with operational objectives. Businesses seek to create products or provide services that meet the needs and satisfy the desires of the marketplace. As our shaping concept highlights, they also seek to instill brand loyalty through a synchronization of word and deed and to combine these with well-integrated promotional activities that are clear and compelling. These business approaches have paid handsome dividends for those who have applied the trade with discipline. Brands such as Starbucks[3] and Apple have captured the hearts and minds of consumers and have reaped financial windfalls in return.

This chapter reviews commercial marketing practices that have been determined to be suitable to shaping civilian populations. Each reviewed marketing practice is followed by its application to operational theaters. Examples from operations in Iraq, Afghanistan, and elsewhere are employed to illustrate these applications, but the recommendations are intended to apply well beyond today's operational environment. Lessons and attendant applications to military shaping operations include the following:

- Know your target audience through segmentation and targeting.
- Apply business positioning strategies to the development of meaningful and salient end states.
- Understand key branding concepts.
- Update the U.S. military brand to reflect operational realities.

---

[2] Commercial businesses rarely operate in environments as complex and dangerous as operational theaters. Their research access to target audiences is relatively straightforward, and, in all but the most rare cases, they do not worry about falling prey to the very customer base they are attempting to serve. In addition, businesses obviously do not need to address complications arising from collateral damage and the use of force.

[3] Starbucks® is a registered trademark of Starbucks Corporation.

- Strategically synchronize the U.S. military brand.
- Synchronize the U.S. military workforce.
- Manage and meet expectations.
- Listen to the voice of the civilian: Make informed decisions.
- Listen to the voice of the civilian: Monitor outcomes.
- Harness the power of influencers.
- Apply discipline and focus to communication campaigns.

Know Your Target Audience Through Segmentation and Targeting

> To win a war you need to know where to attack. . . . We wouldn't have brought the Nazis to their knees if we had landed the Allied forces at Calais instead of the beaches of Normandy.
> —*General Dwight D. Eisenhower*[4]

The Marketing Approach to Segmentation

Through the process called *segmentation and targeting*, modern businesses identify and become intimately familiar with like-minded and well-defined groups of individuals who are most likely to want or need a given product. Businesses then tailor products and promotions to the segment's unique needs, wants, and behaviors. Businesses save valuable resources by not wasting efforts on consumers unlikely to make a purchase.[5]

Sometimes, businesses market a single product to a single group or segment of consumers. Other times, they craft a series of products, each attuned to a different segment. For example, Honda does not develop a single automobile in the hopes of luring a purchase from all prospective car buyers. Instead, it has developed a number of vehicles, including the Civic, Accord, Odyssey, and the luxury Acura line.[6] Each

---

[4] Quoted in Kevin Clancy, "Marketing Strategy Overview," American Marketing Association, 2001.

[5] Clancy (2001).

[6] Honda®, Civic®, Accord®, Odyssey®, and Acura® are registered trademarks of American Honda Motor Company, Inc.

vehicle is targeted to specific segments or groups of people whose life-styles and incomes vary.

Segmentation and targeting involve a three-stage process:

- *Creation of segments:* Researchers employ various techniques, such as one-on-one interviews, focus groups, or online surveys, to collect detailed information on customer needs, interests, and desires. They then divide consumers into smaller groups of buyers who share certain characteristics. These smaller groups are formed on the basis of demographics (e.g., age, gender, income, religion), geography (e.g., national region, country), psychographics (e.g., social class, lifestyle), or behavioral traits (e.g., frequency of product use, attitude toward product). Ultimately, segments must differentiate likely consumer purchase behaviors.[7]
- *Evaluation of segment attractiveness:* Ideal segments for a particular product include the following characteristics: (1) a propensity to purchase the product, (2) a size that makes efforts to market the product worthwhile, (3) reachable through available communication methods, (4) contains a general sample of influencers (i.e., people who like to talk to others about likes and dislikes).[8]
- *Selection of segments to target:* Armed with information about given segments, businesses strategically determine which markets they will enter. A business can target any number of segments with the caveat that the more segments it seeks to lure, the less it may adequately satisfy any one particular segment. Businesses can also apply a differentiated approach, in which they introduce different products to satisfy different segment needs.

ExxonMobil Corporation provides an excellent example in how it has identified a profitable segment for its gasoline service stations. It commissioned a large-scale study that identified five distinct consumer groups of roughly equivalent size:

---

[7]   Philip Kotler and Gary Armstrong, *Principles of Marketing*, 11th ed., Upper Saddle River, N.J.: Pearson Education, 2006, p. 196.

[8]   Kotler and Armstrong (2006, p. 196).

Car Buffs are generally high-income, middle-aged men who drive 25,000 to 50,000 miles a year. They buy a premium gasoline with a credit card, purchase sandwiches and drinks from the convenience store, and will sometimes wash their cars at the car wash.

Loyalists are men and women with moderate to high incomes who are loyal to a brand and sometimes to a particular station. They frequently buy premium gasoline and pay in cash.

Speedsters are upwardly mobile Gen Xers. They are constantly on the go, live in their cars and snack heavily from the convenience store.

Soccer Moms are usually housewives who shuttle their children around during the day and use whatever gasoline station is based in town or along their route of travel.

Price Shoppers generally are not loyal either to a brand or to a particular station and rarely buy the premium line. They are frequently on tight budgets and efforts to woo them have been the basis of marketing strategies for years.[9]

When the data were analyzed, marketers discovered that Car Buffs and Loyalists constituted only 38 percent of the population but represented 77 percent of the potential profitability. They chose these two segments for ExxonMobil's marketing campaign. This research brought an enormous advantage to ExxonMobil, as "once Mobil knew the target, it knew whom to talk to and where to find them, how to communicate with them, in which media, about which products and services, at what price."[10]

Applying Segmentation and Targeting Techniques to Operational Theaters

The United States and its coalition partners should arm themselves with information about their prospective "customers," whose support

---

[9]   Clancy (2001).

[10]   Clancy (2001).

the military requires to conduct effective COIN and other stability operations. Like a business selling a product, the military cannot expect everyone in a given region to accept its presence and message equally. In an occupation-like contingency, there will be at least three general constellations of people: Those who quietly or violently resist coalition objectives and presence; those who quietly or openly support coalition presence and objectives; and those who remain in the middle, unsure of their ultimate allegiance.[11]

A segmentation research program would offer the military several advantages. The specific motivations of each segment can be known in terms of what end states and operational approaches are most likely to increase their respective support and what resources could be devoted to and tailored uniquely for target audiences of greatest opportunity.

To conduct segmentation research in a theater of operations, the military must collect as much information as possible on the population. It can collect this information through individual interviews and enemy prisoner-of-war interrogations, focus groups, and surveys. Where the population is hesitant to speak with coalition force representatives, the military should employ third-party researchers. This research should focus on understanding attitudes related to the previous or current indigenous government, U.S. and coalition forces, and possible end states. Respondents should be asked about their views on real or hypothetical coalition policies, including use of force, soldier-civilian interactions, reconstruction opportunities, and governance. The military should also seek information related to the following variables:

- geographic characteristics (e.g., national region, city location, size)
- demographics (e.g., age, gender, family size, income, occupation, education, religion race, nationality)
- psychographics (e.g., social class, lifestyle, personality)

---

[11] As Table 3.1 suggests, these three segments would likely expand to five segments. "Quiet and violent" resisters would likely be distilled into two segments (e.g., "die-hards" and "skeptics") as would "quiet and open" supporters (e.g., "reformers" and "bandwagons").

- behaviors (e.g., early adopter, influencer, Western buying habits, degree of support for coalition, degree of support for end state, support for adversaries, loyalty to tribal or religious authorities, attitudes toward coalition use of force, reconstruction priorities).[12]

Individuals with segmentation and targeting experience should review the collected data and help the coalition identify ways to group the population according to its level of anticipated support. While attitudes toward the coalition are critical to defining broad segments (e.g., negative, neutral, and positive attitudes), other variables will also play into this, such as education, Western product-buying habits, and early adopter (one who adopts new trends and products ahead of others) and influencer characteristics.[13] Table 3.1 presents a hypothetical construct of segments.

The military must then identify which groups it will target with its shaping campaign. From the hypothetical segments listed in Table 3.1, campaign planners may decide to specifically target the uncommitted, the reformers, and the bandwagons. Ultimately, segments will serve only as a general guide for operations and communication. Unlike a business that sells only a single product to a particular segment, coalition forces will likely make numerous policy and operational decisions, each of which will have a particular impact on popular acceptance of coalition forces. In this regard, the military should consider how these policies will differentially impact each of the identified segments.[14]

---

[12] Adapted from Kotler and Armstrong (2006, p. 196).

[13] John (Jack) W. Leslie, Chair, Weber Shandwick Worldwide, interview with Todd C. Helmus and Russell W. Glenn, New York, February 6, 2006.

[14] Fine-tuned segments are developed once coalition forces are in theater. Military planners will also have to develop tentative segments prior to initiating operations. This is important in that messaging and actions during this stage are critical to shaping audiences for U.S. force entrance. Before the United States enters a theater, the level of direct access to the population may vary according to whether U.S. forces were invited by the host nation, as was the case in Somalia, or whether they arrive via major combat operations. In the first case, the host indigenous government may allow an initial survey team into the country and possibly assist in data collection. In the latter case, direct research access to the population will be very limited. Consequently, segmenting efforts will probably be based on information captured in country studies, interviews with foreign nationals, and other available resources.

Table 3.1
Hypothetical Construct of Theater-Based Segments

Segment Name	Positive Coalition Attitudes (%)	College Educated (%)	Early Adopters (%)	Likelihood of Expressing Opinions to Others	Occasionally Purchase Western Products (%)
Die-hards	10	15	10	High	15
Skeptics	20	20	30	Medium	30
Uncommitted	40	30	45	Low	50
Reformers	60	60	80	Medium	75
Bandwagons	80	80	85	High	95

Apply Business Positioning Strategies to the Development of Meaningful and Salient End States

Coalition force end states should provide an element of hope for the indigenous population, thus motivating popular support for the military intervention. However, the likelihood that the coalition could correctly identify the desires of a foreign population without actively understanding that group seems extraordinarily low. Businesses are similarly challenged in crafting identities for their products. They overcome this problem through a process called *positioning*, which holds valuable lessons for the development and presentation of operational end states.

The Marketing Approach to Positioning

With unlimited time and a consumer's complete attention, marketers could communicate everything there is to know about their products or services. Unfortunately, this is rarely the case, and, at best, busi-

---

It may also be possible to conduct virtual focus groups with members of the population via Internet chat rooms. More sophisticated individual surveys may also be conducted online. In addition, intelligence assets should be directed to fill in data holes and confirm or reject hypotheses.

nesses can develop a core message that the target audience will remember and care about. This core message is encapsulated in the product's positioning.[15] Positioning is a branding concept. While the term *brand* often refers to a product name (e.g., Lexus is a brand name),[16] it is more importantly construed as the collection of perceptions in the minds of consumers (e.g., Lexus may mean different things to different people: expensive, luxury, Japanese, and so on). Positioning is the intended meaning or brand identity a product will have in consumers' minds; it "articulates the goal that a consumer will achieve by using the [product] and explains why it is superior to other means of accomplishing this goal."[17] (Branding concepts are addressed in more detail in the section titled "Branding Concepts Apply to the U.S. Military," later in this chapter.)

A product's positioning is encapsulated in a positioning statement. The content of positioning statements varies from business to business but, in general, includes four key elements. First, they identify the product's target audience (determined via market segmentation). Next, they identify the "point of difference" or brand promise. The brand promise is the brand's central concept and identifies the goal that consumers will achieve by using the product. Wal-Mart, in its tagline, promises "Always Low Prices™," while Subway promises that you'll "Eat Fresh™."[18] Table 3.2 presents positioning promises for an assortment of other brands. Finally, positioning statements often include a "reason to believe." A reason to believe buttresses the point of difference with supporting evidence.[19] Other positioning strategies include

---

[15] Clancy (2001).

[16] Lexus®, a registered trademark, is a division of Toyota Motor Sales, U.S.A., Inc.

[17] Alice M. Tybout and Brian Sternthal, "Brand Positioning," in Alice M. Tybout and Tim Calkins, eds., *Kellogg on Branding*, Hoboken, N.J.: John Wiley and Sons, 2005, pp. 11–26 [p. 11].

[18] Subway® and its tagline are trademarks or registered trademarks of Doctor's Associates Inc.; Wal-Mart® and its tagline are trademarks or registered trademarks of Wal-Mart Stores, Inc.

[19] Tybout and Sternthal (2005, p. 12).

Table 3.2
Brand Positioning Promises

Brand	Brand Promise
Apple	Easy to use and stylish computers and electronic equipment
Charmin	Softness[a]
FedEx	Guaranteed next-day delivery[a] (Absolutely Positively Overnight®)
GE	Improves the quality of life[a] (Imagination at Work™)
Visa	Accepted everywhere[a] (It's Everywhere You Want to Be®)
BMW	Performance for driving enthusiasts[a] (The Ultimate Driving Machine®)
Hefty	Strength[a]
Coca-Cola	Authentic, real, original[a]
Lexus	Luxury
Nike	Athletic performance and competition
Honda	Reliability

NOTE: "Brand promises" are expectations and perceptions of brands extrapolated from advertising and other forms of marketing. Charmin® is a registered trademark of The Procter and Gamble Company. FedEx® and its tagline are registered trademarks. GE® and its tagline are trademarks or registered trademarks of General Electric Company. Visa® and its tagline are registered trademarks of Visa International Service Association. BMW® and its tagline are registered trademarks of BMW Group. Hefty® is a registered trademark of Pactiv Corporation. Coca-Cola® is a registered trademark of the Coca-Cola Company. Nike® is a registered trademark of Nike, Inc.

[a] Adapted from Clancy (2001).

an emotional end benefit that customers will experience by using the product. Black and Decker recently relaunched the DeWalt[20] line of power tools, which is marketed to professionals. It has the following positioning:

---

[20] Black and Decker® and DeWalt® are registered trademarks of Black and Decker Corporation.

To the tradesman who uses his power tools to make a living and cannot afford downtime on the job (*target*), DeWalt professional power tools . . . are more dependable than other brands of professional power tools [*promise*] because they are engineered to the brand's historic high-quality standards and are backed by Black & Decker's extensive service network and guarantee to repair or replace any tool within 48 hours (*reasons to believe*).[21]

Core brand concepts are created with the customer in mind. If the concept is not attuned to how the customer thinks and feels about the brand or what the customer needs and wants, it is doomed to failure. To arrive at the positioning concept, businesses first identify product attributes and benefits that might motivate customers in the identified segment. This research can be conducted simultaneously with the segmentation research.[22] Focus groups and in-depth individual interviews inquire about the different attitudes people have about the brand and the attributes and benefits that they find particularly motivating.[23] Once a list of candidate attributes and benefits is created, marketers then test concepts that have the most widespread appeal. Focus groups are again useful in this regard, as is survey research, which provides consumers with a list of concepts and asks about their likelihood of purchasing the product. Concepts that have the most widespread support are then chosen to represent the brand.[24]

AT&T and State Farm[25] provide classic examples of this approach. AT&T's market research showed that people make calls because they

---

[21] Tybout and Sternthal (2005, p. 13). Emphasis in the original with the exception of bracketed text.

[22] Clancy (2001).

[23] Some marketers use conjoint analysis, a tool that shows different audiences various combinations of attributes and benefits and inquires about their interest in purchasing the product.

[24] Bobby Calder, Professor of Marketing, Northwestern University, interview with Todd C. Helmus, Evanston, Ill., February 21, 2006.

[25] AT&T* and its tagline are trademarks or registered trademarks of AT&T Knowledge Ventures. State Farm* and its tagline are trademarks or registered trademarks of State Farm Mutual Automobile Insurance Company.

want to enjoy the emotional connection of keeping in touch with friends and loved ones. A former AT&T analyst explained that "when we heard that consistently, it led us to the tag line of 'Reach Out and Touch Someone™.'" He continued, "We realized it was something the audience cared about, not what we wanted."[26] Similarly, State Farm listened to its customers and found that they wanted someone to help them if they had a problem. The company realized that its identity was not insurance policies, per se, but as a helpful neighborhood agency. From this insight, State Farm developed the "Like a Good Neighbor™" promise.[27]

In addition to specifying how consumers are supposed to think about the brand, positioning guides the communication strategy and becomes the light that guides all brand behaviors and communications. Consider the example of Hallmark[28] greeting cards. Hallmark is positioned as a provider of "superior quality in communicating sentiments."[29] This positioning guides virtually all aspects of how the company conducts its business. It uses high-quality paper products for its cards, charges a premium price, and distributes its products in its Gold Crown® stores. Its advertising relies on carefully crafted two-minute emotional ads that are nestled among quality family programming. This example gets at the heart of positioning. A properly crafted positioning strategy provides a brand focus that is communicated in virtually every aspect of the marketing campaign. This focus helps ensure that the brand's intended meaning is implanted firmly in potential customers' minds.[30]

---

[26] Anonymous chief marketing officer, interview with Todd C. Helmus, New York, March 1, 2006.

[27] Keith Reinhard, Chair, DDB Advertising, interview with Todd C. Helmus, New York, February 28, 2006.

[28] Hallmark® is a registered trademark of Hallmark Cards Incorporated.

[29] Tybout and Sternthal (2005, p. 26).

[30] Tybout and Sternthal (2005, p. 26).

Applying Positioning to Operational Theaters

Marketing positioning tactics may help the military develop and present meaningful and salient end states. In applying this approach, the military should first seek the end state–related opinions of the indigenous population. Focus groups and in-depth interviews, which could be conducted simultaneously with segmentation research, are an excellent source of information. As Bobby Calder of Northwestern University suggests, it is not major research, as the military might conduct 70 to 80 qualitative interviews for an area the size of Iraq.[31] The goal is to learn people's attitudes and beliefs about U.S. forces and their objectives. Possible end states about which to inquire could include democratically elected government, security, rule of law, economic reforms, or infrastructure development.[32]

Shaping personnel should next seek to make sense of indigenous opinions and form them into candidate positioning concepts. Consultation with marketing professionals might facilitate this task. If concepts are to be of any use, they must be widely shared among the respondents. Other guidelines for concept development should account for operational realities. First, the concepts must not conflict with U.S. end-state interests and messages used to gain international and U.S. popular support. They must correspond to core U.S. values and should be something that U.S. and coalition personnel can actually deliver.[33] They should also be in line with the goals and priorities of key indigenous stakeholders who will likely form an indigenous government responsible for making this end state a reality. Once identified, concepts can be played back to the population via surveys or additional focus groups, with the concept receiving the most support chosen for the campaign.

---

[31] Calder (2006).

[32] Questionnaires with a list of possible end states could also be provided for respondents to rate their respective attitudes on a 0-to-10, negative-to-positive scale.

[33] One reviewer of this monograph commented that the proposed end state should not necessarily correspond to core U.S. values but should focus exclusively on the target audience.

The final concept is articulated in a positioning statement akin to that described here.[34] This positioning would then guide all U.S. force communications and actions concerning U.S. objectives. Importantly, it would introduce clarity to campaign goals and resonate meaningfully with the population.

Understand Key Branding Concepts

An Introduction to Key Branding Concepts

> A brand is the sum of the good, the bad, the ugly, and the off-strategy.
>
> —*Scott Bedbury, brand consultant*[35]

Brands are the associations that surround products' or services' names or symbols. Brands are not the product per se or the factual truth of that product, but, rather, the perceptions people have of that product. People form perceptions about a brand name through all the different interactions they have with it, such as through advertisements, product features, and customer service representatives.[36] These different interfaces between the brand and customer are called *touchpoints*. Northwestern University marketing professor Tim Calkins aptly quotes a marketing executive who observes,

> A brand is the feel of your business card, the way the company's phone is answered, the assistant coordinator who's had one too many after work yet has handed out her business card while at

---

[34] Consider one positioning statement example that is derived from a hypothetical "free from tyranny" concept: To [insert indigenous target audience] who have lived under brutal oppression: U.S. forces will rid your country of tyranny [promise] because we have opposed it for 200 years [reason to believe] and support your living free from tyranny [emotional end benefit].

[35] Quoted in Alex Wipperfürth, *Brand Hijack: Marketing Without Marketing*, New York: Portfolio, 2005, p. 41.

[36] Tim Calkins, "The Challenge of Branding," in Alice M. Tybout and Tim Calkins, eds., *Kellogg on Branding*, Hoboken, N.J.: John Wiley and Sons, 2005b, pp. 1–8 [pp. 1–4].

the bar, the disgruntled salesman who complains to his family and friends that the company he works for is really ripping people off for big profits on the products he sells, the tone of a letter, the employee who doesn't help the customer, the vice president who tells too rude a joke in an inappropriate setting, the package that's almost impossible to open, the receptionist at the corporate office who continues to chat with a fellow worker when a customer arrives, an over-long wait at the cash register, the instructions that are too hard to follow. . . . I could go on and on. The brand is every touchpoint and every thought the customer has about the brand.[37]

Properly managed brands have a unique and clear identity and are defined by a clear and nonconflicting set of associations. Consider the following brands: Apple, Lexus, Porsche, Coca-Cola, Mountain Dew, Starbucks, and Ritz-Carlton.[38] Each brand invokes a unique meaning that is likely shared by many readers. Apple might raise thoughts of style and simplicity, Starbucks a strong brew in a friendly atmosphere, Coca-Cola a refreshing taste, and Ritz-Carlton luxury.

Creating a brand that has a unique and clear identity is enormously difficult, because businesses must synchronize and align every brand-consumer touchpoint to convey a single, clear, and uniform message. To accomplish this, companies first develop an intended brand identity through the positioning process. As suggested previously, the centerpiece of this positioning is the promise the brand makes to consumers about delivering a particular product feature or benefit. This concept must meet a simple reality test of what the product and overarching brand experience can actually deliver, and it must be in tune with the needs and desires of the marketplace. Once an intended identity is created, it must serve as a strict guide to all brand-related behaviors. These brand behaviors include communications, corporate strategy,

---

[37] Calkins (2005b, p. 6).

[38] Porsche® is a registered trademark of Dr. Ing. h.c.F. Porsche AG. Mountain Dew® is a registered trademark of PepsiCo, Inc. Ritz-Carlton® is a registered trademark of the Ritz-Carlton Company L.L.C.

and the words and deeds of the brand's many employees and service representatives.

Branding Concepts Apply to the U.S. Military

Virtually every organization or entity in the public sphere has a brand identity. The U.S. military is no different. During stability operations, the indigenous population will form perceptions of the U.S. military. These perceptions will constitute the U.S. military brand identity and will heavily influence how the population aligns its support. A force that is perceived as helpful and serving the best interests of the population will be far better accepted than a force perceived as hostile, insensitive, and rude.

Two choices confront the military in its approach to managing these perceptions. The military can leave these associations and its corresponding reputation to chance, or it can guide them along a focused path. This is the value of positioning. Positioning articulates the core meaning and purpose of a brand, and, when properly inculcated into the organization, guides all organizational behaviors and communications. If the U.S. military cares about instilling positive indigenous-audience attitudes toward U.S. operating forces in theater, all members of the U.S. force must carry that mindset and be properly aligned to that goal.

What follows is a discussion of how the U.S. military brand identity can be adjusted to suit new operational realities. We subsequently address military applications of commercial brand-synchronization strategies.

Update the U.S. Military Brand to Reflect Operational Realities

The Marketing Approach to Updating Brands

Commercial brands rarely last forever. Although some, such as Budweiser[39] and Coca-Cola, have been around for years, most brands enjoy

---

[39] Budweiser® is a registered trademark of Anheuser-Busch, Inc.

the light of success for a limited period before new competitors, changing social mores, and advancing technology outpace them. The lifespan
of a product or brand is referred to as the *product life cycle* (PLC). PLCs
can apply to a class of products, a particular product brand name, or
a product's positioning. Gas street lamps are a product class that has
largely disappeared from the American landscape. Seventy-five years
ago, Fels Naptha, Octagon, and Kirkman were brand-name leaders in
the powdered laundry soap field. These brands no longer exist.[40] Figure
3.1 depicts a typical PLC. Following a period of slow growth during
the introduction, sales grow rapidly until eventually reaching a state of
maturity, in which growth slows and the brand reaches its peak in sales
and popular acceptance. Sales then decline as the product becomes
outdated or is bested by competition.

**Figure 3.1
Product Life-Cycle Diagram**

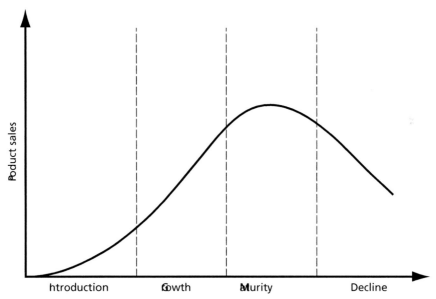

SOURCE: "The Product Life Cycle," *QuickMBA.com*, undated. Used with permission.

RAND *MG607-3.1*

---

[40] Kotler and Armstrong (2006, p. 296).

To maintain or recapture leading market positions, companies must adapt by changing the product's positioning to suit new competitive needs. This new positioning may reflect a modification in different product attributes, such as a change in quality, features, or styling. The slow pour of Heinz[41] ketchup once embodied the brand's positioning of the ketchup as having a thick, rich consistency. Possibly reflecting a new societal focus on speed and efficiency, Heinz still maintains that its ketchup is "thick and rich," but the positioning now focuses more on its new upside-down squeeze packaging that is "always ready when you are."[42] Similarly, McDonald's[43] suffered a tired brand identity, increasing concerns from a health-conscious marketplace, and a saturated fast-food market. It countered this slump with new health-conscious menu items and a hip positioning, reflected in the tagline, "I'm lovin' it™."[44] In highly competitive markets, adaptation is always a key to success in maintaining market leadership.

A New Brand for the U.S. Military

> The United States is fighting the Global War on Terrorism with a mindset shaped by the Cold War. That mindset helped create today's joint force that possesses nearly irresistible powers in conventional wars against nation-states. Unfortunately, the wars the United States must fight today in Afghanistan and Iraq are not of this variety.
>
> —*LTC M. Wade Markel, U.S. Army*[45]

Since before World War II, the U.S. military has developed a brand identity based on a force of might. Like all good consumer brands, it

---

[41] Heinz® is a registered trademark of H.J. Heinz Company.

[42] Heinz, "Heinz Top-Down Ketchup™," *Heinz World*, undated Web page.

[43] McDonald's® and its tagline are trademarks or registered trademarks of McDonald's Corporation.

[44] Shirley Leung, "Arch Support: McDonald's CEO Talks About the Moves That Are Turning His Chain Around," *Wall Street Journal*, classroom ed., April 2004.

[45] Quoted in Aylwin-Foster (2005, p. 8).

was incredibly focused and clear. It served the strategic purpose, like consumer brands do, of imprinting a clear identity on the minds of its intended target, the nation's adversaries. It similarly served as a guiding light for training and corporate behavior and as a reassurance for a second audience, the U.S. public.

More recently, however, the military has been embroiled in numerous smaller conflicts, from Somalia to Haiti and Bosnia. Currently, U.S. and allied forces are engaged in COIN operations in Iraq and Afghanistan. Many U.S. adversaries in these regions have seen the truth behind the brand: The United States cannot be defeated in open-terrain, force-on-force combat. Instead, the new modus operandi is to retreat into complex terrain, don a civilian cloak, and steadily inflict losses that weaken U.S. public resolve. Deftness of touch in interacting with civilians, applying focused combat power, and collecting HUMINT have become the requirements of the day. Addressing these requirements with brute force has hindered operational success in both Iraq and Afghanistan. Some may hope that such operational trends are only a blip on the historical screen and that a U.S. brand focused solely on the application of superior firepower may again carry the day. This is unlikely to be the case.

Like consumer products positioned and branded for a day gone by, so too is the U.S. military brand identity now—at least in part—out of date. A new and more effective U.S. military brand identity is critical to the success of stability operations for several reasons. We posit that engendering positive indigenous attitudes toward U.S. military presence is important in that it will encourage support of the U.S. military, make U.S. forces more approachable to civilians, and enable more effective and trustworthy communications. The perceptions that people hold about the U.S. military (or the U.S. military brand identity) will prove crucial in molding relevant attitudes. Importantly, an effective brand identity also internally guides corporate actions and communication. It is similar to a commander's intent, imbued from boot camp to combat and beyond.

Developing a coherent external and internal branding strategy presents a formidable challenge to the U.S. military. First, what is needed today is a military with an image and capability that addresses both ends of the operational spectrum—and everything in between. The same infantry battalion that fights tooth and nail to establish a foothold in enemy-held urban territory must further conduct kind-hearted and culturally attuned stability-and-support operations while being prepared for the administration of restrained violence directed at insurgents.[46] It is a duality, hard and soft, that does not fit easily into any clear operational concept or brand-like ethos.

Defense strategist Thomas Barnett understands how difficult it is to have a single military force prepared for both ends of the spectrum. In his book, *The Pentagon's New Map*, Barnett recommends bifurcating U.S. forces into the *System Administrators*, light infantry units well capable of defending themselves but specialized to bring order to a nation in chaos, and the *Leviathan Force*, a mix of stealthy submarines, long-range bombers, and extremely well-trained and highly armed combat soldiers.[47] It is classic marketing in the sense that each force holds a unique, clear, well-defined, and focused position in the marketplace. Members of each force know who they are and what is expected of them. Importantly, the application of each force for different contingencies would send a clear signal to civilians and adversaries alike. Regardless, political realities, entrenched organizational structures, and practical matters such as personnel and funding constraints make the implementation of Barnett's recommendations highly unlikely.

U.S. foreign policy presents another branding challenge. During the Cold War, U.S. foreign policy was guided by an overwhelming principle of freedom and human rights that served as a beacon to people oppressed by communist dictators. While these principles still guide the United States, they are often no longer clearly and positively perceived by foreign populations, particularly those in the Middle East. In the minds of virtually any beholder, the U.S. military is closely intertwined with its government. One, therefore, cannot separate the actions of the military from those of the government and the foreign policy it serves. Absent a clear brand identity that guides U.S. for-

---

[46] Krulak (1999).

[47] Thomas P. M. Barnett, *The Pentagon's New Map: War and Peace in the Twenty-First Century*, New York: G. P. Putnam's Sons, 2004.

eign policy, any brand identity applied to the military runs the risk of confusing audiences and failing in communicating desired messages.

These are not insurmountable challenges. A private, nonprofit business group, Business for Diplomatic Action, is currently creating a unique and successful brand-development process for the U.S. Travel Industry Association with the goal of portraying a clear and friendly U.S. identity to those visiting from overseas.[48] Business for Diplomatic Action consults key organizational stakeholders to create an intended brand identity that resonates deeply within those organizations while also being attuned to key consumer audiences.

We recommend that the U.S. military and, ideally, the U.S. government consider undergoing such a branding process. It may reveal previously unforeseen ways to create an internal and external identity that successfully encompasses the operational spectrums that are likely to challenge the U.S. military for years to come.

In suggesting how such a brand strategy might be applied to the United States, Business for Diplomatic Action's chair, advertising guru Keith Reinhard, suggests a simple yet elegant promise: "We will help you." While his recommendation was meant for U.S. foreign policy, the "helping" promise may be a positioning message applicable to the military. It provides an intent for U.S. forces that covers the application of combat power while also meeting the test for a range of other operations. It serves as a message of inspiration for indigenous audiences, one that encompasses—and thus would not conflict with—a wide variety of potential end states. It is a promise that can be kept, and, because it positions the United States as a partner of indigenous populations, it does not usurp their authority, dignity, or responsibility.

MGen. James Mattis created a de facto branding strategy for his 1st Marine Division while readying for OIF in 2003, drawing on the self-written epitaph of Roman general and dictator Lucius Cornelius Sulla Felix (c. 138 BCE–78 BCE): "No better friend—no worse enemy."[49] General Mattis employed this phrase as a way of expressing his intent. He used it to help prepare his forces (and perhaps the

---

[48] Reinhard (2006).

[49] See "Lucius Cornelius Sulla," *Encyclopaedia Britannica*, 2007.

Iraqi public) for upcoming interactions between the two groups. It is a valuable example in that it covers the full operational spectrum faced by U.S. forces and conveys a meaningful message to a broad range of foreign audiences. While there was some disagreement among marketing experts regarding the details of his phrase as a brand, it effectively demonstrates many of the characteristics of successful branding and is a worthy starting point for further consideration.[50]

Strategically Synchronize the U.S. Military Brand

A brand is most effective when it communicates a single, clear message to its target audience. They communicate this message by synchronizing brand-related actions and communications. It is the proverbial "one message, many voices." Ensuring that the brand identity informs strategic decisionmaking is one critical ingredient to brand synchronization.

The Marketing Approach to Strategic Synchronization

Most corporate firms are stratified along one of two lines: a house of brands and a branded house. Proctor and Gamble exemplifies a house-

---

[50] Interviewed marketing experts made the following comments in reference to the "no better friend—no worse enemy" branding strategy:

> Brilliant, but do you have standards that hold yourself to that promise? What is it that supports that? Do you train differently, message differently, act differently? . . . Completely doable. (David Coronna, Senior Counselor, Burson-Marsteller, interview with Todd C. Helmus, Chicago, Ill., February 24, 2006)

> It is a double promise. . . . It would be a lot easier in bifurcated units [akin to that recommended by Thomas Barnett] because it then becomes clear what I'm supposed to do. There would be overall unifying goals in terms of what do I value, what do I fight for. . . . [In "no better friend—no worse enemy"], what do I do? Seems to be I do both. (Reinhard, 2006)

> The front side neutralizes the end. It is threatening. You typically don't win people over with threats. It is better to be focused and single-minded than to have multiple messages. The message can't be crafted around what we have to say, but something that the people care about. (Anonymous chief marketing officer, interview with Todd C. Helmus, New York, March 1, 2006)

of-brands model in that it markets many different products, including Pampers®, Old Spice®, and Olay®. Each branded product has its own positioning, and the product labels lack a prominently visible Proctor and Gamble logo. The house-of-brands concept minimizes corporate risk, as scandals that afflict an individual product will not necessarily tarnish the corporate reputation or that of other brands offered by that corporation.[51]

In a branded-house model, a company applies a single brand identity across multiple product offerings. Dell Inc., for example, offers a variety of products, from desktop computers and laptops to flat-screen TVs. Each product carries the Dell® brand name and fits within with Dell's positioning of value and helpful customer service. Several challenges confront the branded-house model. Scandal that affects one product line impacts the entire corporate image. Branded houses are also limited in their development of new products. New products are called *line extensions* and are exemplified by Apple's successful endeavor to move from personal computers to portable music players. Each line extension can add to or detract from the brand identity. Companies are tempted to introduce products that fail to fit under the overall brand concept.[52] For example, BIC is known for its functional yet inexpensive disposable pens and lighters. BIC was unsuccessful in launching a BIC-branded perfume because the "inexpensive and disposable" brand identity does not lend itself well to perfume. Similarly, the gunmaker Smith and Wesson[53] unsuccessfully launched a line of mountain bikes.[54] Businesses must ensure that a new product fits the original brand's positioning. Apple is known for style and functionality in electronics. The introduction of the Apple iPod® fits extremely well with these themes and maintains the integrity and focus of the corporate brand.

---

[51] Tim Calkins, "Brand Portfolio Strategy," in Alice M. Tybout and Tim Calkins, eds., *Kellogg on Branding*, Hoboken, N.J.: John Wiley and Sons, 2005a, pp. 104–128.

[52] Calkins (2005a).

[53] Smith and Wesson® is a registered trademark of Smith and Wesson Corp.

[54] Calkins (2005a, p. 118).

Managing the U.S. Force Operational Portfolio

The U.S. government operates under a branded-house concept. As such, U.S. forces and the operations they conduct act as a kind of line extension of the parent government. U.S. military actions influence world perceptions of the United States, and U.S. government policies, official or otherwise, carry implications for the U.S. military.

The U.S. military must take pains to ensure that its operations and other actions do not conflict with intended brand identity, shaping themes, or other strategies designed to earn popular support among local populations. However, the United States and its allies must, at times, risk popular support by conducting kinetic operations. Virtually any kinetic operation has the potential to alienate civilians. Global media send uncensored, near-instantaneous visuals of the battlefront, where civilian deaths and the destruction of homes can run high. These actions may appear to contradict U.S. shaping-campaign goals.[55]

In the business analogy, when branded-house firms add new product lines that may not seemingly fit well with the parent brand, marketing experts recommend that businesses help customers understand the basis of the fit.[56] During combat, U.S. shaping operations must thoroughly educate civilians, local government officials, media, and the international community about the necessity for such operations, how they fit into U.S. assistance efforts, and the restraint exercised in lieu of other modes of firepower that could be brought to bear. The burden of responsibility for U.S. force action should similarly be placed directly at the feet of targeted adversaries. Major General (retired) Geoffrey Lambert notes that the United States values civilian life. It is essential that leadership communicate that when U.S. armed forces conduct combat operations. They should, for example,

---

[55] MG (retired) Geoffrey Lambert, Booz Allen Hamilton, Retired Special Operations Forces Mentor, Joint Forces Command, J9, interview with Todd C. Helmus, Tampa, Fla., January 20, 2006.

[56] Bridgette M. Braig and Alice M. Tybout, "Brand Extensions," in Alice M. Tybout and Tim Calkins, eds., *Kellogg on Branding*, Hoboken, N.J.: John Wiley and Sons, 2005, pp. 91–103 [p. 96].

- explain the concept of ROE
- clarify why permissive ROE are necessary
- tell audiences why it is sometimes necessary to destroy buildings
- describe why these actions unavoidably put civilians at risk.[57]

Such an explanation should come with an expression of sincere regret when innocent lives are lost and with promises to rebuild and restore what was broken, when feasible. While certainly not a foolproof means of avoiding the negative consequences of kinetic engagements, such efforts (with promises fulfilled) could be an effective part of a larger campaign seeking to favorably shape indigenous public opinion (one with potential regional and wider implications as well).[58]

Marketing experts Bridgette M. Braig and Alice M. Tybout recommend that businesses assess the impact a line extension has on the parent brand and ensure that the effects are consistent with the brand's long-term goals.[59] U.S. forces should follow a similar strategy by frequently assessing relevant publics' opinions and focusing polls and informal surveys to measure the public relations impact of specific operations. Such information-gathering can have a number of benefits. First, U.S. forces may learn what ROE are deemed more acceptable. It may be that the population is willing to accept less restrictive ROE if they work to defeat an unpopular group. Second, coalition forces may

---

[57] Lambert (2006).

[58] A less kinetic example pertains to U.S. efforts to build and improve military bases in Iraq. Contrary to the intentions of coalition forces, the Iraqi population views many of these construction efforts as attempts to build permanent operational sites. The implications are significant. Recent polling indicates that 41 percent of Iraqis who approve of anticoalition attacks "do not favor a near-term withdrawal." However, a full 90 percent believe that the United States intends a permanent basing presence, and 87 percent believe that the United States would not leave even if so directed by the Iraqi government. Anticoalition attacks might therefore be construed as an effort to motivate an eventual, if not near-term, exit by coalition forces. Consequently, had U.S. and coalition forces thought through the impact of permanent basing, they might have either taken a different approach or better explained their intentions (Program on International Policy Attitudes, *What the Iraqi Public Wants: A WorldPublicOpinion.org Poll*, January 31, 2006, p. 7).

[59] Braig and Tybout (2005, pp. 100–101).

learn how messaging impacts indigenous attitudes, thus allowing them to more effectively address different population segments.

U.S. government policies influence indigenous perceptions toward a U.S. military force presence. Examples of this include U.S. policies regarding Israel and the internment of prisoners at Guantanamo Bay. Policy decisions can impact attitudes for years. U.S. failure to support the Shiite uprising against Saddam Hussein immediately following the 1991 Gulf War left many Iraqis hesitant to support the U.S. presence in 2003. Other events not directly related to theater policies can also influence indigenous views—for example, debates in Washington regarding U.S. force withdrawals from Iraq.

While U.S. government actions and statements can significantly and inadvertently shape indigenous audience opinions, the U.S. military is often powerless to change the situation. The recommendations mentioned here still apply. First, the U.S. military should attempt to measure the impact of these actions on indigenous attitudes toward U.S. forces. When feasible, the military should explain government decisions that generate negative attitudes. U.S. forces could present debates over continued force presence as reflective of a democratic nation's decision process rather than necessarily implying impending withdrawal.

Synchronize the U.S. Military Workforce

> If you are the richest nation in the world, changing structures, systems and platform capabilities is one thing: changing the way your people think, interact and behave under extreme duress is much more difficult.
>
> —*Nigel Aylwin-Foster*[60]

The second critical ingredient of brand synchronization is ensuring that the interactions between brand representatives and customers properly reinforce the intended brand image. The following discussion addresses how businesses align the actions of their representatives and how the U.S. military can follow suit.

---

[60] Aylwin-Foster (2005, p. 3).

The Marketing Approach to Workforce Synchronization

Service firms present a unique challenge to delivering on a firm's brand identity. Such organizations deliver services that range from airline flights to car tune-ups and legal assistance. Unlike products such as blue jeans and laptops, services are intangible (i.e., they cannot be physically handled), unfold in real time (i.e., after the purchase, there is little to show for one's money), and are often complex (i.e., few can tell whether provided legal aid meets acceptable practice standards). Because of these factors, consumers judge services based on the most tangible information available: the interactions they have with the personnel delivering the service. These interactions are so important that marketing experts understand that front-line employees are the drivers of a service firm's brand identity. Front-line employee actions must consistently deliver customer satisfaction and the intended brand identity. Consider a visit to the doctor's office. A given patient interacts with multiple people: the receptionist, the nurse, the physician, and the payment clerk, for example. All of these individuals are variously trained and can have day-to-day variations in mood or demeanor. Consistency is key, because a negative interaction with any single person can spoil the customer's perception of the practice's entire brand.[61] Marketers recommend the following strategies for brand-workforce synchronization to ensure a consistent customer service delivery:

- Create a brand-driven organization.
- Address customer complaints quickly.
- Inventory all brand-customer touchpoints.
- Properly select and train the sales force.

Create a Brand-Driven Organization. Marketing experts recommend that businesses create internal cultures imbued with the intended brand identity. According to Scott Davis of the management consultancy Prophet, "Making the brand the central focus of the organization helps clarify on-brand and off-brand behaviors and decisions for

---

[61] Amy L. Ostrom, Dawn Iacobucci, and Felicia N. Morgan, "Services Branding," in Alice M. Tybout and Tim Calkins, eds., *Kellogg on Branding*, Hoboken, N.J.: John Wiley and Sons, 2005, pp. 186–200.

all employees—whether they're in the field or in the executive suite—which makes it easier to make the right strategic decisions."[62] Frequent and continual communication regarding the brand meaning emanates from corporate executives, middle managers, and key rank-and-file personnel. Employees, especially those on the front lines of customer service, are educated to understand, feel passionately about, and "live" the brand. Employees are further trained to understand their role in delivering customer satisfaction. In addition, individual acts that exemplify the brand and deliver customer satisfaction are properly rewarded.

Ritz-Carlton exemplifies an internally branded organization. Employees who are ultimately responsible for delivering the brand undergo intensive "Gold Standard" training when first hired and receive further instruction throughout their tenure. Regularly held awards dinners celebrate employee feats of customer satisfaction. At Ritz-Carlton, an internal embodiment of the intended brand seeks to ensure a consistent and accurate brand perception for all its customers.[63]

Address Customer Complaints Quickly. Businesses are not perfect. Mistakes are inevitable, given the number of products they sell and the services they deliver. How front-line employees handle these mistakes and any corresponding complaints determines customer brand loyalty. Where employees lack authority to address mishaps, they must ask for higher guidance; the longer the delay between problem and resolution, the less likely a customer's loyalty will remain intact. Firms must therefore empower employees to address customer complaints quickly. Ritz-Carlton meets this challenge by training employees to drop whatever they are doing in order to address customer complaints. Those in some positions are given a $2,000 allowance that enables them to fix problems at their own discretion.[64]

---

[62] Scott Davis, "Building a Brand-Driven Organization," in Alice M. Tybout and Tim Calkins, eds., *Kellogg on Branding*, Hoboken, N.J.: John Wiley and Sons, 2005, pp. 226–245 [p. 228].

[63] See Ritz-Carlton, "Gold Standards," undated Web page; Kotler and Armstrong (2006, pp. 261–262).

[64] Kotler and Armstrong (2006, p. 262).

Inventory All Brand-Customer Touchpoints. Marketing professors Amy Ostrom, Dawn Iacobucci, and Felicia Morgan recommend a process called *service blueprinting*, in which business managers inventory and assess the touchpoints at which customers interact with a brand and its representatives. Service blueprinting diagnoses areas in service delivery that may be slow or prone to mistakes; it makes "all the steps in the service delivery process clear from the customer's point of view."[65] Importantly, the process helps realign all brand-customer interactions so that they convey the intended brand message.

Properly Select and Train the Sales Force. Selecting and preparing sales representatives is another important workforce synchronization step. Sales representative positions require unique skill sets, such as forming relationships with clients and understanding and satisfying client needs. These individuals must also be empathetic, patient, caring, responsive, good at listening, and honest. Businesses have to recruit and select the correct applicants and weed out those who fail to measure up.[66]

Managers often spend anywhere from several weeks to a year training salespeople to interact properly with customers. These efforts can pay handsome dividends: A major telecommunication firm found that its training practices paid for themselves in only 16 days, with an 812-percent return on investment in six months.[67] Training programs have several goals. Sales staff must know and identify with the corporate brand and its range of products. They require in-depth information on customers and competitors. Further, they need in-depth knowledge of the sales process.

Online training programs have greatly reduced the costs and time associated with sales-force education for some organizations.[68] Cisco Systems[69] instituted the Partner E-Learning Connection. This portal allows sales staff to plan, track, develop, and measure their skills and

---

[65] Ostrom, Iacobucci, and Morgan (2005, p. 197).

[66] Kotler and Armstrong (2006, pp. 494–496).

[67] Kotler and Armstrong (2006, p. 496).

[68] Kotler and Armstrong (2006, p. 496).

[69] Cisco Systems® is a registered trademark of Cisco Systems, Inc.

knowledge. Learning aids include audio and video broadcasts, Internet classrooms, and written content. Single training sessions can reach 3,000 staff at once, and sales experts are available to answer individual questions by email or phone. While improving training, the program cut costs by between 40 and 60 percent and increased customer face time with employees.[70]

Synchronization of U.S. Military Personnel

> I do not think you can sell America. I think what you can accomplish is to be less threatening and for the undecideds to give you a shot. That is as good as you can hope for. It starts here with the 18-year-old.
>
> —*Alex Wipperfürth, Plan B*[71]

> Ninety-nine percent of the way your people represent you is the way they conduct themselves everyday. To me, the most effective antidote to Abu Ghraib is to have someone in the village saying, "I know the soldier who was here and there is no way he would stand for that." If your behavior is not right, all the talking in the world will not save your representation.
>
> —*Robert Zeiger, Alticor*[72]

The U.S. military, particularly the ground forces of the U.S. Army and Marine Corps, function very much like a service firm when it comes to conducting stability operations. What is tangible is the way the coalition force conducts itself in theater. The interactions that soldiers have with locals while on patrol, the conduct of cordon-and-search operations, and the engagement decisions soldiers make when confronted with a threat all reflect on the force.

---

[70] Kotler and Armstrong (2006, p. 496).

[71] Alex Wipperfürth, Plan B, interview with Todd C. Helmus, San Francisco, Calif., March 23, 2006.

[72] Robert Zeiger, Chief of Corporate Communications, Alticor, interview with Todd C. Helmus, Grand Rapids, Mich., April 17, 2006.

U.S. force behavior takes on paramount importance when one considers the often-negative initial perceptions of the U.S. government. U.S. forces will enter many theaters behind the proverbial eight ball. The presence of U.S. forces offers a unique advantage in such cases. Jack Leslie, chairman of the public relations firm Weber Shandwick, observed,

> It's all, "Who do you trust to watch out after your interests?" And your interests get defined in many ways, from individual to family to community to country. When you get to the advantage of having people on the ground, you're generally dealing with that basic and most important level. "How do they relate to me, and can I trust them to operate in my best interests?"[73]

Abstract anti-American attitudes can be overcome by intimate and positive experiences with U.S. forces. We recommend four broad strategies for properly aligning U.S. forces to interact with civilian populations:

- Internally brand U.S. force personnel.
- Train and empower U.S. forces to fix mistakes.
- Inventory all U.S. military–civilian touchpoints.
- Select and train U.S. force "sales staff."

Internally Brand U.S. Force Personnel. The U.S. military should conduct an internal branding campaign. To the extent that the U.S. military creates a new brand architecture that encompasses its COIN mission, internal branding campaigns should educate military personnel on the meaning of that new brand and should identify on- and off-brand behaviors.

The internal military culture should be adjusted to fit COIN operational needs. Brigadier Nigel Aylwin-Foster of the British Army observed how the U.S. Army soldier's creed calls on soldiers to "stand ready to deploy, engage, and destroy the enemies of the United States

---

[73] Leslie (2006).

of America in close combat."[74] This focus on *destroy* rules out a host of other options for countering an adversary or interacting with noncombatants. It speaks to the preeminent focus the military has on conducting conventional military operations and leaves soldiers ill prepared to meet the necessary needs of the COIN environment. The military should imbue its soldiers from the very first day of basic training with the understanding that befriending local populations and using force discriminately can be just as great a military achievement as overwhelming employment of firepower. How the military rewards acts of battlefield distinction plays an important role in this regard. The military should ensure that its class of battlefield medals encompasses acts of valor that serve COIN interests. Destroying the enemy is and will remain a vital element of a soldier, sailor, marine, or airman's skills. Training must prepare military men and women to use lethal force when necessary and appropriate. But destruction of a foe is not a soldier's sole task. Training, reward systems, and other components of force preparation should better address his or her full range of responsibilities.

A second, less formal cultural trait what some would say is an overemphasis that many U.S. commanders place on force protection. Observed an anonymous senior coalition officer,

> When you're zipped up in your vehicle . . . soldiers were very safe, but what did they accomplish? If they are not willing to accept any risk, if the nation is not willing to accept any risk, then what are you there for? You need to realize that they may not always come home. . . . Mission accomplishment is so tied to shaking the hand of that local on patrol. . . . There is that balance that commanders need to strike between risk and protection for their soldiers.

The United States should develop doctrine, conduct training, and promote leaders who support a balanced approach to stability operations. The default condition of "full battle rattle" and multiple-vehicle convoys should be reevaluated frequently during each mission. Military leaders understand that loss of life is sometimes necessary to attain vic-

---

[74] Aylwin-Foster (2005, p. 13).

tory in battle. It may also be necessary to risk casualties when shaping civilian populations is a primary mission.

The U.S. military has gone to considerable lengths to instill cultural sensitivity in its troops. Witness the Marine Corps' recently created Center for Advanced Operational Culture Learning. This program teaches marines how they can conduct themselves in culturally attuned ways. However, the military should go beyond cultural dos and don'ts and seek to instill a deeper understanding and respect for indigenous cultures. Psychologist Bella DePaulo aptly observed that U.S. forces "are more likely to act toward Iraqis in likable, trustworthy, and respectful ways if they truly do like and trust and respect them."[75]

Alex Wipperfürth of advertising agency Plan B carries such advice to his clients. Wipperfürth commissioned an ethnographic study of Red Stripe[76] beer drinkers for the sole purpose of helping Red Stripe management understand the cultural characteristics of its consumer base. He instills respect for these values by developing a professionally crafted video. The video is captivating, it shows the many unique and positive characteristics of loyal Red Stripe drinkers, their can-do attitudes, self-reliance, tolerance, authenticity, and creativity. He suggested imagining soldiers being shown a professionally crafted video about Afghan life. The film would highlight the true and positive characteristics of the Afghan culture. Wipperfürth concluded, "The better you can prepare [soldiers] for understanding the other side, the better chance you will have with good will. Prepare [soldiers] to help [local residents] help their [indigenous] culture."[77]

Train and Empower U.S. Forces to Fix Mistakes. In the conduct of operations, U.S. and coalition forces inadvertently destroy civilian property or injure or kill people. Their subsequent response can significantly influence popular support. Colonel Robert Duffy, 321st Civil Affairs Brigade and former leader of a Provincial Reconstruction Team

---

[75] Bella DePaulo, written comments to Scott Gerwehr, RAND Corporation, January 12, 2004.

[76] Red Stripe® is a registered trademark of Diageo plc.

[77] Wipperfürth (2006).

(PRT) in Afghanistan, recalled how a U.S. Army unit went into a village in the vicinity of a recent rocket attack launch. The unit conducted a cordon and search, yelling in English, and left after kicking various homes' doors down. They "didn't repair doors. They didn't seek out the village leader, and there is a leader in every village in Afghanistan." The townspeople later told Duffy, "You're just like the Russians."[78]

U.S. forces should seek to repair damage in a timely manner. (Many better-led units do so.) Where operations leave a dwelling or village in disrepair, efforts should be made to have CA units immediately fix damaged structures and make financial amends as appropriate. Where permitted, CA personnel could accompany infantry units during operations to address damages on the spot (though, at times, a follow-up visit will be necessary).[79]

Civilian casualties present an even greater challenge to coalition forces. Presently, U.S. forces make a $2,500 condolence payment to the family of each Iraqi civilian inadvertently killed by U.S. forces. These payments follow an investigation to determine the nature of the killing. The United States should determine whether the indigenous population and the afflicted families accept the prescribed payment as fair and reasonable. If reasonably higher payments earn greater respect from the population, then such considerations may be necessary. Condolence payments should be made with as little delay as possible when U.S. force culpability is clear.

---

[78] Duffy (2004).

[79] Coalition forces will also make mistakes when it comes to arresting suspected insurgents. In many cases, the wrong individual will be arrested. Brigade commander COL Robert Baker was attuned to the damage done in such cases. He observes, "We have a full-time taxicab driver now. . . . About 70 percent of those we detain we send on for further interrogation. As for the 30 percent we release back, we drive him all the way home rather than just release him to find his own way." Furthermore, given an understanding that mistakes will be made, he takes great efforts to ensure that the families of detained are kept informed: "When we take someone away [i.e., arrest or detain them], we make sure that someone goes back and keeps the family informed regarding what the individual has been accused of, where he is, when he is expected to be back" (COL Robert Baker, U.S. Army, Commanding Officer, 2nd Brigade, 1st Armored Division, interview with Russell W. Glenn and Todd C. Helmus, Baghdad, Iraq, February 21, 2004).

Inventory All U.S. Military–Civilian Touchpoints and Craft "Rules of Interaction." The U.S. military should conduct a service blueprinting of soldier-civilian touchpoints. We recommend the following five-step process:

1. Inventory U.S. military interactions with the civilian populace. Consider interactions related to dismounted patrols, cordon-and-search operations, HUMINT collection, meetings between coalition officers and indigenous tribal or religious leaders, handling questions from families of detainees, mistaken arrests, and as many others as possible. The list could also include cases in which the population may not have face-to-face contact with U.S. personnel but comes into contact otherwise, such as when logistics convoys drive through urban neighborhoods or during firefights between U.S. forces and insurgents.

2. Describe typical ways in which U.S. forces conduct themselves in each setting and identify how civilians perceive such interactions. Remember that not all units conduct themselves similarly in a given situation. (This may indeed be part of the problem.) Consequently, each scenario may require several variants of U.S. force behavior.

3. For each situation, identify the U.S. course of action that would best serve shaping needs, and identify how such an action might lead to positive indigenous experiences. These proposed actions should then be formulated into "rules of interaction." Akin to ROE, rules of interaction would provide specific guidance to U.S. force personnel for their day-to-day interface with the civilian population.[80]

4. Communicate any new rules of interaction to all units and train accordingly.

---

[80] The phrase *rules of interaction* comes from COL Matthew Lopez, who used it to describe his guidance to marines regarding how they were to interact with the local Iraqi populace (Col. Matthew Lopez, U.S. Marine Corps, Commander, 3rd Battalion, 7th Marine Regiment, during OIF, interview with Todd C. Helmus, Suffolk, Va., March 28, 2007).

5.   Conduct systematic reviews of all actions to ensure that they conform to newly drafted guidelines.[81]

Select and Train U.S. Force "Sales Staff." Finally, U.S. forces should understand the special role played by those officers who represent the United States in negotiations with various tribal, religious, and government officials. This is an extraordinarily difficult job, the success of which dramatically impacts the security of U.S. forces and the indigenous population. These individuals should be no less carefully selected and trained than their business counterparts serving in similar roles. Not all individuals are equally adept at negotiation. Rank or position may not be reflective of the skills necessary. The military should evaluate the negotiation skill sets required for different cultural locales and identify personnel meeting those requirements. Next, the military should thoroughly train screened individuals to accurately represent its intended brand identity. It should also train the candidates in indigenous cultural characteristics, appropriate marketing approaches, and negotiation basics. To enhance training effectiveness while decreasing costs, such a program could include an online component.

Achieve Civilian Satisfaction: Meet Expectations, Make Informed Decisions, Measure Success

Customer satisfaction refers to the level of contentment consumers experience after an experience with a product or service. At its most basic

---

[81] A good example of this process comes from an interview with BG Martin Dempsey, commander of the 1st Armored Division stationed in Baghdad during the winter of 2004. General Dempsey observed that Iraqi civilians were becoming angered by U.S. vehicle checkpoints whose poor layouts led to a number of inadvertent civilian shootings. General Dempsey reviewed the problem and ordered that all be constructed to specific guidelines. He then paid personal visits to a number of checkpoints. Despite his clear orders, he found that small-unit leaders continued to make unnecessary adjustments. While intended to fit local needs, the variations served to confuse civilians and held the potential to cause further misunderstandings. In response to these violations, further command emphasis was placed on lower echelons, and, eventually, orders were carried out as advised (BG Martin Dempsey, U.S. Army, Commanding General, 1st Armored Division, interview with Russell W. Glenn and Todd C. Helmus, Baghdad, Iraq, February 19, 2004).

level, it is how a customer feels about doing business with a company. It is the bridge between what the company or retailer does (e.g., processes, policies, products) and the behavior of consumers. When consumers feel good about doing business with a company, that company experiences a number of key benefits.[82] These include increased loyalty, positive word-of-mouth exposure, and a willingness on the part of customers to pay higher prices.[83] Most importantly, customer satisfaction increases business profit margins.[84]

Customer satisfaction also applies to the U.S. military's efforts to prevent or quench an insurgency. Civilians who live in areas where U.S. and coalition forces are conducting stability operations will consciously decide whether to support the coalition or its foes or to maintain neutrality. The degree to which they are satisfied with the various aspects of force presence will be a critical determinant in their decisionmaking.

The previous discussion on internally branding the U.S. force for customer service speaks directly to aligning U.S. force–civilian interactions for achieving customer satisfaction. It is worth addressing three other aspects critical to customer satisfaction: managing expectations, making informed decisions, and monitoring campaign success.

The Marketing Approach to Meeting Expectations

> Good is not good when better is expected.
> —*Thomas Fuller, English clergy and historian*[85]

---

[82] Chris Denove and James D. Power IV, *Satisfaction: How Every Great Company Listens to the Voice of the Customer*, New York: Penguin, 2006, pp. 2–3.

[83] Denove and Power (2006, pp. 2–3).

[84] Denove and Power (2006, pp. 2–3). In one study, J. D. Power and Associates reviewed Nissan dealership close rates, the percentage of shoppers who closed an automobile sale. They categorized the close rates for dealers with low, mid, and high customer satisfaction ratings. High-satisfaction dealers sold a Nissan to 79 percent of customers, compared to low-satisfaction dealers, who closed on only 56 percent of sales. Given that the actual product being sold is held virtually constant across all dealers, these differences in sales were purely a result of the interactions customers had with sales staff. (Nissan® is a registered trademark of Nissan Motor Company Ltd.)

[85] Quoted in Denove and Power (2006, p. xi).

That is what we call the definition of a brand: It's a promise kept. When you make a promise, you create an expectation in someone's mind, and, when you fulfill that, it creates that circle of brand equity. . . . All your actions are built on fulfilling that expectation.

—*David Coronna, Burson-Marsteller*[86]

Customer satisfaction is partly a function of two separate factors: (1) expectations that a customer has going into a business encounter and (2) the actual experience. When customer expectations are high, the bar for meeting or exceeding them is high as well. As Denove and Power observe, the expectations for a stay at a Four Seasons[87] hotel are enormously high, and a single rude bellhop or burnt toast can sour that experience. In contrast, low expectations drop satisfaction standards. A friendly desk clerk at another hotel chain can help create a loyal business traveler.[88]

A customer's expectations are directly proportional to the promises a business makes. When promises go unfulfilled, customers become disappointed and their likelihood of doing business with that company decreases. The most common type of broken promise is made with the intention that it will be fulfilled. J. D. Power and Associates calls these *best-case scenario (BSC) promises*. These promises will be kept if "the supply train arrives on time, all the needed tools are on the truck, ordered parts are in stock, nobody calls in sick, address labels are filled out correctly, and all the planets fall into perfect alignment. In other words, best-case scenario promises are likely to be broken."[89] These promises are often made out of a desire to tell customers what they want to hear. However, J. D. Power cautions its clients to build in a promise safety net. Companies should train front-line personnel to give conservative estimates.

---

[86] Coronna (2006).

[87] Four Seasons® is a registered trademark of Four Seasons Hotels Limited.

[88] Denove and Power (2006, p. 85).

[89] Denove and Power (2006, p. 105).

Another reason promises remain unfulfilled relates to ineffective processes. The same person who makes a promise is not the same person who fulfills it, and, more often than not, many people are involved in the service chain. Businesses should minimize the number of steps a service representative must take before a problem is resolved; empowering front-line employees to handle problems on their own is one way of doing so. Single points of contact should be created for customers, ensuring that they can reach the customer call center operator who is familiar with their problem should an issue involve a telephone complaint.[90]

Information is a powerful weapon. Continental Airlines[91] rose from the bottom of customer satisfaction surveys to the top in part because of its efforts to better inform customers about flight departure delays.[92] As Denove and Power suggest, this is a challenging task because gate personnel often have little idea of when a given mechanical or scheduling problem will be fixed. A common mistake these personnel make is either to leave customers in the dark by not telling them anything or to make repeatedly unfulfilled promises along the lines of "the flight will depart in 15 minutes." Continental CEO Larry Kellner tells his representatives to inform customers of delays and why those delays have occurred. To avoid broken promises, employees are instructed not to give specific departure time information. Instead, they are encouraged to say the following:

> If you leave the gate area, do not be gone for more than ten or fifteen minutes, because as soon as the problem is resolved we're going to board. But we do not want you sit on a cramped plane for long stretches when it is more comfortable here inside where you can get something to eat or use the restroom.[93]

---

[90] Denove and Power (2006).

[91] Continental Airlines® is a registered trademark of Continental Airlines, Inc.

[92] Denove and Power (2006, p. 107).

[93] Denove and Power (2006, p. 107).

Managing Expectations During Stability-and-Support Operations. The U.S. military is no stranger to dashing civilian expectations. In many instances, these dashed expectations are not the fault of coalition forces. In Iraq, the United States has disappointed civilians with the lack of basic infrastructural necessities, such as electricity and clean water. This disappointment is directly linked to unusually high expectations for improvements once coalition forces entered the region. Political leaders promised an improved Iraqi nation to gain wide national and internal support for OIF. These promises made to U.S., UK, and other coalition nations' populations found their way to the Middle East, where many took them to mean that coalition presence would immediately bring about improved standards of living. These expectations were molded by rumor, unfamiliarity with Western politics, and natural human optimism. Major Stuart Tootal, second in command of the British 1st Parachute Battalion during its operations in and around Al Basrah, remembered,

> There was a failure of expectations because they didn't immediately go from three hours to 24 hours [of electricity a day]. But when they only got three hours a day before the war and then they didn't even have three hours, they'd say, "Well, even under Saddam Hussein we had three hours a day."[94]

In conducting day-to-day operations, maneuver forces make an array of promises to civilians. These might range from assurances regarding payments for inadvertent civilian casualties, checking on anti-insurgent tips, or ensuring that a wrongly detained family member is returned from captivity. Promises can go unfulfilled when maneuver units promise civilians a visit from CA but neglect to inform CA units of the promise.[95] The impact of such broken promises is no less

---

[94] Major Stuart Tootal, Second-in-Command, 1st Parachute Battalion during Operation Telic, interview with Russell W. Glenn and Todd C. Helmus, Codford, UK, December 12, 2003.

[95] Duffy (2004).

damaging to the U.S. military's reputation than it is to a neighborhood business. Observed Lieutenant Colonel Peter R. Wreford of the British Army, "A promise not delivered is a catastrophe. It goes around the neighborhood like nothing."[96]

Managing indigenous expectations should be a hallmark of coalition force actions and messages. Where expectations of the civilian populace are not reflective of reality, coalition force IO campaigns must place them in proper perspective. U.S. forces should not set a specific end date for repairs unless they are sure the date will be met. Like the desk representative at Continental Airlines, U.S. representatives should explain the situation and emphasize that all necessary efforts are being undertaken to address the problem. When expectations are the result of messages emanating from Washington, then mistaken or misinterpreted promises should be amended.

Wreford observed, "You must make absolutely sure . . . [that] people never promise what they can't deliver."[97] When coordinating CA follow-on visits, unit commanders should simply forward recommendations to CA units rather than promising visits to members of the population. CA can then credit the maneuver force with the recommendation when making the visit. An alternative course of action is to ensure that there is a single military point of contact for province leaders and other key indigenous personnel. That way, promises made for a particular AO are made by a single person who can ultimately be held responsible—and can deliver on those promises. CA officer Colonel Robert Duffy bluntly warned, "You can't have various leaders in the same uniform making different promises of help for the people."[98]

---

[96] Lieutenant Colonel Peter R. Wreford, British Army, Deputy Chief, Command and Control, V Corps during Operation Telic, interview with Russell W. Glenn, Baghdad, Iraq, July 12, 2005.

[97] Wreford (2005).

[98] Duffy (2004).

Listen to the Voice of the Civilian: Make Informed Decisions

> [To] set up a means to get information . . . you have to proactively go out and get it. The best customer satisfaction companies are in constant touch with their audience.
>
> —*Chris Denove, J. D. Power and Associates*[99]

The Marketing Approach to Customer-Informed Decision-making. Many business owners believe in the motto "build it and they will come." If they create superior and innovative products, customers will come rushing to their door. The graveyard of consumer products is littered with superior products that failed to meet a need in the marketplace or that were out of tune with customer desires. Consider Betamax video recorders. At the time of their introduction, Sony Corporation considered them superior to the late-entry VHS recorders because of their sleeker size and high picture quality. However, Sony never thought that customers would want to record anything longer than an hour, the maximum recording time of the Betamax recorders. VHS met consumer needs with extended recording times and, in short order, dominated the market.[100]

The most successful business endeavors are those that are premised on meeting customer needs and desires. It is an approach driven not by engineers and inventors, but by research that first seeks to gauge the voice of the customer and then designs or modifies products to meet those needs. Denove and Power observe,

> Understanding the needs of your customer provides a filter through which every decision must be screened. Developing a new product or service? Every phase of that process must begin and end with customer needs. Features, options, pricing strategy; they all depend on the wants, desires and concerns of your customers.[101]

---

[99] Chris Denove, Vice President and Executive Director, J. D. Power and Associates, interview with Todd C. Helmus, Westlake Village, Calif., June 5, 2006.

[100] Denove and Power (2006, pp. 235–236).

[101] Denove and Power (2006, p. 239).

Businesses conduct needs-analysis research to determine what factors will motivate the market to purchase their products. Enterprise Rent-A-Car Company knew an opportunity existed when it oriented its business around picking up consumers at their homes or offices, and Starwood Hotels and Resorts introduced its Heavenly Bed® in its Westin® hotels after research showed that superior bedding should bring customers to its door.[102]

Civilian-Informed Decisionmaking in Theaters of Operation. Listening to the voice of the customer, or, in this case, the "voice of the civilian," is just as important in how the military conducts stability operations. The U.S. military, particularly CA personnel, will be charged with rebuilding infrastructure systems, such as water, sewage, and electricity systems. They pave roads; clean streets; and construct schools, government buildings, and soccer fields. Of course, the military is in charge of establishing security and, in the early phases of operations, will invariably provide governance. In performing such services, it is easy to assume that one knows what needs doing. It is the proverbial "build it and they will come" approach. While many coalition decisions will be correct, others will prove meaningless to the population. Consider schools. A commanding officer with the 4th Civil Affairs Group writes,

> We have built so many schools that the Iraqis do not need. You know what happens to them? They get blown up, because no teachers show up, because no students come, no books are there, the [mujahideen] walks in, they blow them up. It happens time and time again, we give them something they do not ask for, they do not need, because it's something that we can do.[103]

Similar misunderstandings can plague larger infrastructural repair projects.

---

[102] Denove and Power (2006, p. 240).

[103] Maj. A. R. Milburn, "Preliminary Report on USMC Civil Military Operations (CMO) in Iraq," report to Director, Security Assistance and Education Training Center, from its representative to the Marine Corps Center for Lessons Learned, November 28, 2004, p. 6.

Consider indigenous input for determining needs and coalition expert input for feasibility. (Adept translators and a not inconsiderable amount of cultural knowledge will be necessary to avoid serving one particular individual's or group's interests over those of others.) Do not limit indigenous input to governmental entities only; incorporate surveys of the local populace and tribal and religious authorities if appropriate. Local U.S. communities provide a useful model in this regard. Zoning boards often combine government, expert, and local opinions in their decisionmaking process. "Ask the locals where they want the dough spent," Brigadier General Peter J. Devlin suggests.

> It needs to be based on the structure that that nation has. If there are corps and divisions and brigades that have relationships with [specific local, regional, or national organizations, then work through them,] ask them how to spend the funds. . . . It has to be tempered with the advice of professionals [within the coalition].[104]

Listen to the Voice of the Civilian: Monitor Outcomes

> If you experience any problems, please call and let us know so we can fix it.
>
> —*Susan, Borders Books sales associate*[105]

> We are sampling public opinion so we know what works and what doesn't work.
>
> —*Brigadier Peter B. Williams, British Army*[106]

The Marketing Approach to Monitoring Customer Satisfaction. Beyond orienting an initial product offering to customer needs, businesses monitor whether their efforts are hitting their mark. Businesses

---

[104]Brigadier General Peter J. Devlin, Canadian Army, interview with Russell W. Glenn, Carlisle, Pa., June 2, 2005.

[105]Comment to Todd C. Helmus, Pittsburgh, Pa., January 5, 2007.

[106]Brigadier Peter B. Williams, British Army, Chief, J3 Operations Support, and Senior Military Advisor to the Regional Coordinator, Coalition Provisional Authority–South, interview with Russell W. Glenn and Todd C. Helmus, Al Basrah, Iraq, February 22, 2004.

consequently must stay in touch with their consumers so that problems can be fixed before they alienate the customer base. Paul Rand of the public relations firm Ketchum talks of the *hear mes*. A hear me is an individual who calls complaint lines to report problems he or she has experienced with products or customer service. If companies fail to listen and address concerns, the hear me can turn into a "reputation terrorist," an individual who will stop at nothing to spread negative word of mouth about the company or product.[107]

J. D. Power and Associates has built a vast empire around listening to the voice of the customer for various clients, most notably Toyota[108] and its subsidiary, Lexus. J. D. Power conducts customer satisfaction surveys across the automotive industry. It not only creates global satisfaction scores, but it also assesses the individual factors that contribute positively or negatively to that satisfaction. For service organizations that sprout multiple branch offices across the country, J. D. Power also evaluates branch-specific customer satisfaction indexes. Enterprise Rent-A-Car monitors satisfaction scores of all its individual branches and uses those scores as promotion criteria for individual managers. J. D. Power and Associates uses branch-scoring systems to help firms understand and fix problems. Sometimes, customer reviews will indicate what ails a particular branch. Other times, J. D. Power and Associates will review operational procedures for the best-performing branches and use those practices to fix internal procedures at lower-performing branches.[109]

Conducting systematic surveys is not the only way to monitor business performance. Many businesses offer customer complaint lines. In-store complaint procedures are another avenue. Denove and Power suggest, "When a customer complains, do not get defensive; savor it as an opportunity to receive free and unfiltered feedback."[110] Lexus sales

---

[107] Paul Rand, Director of Global Technology Practice, Ketchum, interview with Todd C. Helmus, Chicago, Ill., February 24, 2006.

[108] Toyota® is a registered trademark of Toyota Motor Sales.

[109] Gina Pingitore, Chief Research Officer, J. D. Power and Associates, interview with Todd C. Helmus, Westlake Village, Calif., June 5, 2006.

[110] Denove and Power (2006, p. 242).

representatives have created standing "customer advisory boards," from which they receive unfiltered ideas and advice.[111] Ultimately, if complaints are to be helpful, they must be systematically collected, synthesized, and used to enhance performance.[112]

Monitoring Civilian Satisfaction During COIN. Because civilian satisfaction with a U.S. force presence will influence a population's allegiance, we recommend that U.S. and coalition forces use customer satisfaction–like measures to monitor indigenous perspectives on U.S. force actions. Civilian satisfaction should be monitored from multiple perspectives and in different ways. First, because of the varying operating styles of different units and variations in the populations that constitute separate AOs, civilian satisfaction should be measured according to individual battalion or brigade AOs. Surveys should inquire about a range of U.S. and coalition force behaviors, including interactions with U.S. forces, pace and appropriateness of reconstruction, use of force against insurgents, civilian casualties, and other governance issues.[113]

---

[111] Sean Geehan, "Your Customers Can Be Your Most Powerful Advisors," American Marketing Association, 2004.

[112] The challenges inherent in measuring performance should not be underestimated. Managers are often unwilling to receive and forward negative reviews. Denove and Power write of a large European company whose U.S. subsidiary chief of operations would lock up the results of customer satisfaction surveys from the "prying eyes" of his corporate superiors. When the executive left the company and the reports were finally made available to the European chiefs, major quality problems came to light. Only then could the problems be fixed. To prove useful to an organization, customer feedback must be made widely available to all echelons within the business. Because of individual tendency to hide negative performance reviews, information sharing must be systematized and carefully monitored (Denove and Power, 2006, p. 247).

[113] Surveys and opinion polls are an ideal way to systematically collect information for a large cohort of individuals, but they are challenging for several reasons. The danger of walking door to door in a potentially hostile environment is one major impediment. The potential bias involved in opinion surveys is another factor. It is best if surveys are sponsored by an outside, independent organization. The populace may provide more honest appraisals and the results are less prone to influence by the very organization, the U.S. military, whose performance is being evaluated. That said, it would be wise to validate the findings through skilled qualitative interviews (Denove, 2006).

Interpreting satisfaction results may be difficult.[114] Depending on survey construction, satisfaction measures may not inform the military about why a particular problem exists. It may know that the population is dissatisfied with soldier-civilian interactions, but the fix may not be apparent. Focus groups that permit more detailed follow-on questioning may be helpful in this regard. Finally, the military should compare operational procedures of units that achieve high versus low satisfaction scores. "Separate the wheat from the chaff," says Chris Denove. He suggests doing so by comparing the tactics of units that successfully pacify major urban AOs with those of less successful units. The lessons of the former can then be used to improve the latter.[115]

Set procedures should be established for collecting information via dismounted patrols.[116] U.S. forces in Iraq have conducted beneficial town hall–style meetings with civilians. These meetings are potential venues for collecting intelligence and operational feedback. They should be conducted at regular intervals across AOs where security conditions allow. U.S. forces can further employ customer advisory boards that provide finer-grained observations and suggestions. These boards should incorporate indigenous personnel who represent a range of different AO-specific ethnicities and backgrounds.

Finally, the information collected must be put to use. It should be provided to relevant units and used to improve operational success. While civilian satisfaction scores may not reach the heights that

---

[114] "Virtually every data set comes with an inherent bias or is not representative of [an operational theater's] population's attitudes, opinions and behaviors. For the sake of monitoring we have found it valuable to collect a multitude of independent datasets. After fusing the sets this usually gives a reasonably accurate picture of the situation. The big thing is understanding how to weight the data sets properly—Polls, surveys, ethnographic studies, focus groups, structured interviews, media monitoring, intelligence, PSYOP/CA reporting" (Blum, 2007).

[115] Denove (2006).

[116] There will be a natural tendency on the part of patrol leaders and their unit commands not to forward opinions that reflect poorly on command or unit performance. They may also withhold responses that they think are unjustified or lack merit. Getting around this problem is a challenge, as few outside a company will come in contact with that unit's indigenous residents. Higher-echelon commanders can partially overcome the problem by including their own representatives on patrols to ensure that feedback is optimal.

Lexus achieves with its customer base, they can help monitor shaping progress, identify operational problems before they cause widespread alienation, and otherwise help coalition forces achieve the most they can given baseline population attitudes.

Harness the Power of Influencers

> You can't use Internet, blogs, podcasting to shape people. You can use them to tap people, to tap their energies and include them in a conversation or dialogue and expose them to things. . . . What makes a blog so powerful? It's an expression of a group of people around a personality or a purpose.
> —*Thomas Goetz, Deputy Editor,* Wired[117]

The Marketing Approach to Influencers

Beyond broadcasting messages on a mass scale, a number of marketers are starting to see the value in harnessing the power of influencers who speak and write about their product observations. These influencers include social nodes or those whose position in society affords them a megaphone and the respect and admiration of key population segments. Examples of these social nodes include authors, academics, celebrities, and researchers.[118] Influencers are also regular individuals who speak to friends and family about their likes and dislikes. A study by market research firm Roper ASW reports that 10 percent of Americans have the "power to influence the habits of the other ninety percent."[119] Since 1977, the estimated value of word of mouth has grown by 1.5 times annually, and two-thirds of the U.S. population report being influenced by word of mouth in their purchase decisions.[120] These purchase decisions range from such mundane purchases as checking out a movie

---

[117] Thomas Goetz, Deputy Editor, *Wired*, interview with Todd C. Helmus, San Francisco, Calif., March 22, 2006.

[118] Rand (2004).

[119] Rand (2004).

[120] Rand (2004).

at a friend's recommendation to more costly endeavors, such as choosing a new car based in part on neighborly conversations.

Ultimately, fostering customer satisfaction is the most critical ingredient to getting social nodes and everyday influencers to speak well of a business' products and services. However, businesses employ several tactics to increase positive word of mouth. Delta Air Lines[121] asked its executives to write customized letters to a list of social nodes from media outlets who cover ecommerce-related industries. The social nodes were strategically addressed as key sources of "information and expertise." The campaign was highly successful, and Delta received significant and positive attention in the ebusiness industry.[122]

Many companies foster customer evangelism. According to James Pethokoukis, companies should "find and identify those customers who are already crazy about your product or service . . . who then spread the word to others."[123] Recommendations include flying evangelists to corporate headquarters, where they can receive a tour of the plant, learn new product information (which they can then pass on to their audiences), and speak with executives about "what they're doing well and how they're screwing up."[124] This feedback provides the company with important market observations while also empowering the individual influencer with new sources for content.

Cultivating relationships with customers is another approach to customer evangelism. Betsy Weber is the chief evangelist of software developer TechSmith. She says, "My job is about relationships."

> Weber estimates that she chats with 400 customer evangelists several times a month via E-mail, instant messaging, phone, private forums, and meet-ups on the road. . . . She tries to reply to each and every E-mail, forwards problems or complaints to product

[121] Delta Air Lines® is a registered trademark of Delta Air Lines, Inc.

[122] Rand (2004).

[123] James M. Pethokoukis, "Spreading the Word: Corporate Evangelists Recruit Customers Who Love to Create Buzz About a Product," *U.S. News and World Report*, December 5, 2005.

[124] Pethokoukis (2005).

specialists, [and] invites the customer evangelists to groups beta-testing new products. . . . [125]

Observes one of her contacts, Tim Fahlberg, who uses TechSmith software for his business, "I'd say that there are . . . few people—outside of my family—on our planet who I appreciate more than Betsy Weber."[126]

The power of word of mouth has increased with growing Internet use and especially with the introduction of the blog. Blogs are journal-style Web sites that provide commentary on a particular topic, such as news, politics, entertainment, or commercial products. Today, there are 74.3 million blogs, and approximately 175,000 new blogs are created daily.[127] Blogs have proven extremely influential and have had both a positive and negative impact on the products they discuss. Former TV critic Jeff Jarvis blogged about his displeasure with Dell's inability to service a broken computer. This diatribe was visited 10,000 times daily.[128] Other blogs have positively addressed the value of such marquee brands as Starbucks and Wal-Mart.

A challenge for businesses has been to determine how best to harness this influential power and, if possible, insert themselves into everyday Web conversations. It is no small challenge. According to Kevin Allison of the *Financial Times*,

> Bloggers are an anti-establishment lot, and messages from big business are automatically suspect. In bloggers' eyes, most companies' attempts to insert themselves into online conversation come across as ham-fisted at best, and disingenuous at worst.[129]

---

[125] Pethokoukis (2005).

[126] Pethokoukis (2005).

[127] Technorati, "About Technorati," undated Web page.

[128] Louise Lee, "Dell: In the Bloghouse," *Business Week Online*, August 25, 2005.

[129] Kevin Allison, "Who's Afraid of the Big, Bad Blog?" *Financial Times*, November 4, 2005, p. 12.

Vespa,[130] the scooter company, for example, recently tasked two devoted fans to write unpaid blog submissions for its corporate Web site. Online marketing strategist Steve Rubel says, "Vespa has incredible fans, and we thought the best approach was to let the customers tell their stories online."[131]

Other companies empower employees to espouse their views on the Internet. Observed Mark Jen, a computer programmer in Silicon Valley, "When you go to an individual's blog and read the content . . . people will actually take the perception they get from an individual and project it on to the company they work for. . . ."[132] Similarly, a recent international poll conducted by the PR firm Edelman suggested that its regular employees hold levels of popular trust and credibility far surpassing those of CEOs and corporate spokespeople.[133] Brutal honesty and independence are key requirements for blog credibility. Robert Scoble, a Microsoft computer specialist, frequently promotes Microsoft products on his blog but does not shy from criticism. He once wrote that he loves his Microsoft SmartPhone,[134] but that "you can't compare that to the iPod."[135] As Robert Zeiger, communication chief for Alticor, told us, "They've got to hear some elements of doubt, elements of criticism. That is the homeopathic dose that gives the rest credibility."[136] Capitalizing on the opportunity, IBM has begun to encourage its employees to write blogs. At IBM's request, employees developed their own set of blogging principles. These are as follows:

Know and follow IBM's internal conduct guidelines.

Be mindful of what you write. You are personally responsible for your posts.

---

[130]Vespa® is a registered trademark of Piaggio and C., S.p.A.

[131]Quoted in Pethokoukis (2005).

[132]Quoted in Allison (2005).

[133]Edelman (2006).

[134]Microsoft® Smartphone® is a registered trademark of Microsoft Corporation.

[135]Allison (2005).

[136]Zeiger (2006).

Use your real name and state your role at IBM when writing about IBM-related matters.

Use a disclaimer stating that your postings do not necessarily represent IBM's positions, strategies or opinions.

Respect copyright, fair use, and financial disclosure laws.

Do not leak confidential or other proprietary information.

Do not talk about clients, partners or suppliers without their approval.

Respect your audience. Do not use profanity or ethnic slurs.

Find out who else is blogging about your topic and cite them.

Do not pick fights, and correct your own mistakes.

Try to add value. Provide worthwhile information and perspective.[137]

Using Influencers for Campaign Success

U.S. forces must impress people with who they are and what they are doing in order to motivate civilians to think well of them and communicate those thoughts to others. U.S. forces should also seek additional routes to increase the probability that social nodes and everyday influencers speak well of the coalition and its objectives. A certain caveat is worth noting: Overt manipulation of word of mouth can ultimately work against coalition forces. Observes Ed Keller of Roper ASW, "It has to be real or people will get turned off. Marketers can't go over the line or they're going to blow it. If you do something overly manipulative, you're going to get found out and it's going to work against you."[138] We recommend three specific avenues for fostering influencers in operational venues:

- Cultivate relationships with social node influencers.
- Use blogs to harness the influencing power of everyday people.
- Open Internet access to indigenous populations.

---

[137] Allison (2005).

[138] Quoted in Rand (2004).

Cultivate Relationships with Social-Node Influencers. Social nodes in present and future theaters of operation might include tribal, religious, civic, and other leaders. Coalition forces should seek to develop and sustain personal relationships with these and other social nodes and cull their opinions on policy and operations. One chief marketing officer stated,

> I would try to bring together more of the clerics. . . . The way to engage them is through dialogue. Talk about the violence. . . . "What are positive steps we can take?" "We really took to heart what you said and here are the action steps from our conversation." That has to happen because they control so much of society.[139]

The extent to which these individuals can come to view coalition forces as partners rather than overlords and the extent to which they see their ideas taken seriously will influence how they speak of U.S. initiatives.

Similar advice holds for those influencers who appear friendly to U.S. forces, but the coalition should take these individuals one step further. Like customer evangelists, relationships between coalition forces and selected social nodes should be strengthened with access and information. Two Iraqi dentists began writing a blog about the new Iraq several years ago. The nonprofit organization Spirit of America, whose efforts helped give these individuals Arabic blogging tools, brought them to the United States where they held an audience with President George W. Bush. This meeting and their overall trip no doubt left these individuals better educated regarding U.S. efforts, and it likely gave them many new insights that could be included in future blog entries. While meetings with the President of the United States are beyond the general reach of most individuals, the U.S. military may give unusually resourceful and positive influencers access to higher-echelon commanders or other U.S. and indigenous leaders.

---

[139] Anonymous chief marketing officer, interview with Todd C. Helmus, New York, March 1, 2006.

Use Blogs to Harness the Influencing Power of Everyday People. There are other individuals who have a propensity to speak their mind but lack the requisite social status to reach broad sectors of society. U.S. forces should empower them with the skills and technology to reach an audience broader than their local coffee shop. This is the power of the Internet, and it has revolutionized American society by flattening the communication architecture such that the power of the voice is no longer restricted to media moguls and politicians. In many areas where U.S. forces conduct operations, freedom of speech and economic revitalization and deregulation will open Internet access to millions of people. The United States must take advantage of this opportunity.[140]

The Internet, blogs, and podcasting offer another advantage. In locales marked by deleterious security situations, those who openly and visibly voice their support for U.S. forces and newly established democracies risk incrimination and retribution from insurgents and other adversaries. People's views are impacted by prevailing social attitudes and the groups to which they belong. If one thinks they are alone in their ideas, then those ideas are likely to remain sheltered and risk a quiet death.[141] Blogs provide an alternative space in which thought and opinion can be freely, openly, and safely expressed.

The United States should use this tool not to create fake and deceitful voices of support, but rather to tap broader segments of an otherwise quiet society. Business blogging practices provide a unique blueprint for action. Consider the potential power of a blog written by an indigenous soldier who fights alongside U.S. soldiers and marines. The soldier writes of his exploits fighting insurgents. Interspersed are discussions of a wife he dearly misses, off time with comrades, and associations with U.S. colleagues. He is no lackey of the coalition or

---

[140] Observes Thomas Goetz (2006),

> The reason American culture has become so powerful is because it's completely authentic and a blending of so many elements. It is a bubbling-up culture, from rock music to the Internet itself. It is about decentralized nodes that emerge and have much broader relevance. It's a culture of niche interests and expression, and sometimes those things blow up and you have Elvis.

[141] Myers (2005).

his superiors. He occasionally criticizes his government, the army, and the coalition, but these criticisms serve only to enhance his credibility. Not unlike the blogs written by U.S. personnel and eagerly consumed by the U.S. public, these dispatches from the front could make for popular reading.

We recommend that U.S. forces empower indigenous soldiers, government employees, and others with blogging tools that enable them to convincingly voice their messages to large sectors of the population. Like employee blogs, they require autonomy and freedom to spread their messages independent of the coalition and governing authorities. Guidelines should be established and monitored for compliance to prevent misuse and lapses in operational security. A selection process could be instituted to assist in ensuring that bloggers write with requisite ability. Of course, adequate Internet penetration in the host environment is a must for success and should be evaluated prior to program initiation.

It is worth noting that businesses strive to control their messages. They create well-crafted positioning statements and do all within their power to properly synchronize corporate actions and messages. Influencers present a challenge to these best-laid plans, as they are not beholden to corporate message platforms. They will find their own product attributes to praise, and they may advocate product uses unanticipated by corporate executives. Businesses have learned through the years to not fight these efforts and to let go of control of the message. The United States will have to take a similar approach, allowing social nodes and everyday influencers to reach their own conclusions and find their own voices.

Open Internet Access to Indigenous Populations. The previous discussion of blogging brings to mind another key question. Should the United States foster greater Internet use in areas where they conduct stability-and-support operations? It is not an easily answered question, given the degree to which the United States' adversaries have thus far dominated the medium. Expansion of indigenous Internet use runs the risk of enhancing enemy IO capabilities.

The Internet offers other possibilities. It connects individuals who have been shielded from globalization's advance by providing access to new and liberal ideas, international commerce, and education. If coalition forces see that the benefits of wide and equal Internet access outweigh the risks, there are several avenues of promotion. MIT professor Nicholas Negroponte stands on the verge of introducing a rugged, wireless-enabled $100 laptop. (See Figure 3.2.) The U.S. military should consider this tool and other related technologies as a means to provide low-cost computer access to children and adults who live in areas where the U.S. military conducts operations.[142]

Figure 3.2
The $100 Laptop

©UⒹDesign Ⓒntinuum for One Laptop per Ⓒild.Used under the conditions of the Ⓒeative Ⓒmmons License.
RAND MG607-3.2

---

[142]Recently developed technology, such as Novatium NovanetTV, enables TVs to be effectively used as very low-cost, Internet-connected computers (Jason Overdorf, "The $100 Un-PC," *Newsweek*, international ed., February 12, 2007).

Computers are important, but they must be linked to the Internet to reach their full potential. John Rendon of the Rendon Group sees the potential of installing wireless fidelity (Wi-Fi) clouds around U.S. military installations in the developing world:

> You want people connected to technology . . . broad-based and not micromanaged. Strategically, our goal is to get the street to be an active ally in GWOT. So every place U.S. forces go overseas in training or deployment, we should set up a Wi-Fi cloud and leave it there so schools and community centers [benefit from] our presence. . . . If you think about Air Force bases overseas, we own everything inside the gate [and nothing outside]. If we put access to the future in the community . . . the perimeter will be pushed out psychologically.[143]

Apply Discipline and Focus to Communication Campaigns

During counterinsurgency and other stability operations, U.S. and coalition forces must elicit specific changes in behavior from indigenous populations. These behaviors may include providing intelligence about adversaries, engaging in interethnic reconciliation, or participating in elections.

Social marketing applies well-grounded commercial marketing techniques to influence noncommercial behavioral change in a target audience. Past campaigns have sought to reduce littering, increase blood-drive participation, and promote an array of health-related behaviors. A growing body of scientific research attests to the effectiveness of these social marketing interventions, even those transported to the developing world.[144]

---

[143]John Rendon, Rendon Group, interview with Todd C. Helmus and Christopher Paul, Washington, D.C., December 15, 2005.

[144]Steven Chapman and Hibist Astatke, "Appendix to Annex 5: The Social Marketing Evidence Base," *Review of DFID Approach to Social Marketing*, Annex 5: *Effectiveness, Efficiency and Equity of Social Marketing*, London: DFID Health Systems Resource Centre, April 2003.

Like commercial marketing, social marketing is oriented to the specific needs and wants of the target audience. The exchange theory is applied such that the perceived benefits of making the specified change in behaving are at least equal to or exceed the costs of adopting that change. In addition, audiences are segmented into like-minded and like-behaving groups so that marketing efforts can be uniquely tailored to a target audience. Social marketing also calls for the crafting of a holistic offer through the application of the "4Ps"—product, price, place, and promotion. Finally, results of the campaign are measured to enable continual program improvements.[145]

Social marketing provides a useful framework for motivating civilian adherence to U.S. campaign objectives. The framework consists of the 10 steps presented below. They and much of their descriptions are adapted from *Social Marketing: Improving the Quality of Life* by researchers Philip Kotler, Ned Roberto, and Nancy Lee.[146] To illustrate the application of these steps in an operational theater, we utilize a running example of a "tip" program. A tip program is a hypothetical information campaign that seeks to motivate indigenous populations to provide intelligence to coalition forces.

- Step 1: Know your program focus.
- Step 2: Move the movable.
- Step 3: Clearly delineate your objectives and goals.
- Step 4: Know your market and competition.
- Step 5: Design a product just for them.
- Step 6: Make prices as low as they go.
- Step 7: Place the product: location, location, location.
- Step 8: Create messages that stand out and are motivating.
- Step 9: Get the message out.
- Step 10: Monitor and evaluate the success of the campaign.

---

[145] Philip Kotler, Ned Roberto, and Nancy Lee, *Social Marketing: Improving the Quality of Life*, 2nd ed., Thousand Oaks, Calif.: Sage Publications, 2002, pp. 10–11.

[146] Kotler, Roberto, and Lee (2002).

Step 1: Know Your Program Focus

Campaign planners must first select a program focus. The highway and transportation division may seek to reduce traffic fatalities by focusing on seat belt use, while the U.S. military may want to reduce insurgent violence by concentrating on the indigenous provision of intelligence. Next, it will be necessary to conduct an analysis of strengths, weaknesses, opportunities, and threats. Strengths and weaknesses evaluated should be those internal to the marketing program, such as available resources. Opportunities and threats are external factors, such as cultural, economic, political or demographic forces, that could assist or impede the program. Knowing these factors prior to program development will enable planners to take advantage of opportunities and mitigate the impact of foreseeable problems.[147]

Step 2: Move the Movable

This chapter began with a discussion of business segmentation techniques and their application to a theater of operations. These recommendations pertained to the overarching campaign plan. This process requires refinement when it comes to eliciting behavior change for specific message campaigns. Social marketers recommend audience segmentation based on the behavior addressed by the campaign's focus.[148] In a tip program, this would involve segmenting according to the willingness of the population to provide intelligence on adversaries. The stages of change model developed by Prochaska and DiClemente presents a useful paradigm. The model addresses five behavior stages:[149]

- Precontemplation: An individual has no intention of changing behavior in the near future.

---

[147] Kotler, Roberto, and Lee (2002, pp. 99–102). The stages of change model describes the degree to which an individual is willing to engage in a change of behavior.

[148] Kotler, Roberto, and Lee (2002, pp. 117–121).

[149] Kotler, Roberto, and Lee (2002, pp. 121–122).

- Contemplation: An individual acknowledges that there is a problem and is considering a change in behavior but has not yet made a commitment to change.
- Preparation: An individual has decided to change behavior but has not yet initiated that change.
- Action: The first steps of change are made.
- Maintenance: An individual consolidates the gains made during the action stage and attempts to prevent a relapse.

Those population segments most likely to respond to the campaign should be selected for targeting. This would likely involve those in the contemplation or preparation stages. New segments can be added as the campaign progresses.[150]

Step 3: Clearly Delineate Your Objectives and Goals

During this step, program objectives and goals must be established. *Objectives* refers to the specific behaviors the audience is "to accept, modify, abandon, or reject."[151] These behaviors should be simple, clear, and doable. Knowledge and belief objectives are also advised.[152]

Goals identifies specific behavior, knowledge, and belief outcomes that serve as benchmarks for campaign success. Table 3.3 summarizes the objectives of a hypothetical tip campaign.[153]

---

[150] Kotler, Roberto, and Lee (2002, pp. 128–129).

[151] Kotler, Roberto, and Lee (2002, p. 142).

[152] *Knowledge objectives* might involve the following: statistics on the risks of performing the current behavior, statistics on the benefits of the proposed behavior, facts that can help correct misconceptions, or information on how an audience might perform the behavior. Similarly, *belief objectives* might cause the target audience to believe that it is at risk, that it will benefit from adopting the new behavior, that it can successfully execute the desired behavior, or that the negative consequences associated with the new behavior are minimal (Kotler, Roberto, and Lee, 2002, pp. 142–148).

[153] Kotler, Roberto, and Lee (2002, pp. 148–150).

Table 3.3
Behavior, Knowledge, and Belief Objectives and Goals for a Hypothetical Tip Campaign

Problem	Objective and Goal		
	Behavior	**Knowledge**	**Belief**
Insurgent activity	Provide intelligence to coalition forces	All coalition force personnel will accept intelligence from the populace.	"I can safely provide intelligence to coalition authorities."
	Increase tips by 50%	Increase this knowledge by 75%	Increase this belief by 50%

SOURCE: Format adapted from Kotler, Roberto, and Lee (2002, p. 308).

Step 4: Know Your Market and Competition

Campaign planners must offer product, price, place, and promotional strategies that are attuned to their target audience. Planners must consequently understand target audience views regarding both the campaign's intended behavior and the behavior the campaign hopes to replace or otherwise influence (e.g., the competing behavior). Sample questions related to competing and desired behaviors are listed below. Hypothetical responses for a theater-based tip program appear in parentheses. Behavior, knowledge, or belief objectives and goals might have to be revised based on responses to these questions.

- In contrast to the behavior the campaign intends to influence, what would the target audience rather do (i.e., what is the preferred behavior)? (In a tip program, the populace may wish to remain silent.)
- What benefits does the target audience attribute to its preferred behavior? (Not providing intelligence to the coalition will keep civilians safe from insurgent retribution.)
- What costs does the target audience attribute to its preferred behavior? (Failure to provide intelligence may exacerbate violence.)
- Does it know how to perform the desired behavior? (The populace may not know what types of information it should provide.)

- What benefits does it attribute to the desired behavior? (Providing intelligence may help decrease violence.)
- What costs does it attribute to the desired behavior? (Providing intelligence may cost civilians their lives.)
- What barriers exist to performing this behavior? (The populace may not know to whom it can safely provide information.)[154]

Step 5: Design a Product Just for Them

There are three levels associated with the product the campaign intends to promote. These include (1) the actual product or the behavior the campaign intends to promote, (2) the core product or the benefits of performing the campaign's desired behavior (i.e., the benefits of the desired behavior), and (3) the augmented product or any tangible objects or services the campaign develops to support the target audience's behavior change. Tip program applications to this multifaceted "product" are depicted in Table 3.4. The core product or benefit of the desired behavior is determined partly through understanding a target audience and the benefits it associates with the desired behavior. (See step 4, "know your market and competition.") The augmented product is optional, but providing tangible objects and services can be critical in helping the audience overcome barriers.[155]

This product information is used to define the behavior change's positioning. The positioning is simply the benefit the customer is supposed to associate with a given product. Importantly, the intended benefits must be greater than the benefits the target audience associates with its current behaviors. Positioning statements are derived by filling in the blanks of the following statement:

> I want my target audience to see ____ (desired behavior) as _____ (positive benefits of adopting the behavior) and as more important and beneficial than ____ (the competing behavior).[156]

---

[154] Kotler, Roberto, and Lee (2002, pp. 167–168).

[155] Kotler, Roberto, and Lee (2002, pp. 194–203).

[156] Adapted from Kotler, Roberto, and Lee (2002, p. 203).

Table 3.4
Products in a Campaign Designed to Motivate Indigenous Populations to Provide Intelligence on Anticoalition Insurgents

Product	Description
Desired behavior	Provide information on insurgents or criminals to local, national, or coalition authorities
Associated benefits	Reduced violence and crime in the neighborhood
Tangible object	Free text-messaging software so that residents can text their tips anonymously
Service	Local town hall meetings that explain how the tip program works

Someone using the tip program might fill the blanks in the following way:

I want my target audience to see that providing authorities with accurate information on insurgents and criminals (desired behavior) as a way to reduce crime and violence in their neighborhood (positive benefits of adopting the behavior) and as more important and beneficial than protecting insurgent and criminal identities (the competing behavior).

Step 6: Make Prices as Low as They Go

The price in social marketing is the cost that the target audience associates with performing the new behavior. Nonmonetary costs are "associated with time, effort, and energy to perform the behavior; psychological risks and losses that might be perceived or experienced; and any physical discomforts that may be related to the behavior."[157] Exchange theory must guide the campaign: The benefits associated with the campaign's intended behavior must be equal to or greater than the costs the target audience must pay to perform the behavior.[158] Campaign planners must craft a price for behavior change that is acceptable to target

---

[157] Kotler, Roberto, and Lee (2002, p. 217).

[158] Kotler, Roberto, and Lee (2002, p. 217).

audiences. The following four approaches are described by Kotler, Roberto, and Lee:[159]

1. Decrease nonmonetary costs. Decrease time, effort, physical, or psychological costs. In the tip example, consider the following strategies:
    a. Decrease physical risks by ensuring anonymity.
    b. Decrease psychological risks related to social norm violations by communicating high tip-call volume (thus demonstrating that "everyone is doing it").
    c. Decrease time by having soldiers or marines request tips from citizens when they are on patrol.
2. Decrease costs relative to the competition. Compare the costs of performing the intended behavior with those of the target audience's preferred behavior. A tip message campaign can include an ad comparing the simple task of calling a tip line versus expressions of grief over a loved one lost to violence.
3. Increase monetary benefits. Provide participating neighborhoods with exceptional benefits beyond the support normally made available or provide monetary rewards to those performing the intended behavior.
4. Increase nonmonetary benefits. Recognize and appreciate those who perform the intended behaviors. In a tip program, representatives who receive information can certainly heap praise on individuals who provide information while preserving their anonymity. Information campaigns can likewise express gratitude.

Step 7: Place the Product: Location, Location, Location
Behaviors intended by the campaign must be performed at a certain time and in a certain place. This time and place should be as convenient as possible for target audiences.[160] Four approaches to accomplishing this, with relevant examples, are as follows:[161]

---

[159] Kotler, Roberto, and Lee (2002, pp. 220–228).

[160] Kotler, Roberto, and Lee (2002, p. 243).

[161] Kotler, Roberto, and Lee (2002, pp. 244–253).

1. Make the location closer. For example, create hotlines so that the population can call in tips rather than visit a forward operating base. Can the time it takes to place a tip call be reduced? Can dismounted patrols be increased so that coalition and indigenous troops can interact with the populace?

2. Extend hours. For example, is the tip hotline available for only a few hours a day? Can this period be increased?

3. Make the location more appealing. Can visits to forward operating bases be made more discreet or pleasant?

4. Be there at the point of decisionmaking. Local townspeople may be more apt to provide intelligence immediately after witnessing an attack, thereby requiring a timely canvassing of targeted neighborhoods by U.S. forces. Members of the 1/15th Stryker Brigade Combat Team would enter a neighborhood immediately after the detonation of a mortar or other munition, canvassing the affected neighborhood to learn what residents might know about the event and to inquire about the welfare of their families. The combination of timely arrival and expressions of concern often resulted in valuable information being provided to the soldiers.[162]

Step 8: Create Messages That Stand Out and Are Motivating

Message campaigns must raise awareness of the campaign, convince the target audience that it will benefit from the behavior change and motivate it to act.[163] Crafting messages is a complex process, and it is beyond the scope of this monograph to provide an in-depth discussion of its practice.[164] We do address two elements critical to the message formulation process: the creative brief and the pretesting of messages.

---

[162]LTC Michael E. Kurilla, U.S. Army, interview with Russell W. Glenn, Mosul, Iraq, July 9, 2005.

[163]Kotler, Roberto, and Lee (2002, p. 264).

[164]For more information about message campaigns, see William Wells, Sandra Moriarty, and John Burnett, eds., *Advertising: Principles and Practice*, 7th ed., Upper Saddle River, N.J.: Prentice Hall, 2006; and John Caples, *Tested Advertising Methods*, 5th ed., Paramus, N.J., Prentice Hall, 1997.

A creative brief must be formulated before any message-crafting can begin. Creative briefs are usually only a couple of pages in length but are critical to effective synchronization and coordination among disparate parties responsible for executing a campaign. The key characteristics of a creative brief, as presented by Kotler, Roberto, and Lee in *Social Marketing: Improving the Quality of Life*, are as follows:[165]

- *key message:* a single statement that details the primary message
- *target audience:* audience demographics; geographic profile; current knowledge, beliefs, and behaviors; and desired and competing behaviors and stage-of-change profiles (step 2)
- *communication objectives:* detailed behavior, knowledge, and belief objectives (step 3)
- *benefits to promise:* what the target audience hopes to achieve through performing the intended behavior (step 5)
- *support for promise:* additional benefits highlighted in step 5 and the developed product, price, and place strategies
- *openings:* when (times) and where (places and situations) the target audience is most receptive to the message and most likely to act on it (steps 3 and 4)
- *position:* reinforcement of the positioning statement crafted in step 5.[166]

Once a message is crafted, it should undergo pretesting to verify that it connects with the target audience in a convincing, effective, and inoffensive manner. This is particularly important for ads running in foreign markets, as intuition is a particularly poor evaluation method given the unfamiliarity of the cultural landscape.[167] Qualitatively, ads can be pretested by being shown to focus groups consisting

---

[165] Kotler, Roberto, and Lee (2002, pp. 264–266).

[166] The positioning statement presented in step 5 is as follows:

> I want my target audience to see _____ (desired behavior) as _____ (positive benefits of adopting the behavior) and as more important and beneficial than _____ (the competing behavior). (Adapted from Kotler, Roberto, and Lee, 2002, p. 203)

[167] Wells, Moriarty, and Burnett (2006, p. 549).

of members of the target audience. Though yielding rich diagnostic information, small sample sizes increase the risk for biased information. Quantitatively, there are several methods for both pre- and post-testing. Viewers can be queried as to their recall of the ad's story line (after the message is shown amidst other ads or programming), their attitudes toward the ad (e.g., likability, uniqueness, believability), and its persuasive appeal.[168]

The specific measures used will likely be determined by various factors, including the goal of the ad campaign. A new campaign seeking to increase brand awareness may be most interested in memory recall, while established campaigns may be most interested in likability.[169]

Step 9: Get the Message Out

Shaping-campaign planners next need to identify the media that will convey the message. Ideally, they will know the media habits of targeted segments, enabling pinpoint accuracy in their selection.

Kotler, Roberto, and Lee recommend that planners consider three major approaches when determining media channels: mass, selective, and personal. Mass media (e.g., television, radio, billboards, newspapers) target large groups of people and are especially helpful when it is important to quickly inform a broad cross-section of a population. Selective media (e.g., direct mail, flyers, posters, telemarketing, Internet) are generally more cost-effective than mass media area and allow planners to communicate more information to a more narrowly defined target audience. Finally, personal media (i.e., one-on-one interactions with the target audience, such as soldier-civilian interactions, seminars, or training sessions) are more expensive than mass or selective media are but permit personalized interaction with the target audience and provide it detailed information while also building trust and addressing individualized target-audience barriers to message accep-

---

[168] David Olson, "Principles of Measuring Advertising Effectiveness," American Marketing Association, 2001.

[169] Olson (2001).

tance. Integration of all three approaches allows for mutually reinforcing messages.[170]

Decisions related to reach and frequency must be addressed next. *Reach* measures the percent of people in a target market who are exposed to the message in a given period. *Frequency* is the number of times the average person in the target audience is exposed to the message. Planners of a smoking-cessation campaign, for example, might determine that they want to reach 50 percent of 20- to 30-year-old adults at least 10 times in a six-month campaign. Ensuring adequate penetration of the marketplace is a challenge in markets with many media choices. In the United States, for example, 80 percent of Americans could be reached with three TV spots in 1965, whereas 97 spots would be required to reach that percentage today.[171] New campaigns likely require greater levels of reach and frequency than do more established campaigns. A new commercial brand will spend as much as 40 percent of its budget in the first few months after product launch.[172]

With media determined, specific media vehicles must also be evaluated. Media vehicles are the particular TV shows or magazines in which the ad will be placed. Again, this will require an understanding of the target audience so that identified vehicles are those most likely to be viewed by that target audience.[173] Related to this is the current trend in advertising to customize messages to specific audience demographic

---

[170] Kotler, Roberto, and Lee (2002, pp. 304–305).

[171] Brian Sternthal and Angela Y. Lee, "Building Brands Through Effective Advertising," in Alice M. Tybout and Tim Calkins, eds., *Kellogg on Branding*, Hoboken, N.J.: John Wiley and Sons, 2005, pp. 129–149 [p. 129].

[172] Sternthal and Lee (2005, p. 143).

[173] Vehicles with high exposure will also have relatively expensive advertising fees. Consequently, media planners will calculate the cost per thousand persons reached by a particular vehicle. In a commercial marketing paradigm, a 30-second television spot during one of CBS' CSI programs may cost $100,000 and reach 1 million people, while a Golf Channel spot might cost $100,000 but reach 500,000. Thus, the CBS spot would cost $100 to reach 1,000 people, while the Golf Channel ad would cost $200 to reach the same number. However, while the Golf Channel program is more expensive, it may be that the target audience (e.g., golfers) is far more likely to watch the Golf Channel than a *CSI* show, and research may also suggest that, by virtue of making more money than the CSI-viewing demographic, the target audience is more receptive to making the intended purchase.

groups that are more likely to tune in to a particular TV channel or show or read specific magazines. Consequently, the same business may produce ads for both the Golf Channel and CBS' *CSI* drama series franchise, but the ads will have story lines specifically suited to different viewerships.[174]

Finally, media timing must be determined. This is simply the time of year and time of day that the ad is placed. Once again, specific media timing is determined through an understanding of the media habits of target audiences. If demographic, geographic, and psychographic data suggest that the target audience will be most attuned to a particular medium during a certain time of the day, planners should pursue slots in that period. Another factor related to timing is the need to be present "in the event of."[175] Where certain events are likely to raise awareness of problems the campaign intends to address, there may be value in increasing the reach and frequency of campaign messages. For example, in the hypothetical tip program, events such as an insurgent or terrorist attack that has caused civilian casualties may be an ideal time to ensure that the local populace is aware of the campaign.

Step 10: Monitor and Evaluate the Success of the Campaign

Campaign planners should monitor and evaluate the success of message campaigns. *Monitoring* refers to an ongoing assessment of campaign outcomes and enables the early detection and correction of problems. *Evaluation* involves a single and final campaign assessment and allows for collection of lessons learned critical to improving subsequent campaigns. Both are measured via outcome and process measures. Outcome measures evaluate the specific behavioral, knowledge, and belief changes that a campaign is intended to promote.[176] Potential indicators for outcomes are as follows:

---

[174] Brian Steinberg, "Speaking Up Through Bespoke Ads," *Wall Street Journal,* February 11, 2005b, p. B5.

[175] Kotler, Roberto, and Lee (2002, pp. 310–311).

[176] Kotler, Roberto, and Lee (2002, p. 327).

- Behavior: Specific behavior changes can be measured by a percentage increase or decrease or by a change in raw numbers.
- Behavior intent: Where specific behavioral changes cannot be measured, it may be possible to question the target audience about its intention to adopt the desired behavior.
- Knowledge: The population can be surveyed about important facts and recommendations.
- Beliefs: Beliefs can be measured through the evaluation of attitudes, opinions, and values.
- Campaign awareness: Campaign awareness measures the extent to which the target population notices or recalls the campaign.[177]

Process measures evaluate campaign efforts to reach the target audience. These include the following:

- Reach and frequency: Campaign planners can estimate the number of people exposed to the campaign and the number of times they were exposed.
- Media coverage: Media and public relations coverage of a campaign can evaluate newspaper and magazine coverage (number of column inches related to the campaign), television and radio coverage (minutes of airtime), and exposure to program-related seminars (number of people in attendance).
- Total number of impressions and cost per impression: This measure evaluates the total campaign costs and divides them by the number of people exposed to the campaign.[178]

Outcomes will ideally be surveyed at the following three points in time: prior to the launch of the campaign, so that baseline measures can be obtained; during the campaign, so that midcourse adjustments can be made; and after the campaign's conclusion.[179] The pri-

---

[177] Kotler, Roberto, and Lee (2002, pp. 328–329).

[178] Kotler, Roberto, and Lee (2002, pp. 330–331).

[179] Baseline measures are critical in that they ultimately provide a benchmark with which the rest of the campaign can be compared.

mary measurement tool will ideally be surveys of the target audience, though other options are available.[180] In the case of the tip program, the number of incoming tips can be catalogued for a precampaign baseline period, monitored throughout the campaign, and measured again after its conclusion.

A Concluding Comment on Integration

> When armed insurgents moved into her southern Baghdad neighborhood last spring and started threatening Shiite families like hers, Umm Hussein called Iraq's widely publicized 24-hour terrorism hot line. Nobody answered.
>
> —*Kirk Semple*[181]

The message campaign will be a central feature of this effort and, as such, will likely require support from IO and PSYOP. However, a well-synchronized campaign will demand the coordinated efforts of the entire friendly force. PSYOP will likely craft specific program goals and objectives and create broadcast messages. Message campaigns will require considerable intelligence support. In addition, ground forces will ultimately be charged with backing the implied promises made by the media campaign. In the tip program paradigm, all U.S. ground personnel, including those whose tasks are limited to convoy and other support operations, must understand their roles in accepting intelligence from the indigenous population. These forces must similarly make themselves more approachable to civilians, learn and apply discreet collection methods so as not to jeopardize the lives of informants, and uniformly express appreciation for assistance. Conversations with civilians should convey themes similar to those broadcast by the PSYOP element of the campaign (e.g., benefits associated with providing intelligence). Soldiers supporting the Regional Assistance Mission to Solomon Islands (RAMSI) in late 2003 were issued cards before going out on patrol to ensure that they were "on message" with

---

[180]Kotler, Roberto, and Lee (2002, pp. 332–334).

[181]Kirk Semple, "U.S. Backs Hot Line in Iraq to Solicit Tips About Trouble," *New York Times*, November 5, 2006, p. 14.

operational objectives.[182] Unity of message will never be perfect, but it is essential to achieve it to the extent possible.

Integrated marketing communication is a marketing concept that calls on a company to coordinate communication activities to "deliver a clear, consistent, and compelling message about the organization and its products."[183] Integration activities are addressed in greater detail in Chapter Four, but Kotler, Roberto, and Lee's observations provide a useful frame of reference for the U.S. military:

> Integrated marketing communications means achieving consistency in the use of slogans, images, colors, font types, key messages, and sponsor mentions in all media vehicles. It means that statistics and facts used in press releases are the same as those in printed materials. It means that television commercials have the same tone and style as radio spots and that print ads have the same look and feel as the program's Web site.
>
> In addition, [integrated marketing communication] points to the need for a graphic identity and perhaps even a statement or manual describing graphic standards. The integrated approach also addresses the need for coordination and cooperation between those developing and disseminating program materials and, finally, calls for regular audits of all customer contact points.[184]

Summary

This chapter has reviewed various business marketing tactics that may guide U.S. military efforts to shape the attitudes and behavior of indigenous populations. Business-based segmentation and targeting practices can help the U.S. military identify the target audiences

---

[182] Russell W. Glenn, *Counterinsurgency in a Test Tube: Analyzing the Success of the Regional Assistance Mission to Solomon Islands (RAMSI)*, Santa Monica, Calif.: RAND Corporation, MG-551-JFCOM, 2007.

[183] Kotler and Armstrong (2006, p. 430).

[184] Kotler, Roberto, and Lee (2002, p. 308).

most likely to support U.S. force presence. Business positioning strategies can guide creation of end states that are meaningful and salient. Branding concepts are especially important to the military, as they seek to mold indigenous opinions of a U.S. force and create a synchronized approach to shaping operations and soldier-civilian interactions. While businesses strive to create satisfied customers, so should the military understand the importance of satisfaction in inculcating positive civilian attitudes. Management of expectations, basing operational and reconstruction decisions on the civilian voice (at least to an extent), and monitoring outcomes through measures of satisfaction are three critical approaches. Because U.S. forces often lack the requisite credibility with a host-nation populace, it is critically important that they harness the power of indigenous influencers. U.S. forces should also employ discipline and focus to communication campaigns by applying a systematic social marketing framework.

CHAPTER FOUR

Shaping Solutions Based on Recent Operational Experiences

The commercial marketing industry cannot provide all the relevant lessons for today's complex operational environment. Many facets of U.S. operations fall outside those anticipated or experienced by the U.S. business community. Managing use of force, exigencies of troop rotations, and shaping in preparation for future conflicts are but a few examples. In addition, there are unique requirements for specific entities involved in U.S. shaping operations, such as maneuver units, CA, IO, and PA. This chapter addresses those topical areas otherwise unattended by commercial marketing. These lessons for shaping the perceptions and behaviors of indigenous audiences are based on recent operational experiences (primarily in Afghanistan and Iraq, but also from peacetime operations in Southeast Asia, Europe, and elsewhere in the world). The format is akin to a lessons-learned analysis. The chapter is organized by recommendation area. Following from the central premise of this monograph—that, in many foreseeable operations, shaping will be a major component of the mission—the following 11 general recommendations are presented:

- Pursue anticipatory shaping.
- Better leverage CA/CMO activities.
- Manage use of force for shaping.
- Establish and preserve credibility.
- Integrate communication.
- Improve communication resource allocation, grade structure, joint training, and processes.
- Address shaping intelligence requirements.

- Establish and maintain the relationships that shaping requires.
- Better respond to mistakes.
- Counter adversary shaping efforts.
- Improve relations with news media.

Pursue Anticipatory Shaping

> The most popular toy in Pakistan today is the little plastic Army
> Chinook. . . .
> —*GEN Peter Schoomaker, U.S. Army Chief of Staff*[1]

The United States may have already missed a vital opportunity to shape indigenous populations by the time international contingencies required full-scale military operations. Proactive shaping efforts should be undertaken before major security problems arise. Not only can they lay the essential groundwork for operational success, but they may completely forestall the need for such operations in the first place. This preconditioning is referred to as *phase 0 operations* or *anticipatory shaping.* Several U.S. COCOMs currently conduct anticipatory shaping as part of GWOT with the goal of limiting the burgeoning influx of radical ideology and popular support for terrorist organizations. Future shaping efforts can benefit from lessons learned during these operations.

Contemporary anticipatory shaping efforts consist largely of foreign internal defense (FID) and "doing good" through CA activities. FID operations include direct instruction of foreign military security forces and the conduct of joint training exercises. These efforts enable indigenous prosecution of GWOT and form the backbone for strong military-to-military relationships. M. A. Thomas of the 4th PSYOP Group helps conduct joint U.S.-Thai PSYOP exercises. He observed a direct correlation between the number of U.S. visits to Thailand and

---

[1]   Quoted in MountainRunner, "DoD as Our Public Diplomat in Pakistan," blog entry, *MountainRunner*, January 13, 2006.

the quality of interaction between U.S. and Thai military personnel.[2] Such relationships are crucial, in part because young military officers with U.S. contacts often advance in rank to ultimately hold positions as key influencers.

CA and other efforts fall under the rubric of "doing good." In the horn of Africa and the Philippines, CA units build schools, dig clean wells, and provide medical care via MEDCAPs. These efforts and corresponding interactions show the local population a positive side to U.S. forces that is otherwise not projected in local media. After a CA-sponsored project to remove garbage from the streets of the Kenyan town of Mokowe, news reports quoted a local observing, "We're used to only hearing about the American soldiers fighting. . . . They are friendly. We appreciate it. We like them to come here."[3]

CA activities further seek to thwart militant recruitment through economic development. One observer with whom we spoke mentioned the huge success of Joint Task Force 5-10 in the Philippines, during whose time a lawless region was reportedly made fairly stable through a joint U.S.-Filipino CA venture.[4]

While U.S. forces conduct military training and CA work, their presence also allows them the opportunity to conduct other critical shaping tasks. For one, they cultivate relationships with U.S. embassy and USAID personnel, helping to establish a framework for future interagency coordination. In addition, U.S. forces collect cultural intelligence critical to operational success and learn the identities of indigenous influencers.

Major Lawrence Tessier of the 6th PSYOP Battalion, part of the 4th PSYOP Group, detailed a campaign to immunize African children. He observed that the campaign provided benefits beyond positive public exposure:

---

[2]   M. A. Thomas, Area Analyst, 4th Psychological Operations Group, interview with Todd C. Helmus and Christopher Paul, Ft. Bragg, N.C., December 14, 2005.

[3]   Quoted in Kevin Maurer, "Fort Bragg Troops Are on a Goodwill Mission in Africa," Fayetteville (N.C.) Observer, August 6, 2006.

[4]   McDonald and Brown (2006).

[The] point of immunizations was getting access to key commu-
nicators. [This, in turn, provided answers to key questions. For
example,] what type of sway do these locals have to communicate? Is it word of mouth or radio broadcast? What are people
listening to up north? At the lowest common denominator, it is
to identify leaders to influence them.[5]

The campaign additionally provided the United States with the
opportunity to form relationships with established NGOs.

Disasters in foreign lands provide other shaping opportunities. In
2005, calamity struck Indonesia, Thailand, and Pakistan. The tsunami
that hit Indonesia and Thailand killed upward of 200,000 people and
left thousands more without food or shelter.[6] Pakistan's massive earthquake took the lives of more than 79,000 people.[7] In both instances,
the United States responded with humanitarian aid to feed and shelter the afflicted and provided needed medical aid. This assistance was
a manifestation of U.S. goodwill and an understanding of the nation's
global responsibility. However, the strategic shaping consequences
cannot be overlooked. In Indonesia, post-tsunami polls indicated that
79 percent of the populace reported increased favorability toward the
United States.[8] Favorable opinion of the United States increased from
23 percent to 46 percent in the span of less than a year after the Pakistan earthquake.[9]

While these anticipatory shaping actions are extraordinarily helpful to U.S. interests, stronger efforts are needed to maintain their gains,

---

[5]　MAJ Lawrence Tessier, Assistant Operations Officer, 6th Psychological Operations Bat-
talion, 4th Psychological Operations Group, Psychological Operations Support Element in
Nigeria, in Kuwait in support of OIF, interview with Todd C. Helmus and Christopher Paul,
Ft. Bragg, N.C., December 14, 2005.

[6]　UN Office of the Special Envoy for Tsunami Recovery, "The Human Toll," undated.

[7]　Associated Press, "New Figures Put Quake Toll at More Than 79,000," *MSNBC*, October
19, 2005.

[8]　Nicole Speulda, "Documenting the Phenomenon of Anti-Americanism," The Princeton
Project on National Security, posted November 7, 2005.

[9]　Terror Free Tomorrow, "Poll: Dramatic Change of Public Opinion in the Muslim World,"
2005.

lest the benefit fade. For CA, humanitarian missions, and military-to-military relationships, John Rendon cautions that

> it has to be enduring. When you look at how the U.S. military functions overseas, the ways they engage [are] all treated as one-offs. We will go to Honduras and do [a medical mission.] . . . we need someone to go back a year later and another year [later] so it's an enduring relationship.[10]

He similarly suggests the need to maintain relationships with indigenous militaries. He notes that U.S. flag officers traveling overseas could sit down for dinner with six officers previously trained by the U.S. military. "If you did that for six months," he told us, "you'd have 10,000 third-party validators."[11] Bruce Gregory, director of George Washington University's Public Diplomacy Institute, concurs and maintains that the United States needs to keep track of the identities and locations of military exchange program graduates so that they can be contacted after they complete their training.[12]

Anticipatory shaping demands advance planning for communication and other in-theater shaping activities. Christopher Lamb's 2005 PSYOP lessons-learned study finds that "PSYOP [and other shaping] must be involved early in the planning stage of operations in order to maximize its effects."[13] A UK report on OIF also noted, "An information campaign, to be successful, needs to start as early as possible and continue into the post-conflict phase of an operation."[14] Shaping success requires sufficient lead time in planning. Military leaders need to establish shaping objectives early, attach shaping themes and actions to them, and keep them consistent to the greatest extent possible.

---

[10] Rendon (2005).

[11] Rendon (2005).

[12] Bruce Gregory, Director, Public Diplomacy Institute, George Washington University, interview with Todd C. Helmus, Washington, D.C., December 26, 2005.

[13] Lamb (2005, p. 16).

[14] UK Ministry of Defence, *Operations in Iraq: Lessons for the Future*, London: Directorate General Corporate Communication, December 2003, p. 57.

Former Assistant Secretary of Defense for Public Affairs Torie Clarke concurs:

> As they say, "To help you on the landing, I need to be there at the takeoff." . . . If they're in the mix, the communications staff can push hard on policy or operations people who may not have thought through all the potential consequences of a decision. Good communications people tend to be a paranoid lot. They can often spot a truly awful disaster before it occurs.[15]

Better Leverage CA/CMO Activities

> We all have war stories [about] how we won over [the] local villager with aid. . . . I get emails to this day from the Shia tribesman from Hilla. . . . You win over a town and that has force protection value. . . . The town will look out for you. In Hilla, villagers put themselves at risk to protect the military compound.
> —*LtCol. Alan Burghard, U.S. Marine Corps*[16]

> Cooperate with us and the PRT will come quicker. Do not and the PRT may never come.
> —*COL Robert Duffy, U.S. Army*[17]

CA activities have enormous potential for positive shaping. U.S. forces are seen doing good works. They also improve the life and well-being of indigenous residents through activities such as infrastructural repairs, economic revitalization, and employment programs. The U.S. military should expand the scope and reach of these operations. Beyond this, U.S. forces could better capitalize on existing CA operations by ensuring that CA actions receive greater publicity, integrating the short- and long-term benefits of their actions, and, with caution, using CA as a

---

[15] Torie Clarke, *Lipstick on a Pig: Winning in the No-Spin Era by Someone Who Knows the Game,* New York: Free Press, 2006, p. 178.

[16] LtCol. Alan G. Burghard, U.S. Marine Corps, Civil Affairs Officer during OIF, interview with Todd C. Helmus, Santa Monica, Calif., March 23, 2006.

[17] Duffy (2004).

reward for indigenous behavior that meets coalition shaping-campaign goals. CMO and the good they do should unfailingly be integrated parts of shaping efforts.

Enhance the publicity given CA accomplishments. One Marine Corps briefing on humanitarian assistance and CMO observes, "It is not enough to do good things for the local populace. You must also broadcast that fact to a wider audience than the direct recipients of your assistance."[18] To this end, the United States must integrate communication-shaping assets with CA units. Combat camera personnel can photograph CA operations, and the photographs can, in turn, be offered to local media by PA representatives.[19] PSYOP personnel should similarly apply their tradecraft to broadening the message of CA assistance. Given the need to train as you fight, Army and Marine CA units and the U.S. Naval Construction Battalion Force (Seabees) should conduct regular exercises with combat camera, PA, and PSYOP personnel prior to deployment.[20] This will improve coordination and working relationships and will enhance mutual trust. Because indigenous media have greater credibility with local populations, CA units should facilitate the embedding of local media or otherwise encourage local coverage of operations.[21]

CA personnel shared two additional successful practices for publicizing CMO. The first is to stimulate local awareness and participation by employing indigenous populations. Maj. Amber Lehning suggests, "Say it's not a MEDCAP; say it's [construction of a] building. How many people do you need to [build] a building? Triple it and bring in other villagers to help."[22] Second, as CA physician Alan "Doc"

---

[18] U.S. Marine Corps Security Cooperation Education and Training Center, "Perspectives on HA/CMO in Iraq," briefing notes, undated.

[19] COL John Davis, U.S. Army, Special Operations Command, interview with Todd C. Helmus, Tampa, Fla., January 19, 2006.

[20] Champagne (2005).

[21] Bill Mendenhall, President, Mendenhall and Associates, interview with Todd C. Helmus, Holland, Mich., November 28, 2006.

[22] Maj. Amber Lehning, U.S. Marine Corps, Civil Affairs Officer during OIF, interview with Todd C. Helmus, Santa Monica, Calif., March 23, 2006.

Spira suggests, conduct multiple MEDCAP (or related) missions in a similar location and enhance publicity by allowing inhabitants of neighboring locales the opportunity to learn of and plan for subsequent attendance:

> You do a MEDCAP successfully. You do not end it there. You come back at regular intervals so, between those times, the word spreads and you find more people. [In previous operations,] we did three rounds. . . . By the third week, we had people walking for six hours to come to us. That was very successful.[23]

Beyond increasing publicity for CA actions, the United States should balance the short- and long-term impact of CA operations and reconstruction. After the cessation of hostilities, there is a critical window in which restoration attempts can have an unusually pronounced effect on shaping the population. Many reconstruction projects take several months to be completed; their impact is all but invisible to the majority of the indigenous population until that time. Implementing projects that have immediate impact and high visibility is critical to establishing U.S. force credibility and presence. There is a need to integrate near-term projects with longer-term efforts in a program that demonstrates consistency in provision of aid.

Commander Emergency Relief Program (CERP) funds that permit discretionary spending by maneuver commanders have proven to be a critical ally in CA efforts. These funds can immediately fill in the gap between cessation of major hostilities and the completion of major reconstruction projects. Anthony Cordesman observes,

> The civilian aid program at best is far too slow and cumbersome for hearts and minds and unfocused in terms of security and local objectives. If the military had not had major CERP funds, and spent them quickly, it seems almost certain that Iraqi hostility would today be far greater and the civil aid program and nation building effort would never have had time to take hold. The mili-

---

23 CDR Alan M. Spira, U.S. Navy, Civil Affairs Officer, interview with Todd C. Helmus, Santa Monica, Calif., March 23, 2006.

tary may not like armed nation building, but it seems clear that it is the most vital aspect of the aid effort in asymmetric wars and it seems unlikely that civil or contractor efforts can ever be a substitute.[24]

CA units, interagency organizations, and civilian contractors should follow closely behind tactical units so that they can begin restoration efforts immediately after major combat operations have ceased. These projects should have extensive reach and high visibility. Commanders could be similarly prepared to provide humanitarian relief and postcombat restoration immediately after (or even prior to) the cessation of combat operations. To facilitate this, commanders must be allocated ample CERP funds, the use of which is coordinated with CA efforts. Instruction regarding their use should be provided during officer and NCO development courses.

U.S. forces can further use CMO and CERP funds to encourage civilian behaviors that are key to counterinsurgency success. CA projects may be allocated or strategically withheld based on adherence to U.S. operational goals. To work effectively, the United States must set forth clearly defined rules that identify expectations for the population. For example, LtCol. William Costantini observed a marine colleague using CA incentives to direct relationships with local tribal and civic leaders in Iraq: "[A marine associate] came down and said, 'I'm not giving you anything because every day I drive by someone shoots at me. Next time I drive by [and] no one shoots at me, you get something.'"[25]

Likewise, use CMO "rewards" to highlight the benefits of compliance. Communities that do well then become positive examples to those behaving poorly:

> In a counterinsurgency, you need to spend money on your friends as well as those you want to have be your friends. . . . It doesn't work when you're only spending money after you've devas-

---

[24] Cordesman, Anthony H., *The "Instant Lessons" of the Iraq War: Main Report*, third working draft, Washington, D.C.: Center for Strategic and International Studies, April 14, 2003.

[25] Costantini (2005).

tated everything. You're just rebuilding something after you've destroyed it. . . . Rather than be asked to sustain, we should have been asked to reinforce success. Money should have flowed into Kurdistan and areas in the south. That would have given the government in Baghdad a lever.[26]

Note that this approach must be used with caution. An insurgent group may take action in an area with the deliberate intention of denying it coalition aid, thereby reducing the likelihood of local support for friendly force efforts. It may be advisable to provide aid despite negative events to show that the enemy is the insurgent rather than an innocent member of the population. Alternatively, all communities can be given a base level of support, with those that are more supportive receiving extraordinary benefits. It is critical, in these and other approaches, not to neglect those communities that continue to support the coalition by concentrating resources on efforts to make progress elsewhere.

Manage Use of Force for Shaping

In the web of interconnected actions and communications that contribute to shaping, kinetic actions are among the most significant. Civilian casualties and infrastructure damage inflicted at the hands of U.S. and coalition forces inflame local opinions of U.S. forces, contribute to an increasing pool of adversaries, and undermine U.S. shaping-campaign themes of good will and protection for civilian residents. Circumstances will still demand the application of U.S. firepower and will, in fact, serve shaping goals by communicating U.S. determination to pursue adversaries, but use of force must be well managed.

Close attention should be paid to the selection of weapon systems; indirect-fire munitions and aerial bombardment may need to be put aside in favor of snipers, AC-130 engagements, and other capabilities that can at once deliver greater accuracy and more controllable effects.

---

[26] Anonymous interview.

As suggested in Chapter Three, ensure that the shaping campaign clearly articulates the need for force, how force applications benefit the civilian populace, and how the onus of its application falls directly on coalition adversaries. Conduct procedural reviews of vehicle control points and other operational settings where noncombatants frequently fall victim to U.S. fire. The number of civilian casualties should be continually monitored as a measure of the success of these efforts.

Beyond cautions regarding kinetic force, persuasion can be accomplished both by the carrot and the stick. Effective shaping campaigns will consider the possible application of both. Consider these examples from Iraq:

> The bombs did not stop, so Col. [Steven] Salazar implemented a strategy he has used throughout his area of operations, the western half of Diyala, just north of Baghdad: shut down the road on which any roadside bomb is found for 24 to 48 hours. It is a matter of safety, but also one of spreading the pain. If the local community is inconvenienced by a road closure, goes the theory, perhaps they will put pressure on the insurgents to stop.[27]

> This is before we knew who the local sheik was. . . . Andy [LtCol. Andy Kennedy, Commanding Officer, 3/4 Marines] was sending his guys into this area and rooting through peoples' houses every night. And the sheik came and said, 'What will it take to stop your guys from rooting through our houses?" And Andy said, "Stop IEDs." It wasn't overnight, but they did significantly reduce the number of IEDs.[28]

Efforts to shape with the stick can be dangerous and may backfire, increasing public resentment against coalition forces. U.S. forces need to apply such measures with extreme caution and continually monitor the population's willingness to accept U.S. force demands.

---

[27] Pamela Hess, "Officer Commands Respect from Locals: 'Sledgehammer' Strategy Working," *Washington Times*, September 26, 2005.

[28] Col. Charles M. (Mark) Gurganis, U.S. Marine Corps, Commanding Officer, Regimental Combat Team 8, interview with Russell W. Glenn, Fallujah, Iraq, July 13, 2005.

Nonlethal Use of Lethal Systems

Lethal systems can be used in nonlethal ways for shaping. This can range from using heavy armored vehicles to intimidate individuals to fixing bayonets as a means to convince a crowd that coalition forces mean business. LTC Dallas Eubanks provided the following example from OIF:

> In the city of Balad, we put up Apaches [attack helicopters] and the Abrams [tanks] to show force, because they respected power and force. . . . We used a lethal system in a nonlethal way, never intending to fire. We knew from being there a month or two which weapons systems they were afraid of. They weren't afraid of Bradleys [fighting vehicles].[29]

The threat or actual use of lethal fire can also influence those witnessing their effects. Consider the hard-fought nature of the second battle of Fallujah, which may have, at least briefly, persuaded civilians in other local areas to be less hospitable to insurgent forces. One British officer observed that, during a period of civil unrest in Al Basrah, "the provincial council came to me and asked me not to turn Basrah into another Fallujah."[30] Other evidence suggested that, at least temporarily, residents in Ramadi were becoming similarly restless, believing that the United States might take a similar tack with them.[31] Since the time of Alexander the Great, demonstrations of force have proven effective in influencing unaffected urban areas. The United States should take advantage of this by designing and conducting shaping activities to maximize the desirable consequences of urban combat operations.

---

[29] LTC Dallas Eubanks, U.S. Army, G-3 Operations Officer, 2nd Brigade, 4th Infantry Division during OIF (July to April 2004), interview with Russell W. Glenn, Ft. Leavenworth, Kan., April 27, 2005.

[30] Brigadier Andrew C. P. Kennett, British Army, interview with Russell W. Glenn, Warminster, UK, December 15, 2004.

[31] John Hillen, "Our Best and Bravest," *National Review Online*, February 28, 2005; Karl Vick, "Iraqi Security Forces: Hunters and Hunted," *Washington Post*, January 11, 2005, p. A1.

Lethal fires are also influential from a standpoint of deterrence. That is, few will engage in behaviors that are *certain* to provoke a lethal response. Of course, individuals coerced in this way may be more likely to behave in ways inimical to the friendly force once the coercive threat is removed. Like all shaping activities, kinetic shaping requires careful consideration of second- and higher-order consequences and unintended effects.

Attacking Symbolic Targets Can Communicate, Too

Kinetic attacks against symbolic targets offer unique shaping opportunities. When conducted with precision, they can strike at the heart of regime authority, communicate the true intentions of coalition force adversaries, and convey themes of liberation to the indigenous population. When U.S. forces moved into Baghdad in April 2003, symbolic targets were struck heavily, "maintaining a visible and audible example of targeting the regime rather than the people."[32] British units in the south applied a similar strategy, as the following examples illustrate:

> [British forces destroyed the city landmark where the fedayeen executed civilians.] It had no military purpose, but, for the civilians, it did a lot.[33]

> [The British could have taken Al Basrah earlier, but it] would have been a mess, so they held back and did not riddle Basrah with bullets. [Instead, they decapitated Iraqi command in the city, the Baath party. They put out the message that Al] Basrah is not the enemy. The leadership is the enemy.[34]

---

[32] Michael Knights, "'Iraqi Freedom' Displays the Transformation of U.S. Air Power," *Jane's Intelligence Review*, May 2003, p. 18.

[33] Medhurst-Cocksworth, Captain Christopher R., British Army, Intelligence Officer, Grade 3, G2 (Intelligence) Brigade during OIF, interview with Russell W. Glenn and Todd C. Helmus, Bergen, Germany, December 10, 2003.

[34] Bailey, Major General Jonathan, interview with Russell W. Glenn and Todd C. Helmus, Upavon, UK, December 3, 2003.

Establish and Preserve Credibility

War is based on deception.

—*Sun Tzu*[35]

Best PSYOP is based on truthful, credible information.

—*LTC Jerry Orban, U.S. Army,*
Special Operations Command[36]

Everyone involved in this argument would do well to heed Gen. [Richard B.] Myers' [Chair of the Joint Chiefs of Staff] warning against mixing the liars and the truth-tellers in one pot. That distinction was blurred during the Vietnam War, and the image the American public carried away was of the Five O'Clock Follies, the daily official news briefing in Saigon where lies and spin were dispensed along with the facts. Believe me, we do not want to go there again.

—*Joseph L. Galloway*[37]

A loss of credibility significantly reduces the likelihood that the indigenous population will heed coalition messages. Credibility is damaged in many ways, most notably by being caught in a lie. A debate about the role and place of deception in the stability-and-support operating environment is in order.

One ill-conceived deception at the tactical level could do lasting and widespread damage to U.S. credibility. Consider the fallout from the false announcement that operations in Fallujah had begun in October 2004, when in fact they had not.[38] Following this decep-

---

[35] Sun Tzu, *The Art of War*, New York: Oxford University Press, 1963, p. 106.

[36] LTC Jerry Orban, U.S. Army Special Operations Command, Concept Developer, Army Futures Center, interview with Todd C. Helmus and Christopher Paul, Ft. Bragg, N.C., December 14, 2005.

[37] Joseph L. Galloway, "Lies Are a Part of War Strategy," *Miami Herald*, December 10, 2004.

[38] Mark Mazzetti, "PR Meets Psy-Ops in War on Terror: The Use of Misleading Information as a Military Tool Sparks Debate in the Pentagon; Critics Say the Practice Puts Credibility at Stake," *Los Angeles Times*, December 1, 2004, p. A1.

tion, considerable media air time and print space were consumed with recriminations about the inappropriateness of deliberately deceiving the media, the questionable legality of doing so, and calls for punitive action against whoever approved the deception. More insidiously, this deception raised the specter that the next time a U.S. military spokesperson announced that an operation had begun, the press would wonder, "Is that so, or is this another Fallujah?"

While many interview respondents lauded the importance of credibility, they additionally noted the military value of deception. Respondents discussing this apparently contradictory point revealed the inexactness of its application: First, different respondents drew the line between acceptable and unacceptable deceptions at different points. Second, "unacceptable" deceptions are acceptable only *if you do not get caught*.

Imagine a spectrum for deception (see Figure 4.1). At one end lies the universally accepted military undertaking, "deception by maneuver"—the feint, the effort to seize the initiative or surprise the enemy by attacking after appearing to be attacking from elsewhere. At the other end of the spectrum lies bald-faced, false propaganda, broadcast publicly, such as the ridiculous claims of Iraqi Information Minister Mohammed Saeed al-Sahaf during the first few weeks of OIF.[39] Somewhere between those endpoints is a line that demarcates acceptable deceptions from the unacceptable ones, with many gradations in between. The line's location is dependent on both the situation and personal judgment.

Near the "deception by maneuver" end of the spectrum is a commander's use of "false forces"—the inflatable tanks and planes deployed in England in support of the World War II D-Day invasion or the more recent use of PSYOP loudspeaker trucks that broadcast sounds mimicking an armored column or close air support aircraft. Some would argue that planning the "left hook" of the first Gulf War and accompanying it with invitations to reporters to witness marines preparing for an amphibious operation they would never execute is closer to the middle of the spectrum. Similarly, U.S. contractors paying

---

[39] BrainyQuote, "Mohammed Saeed al-Sahaf Quotes," undated.

Figure 4.1
Gradations of the Acceptability of Deception

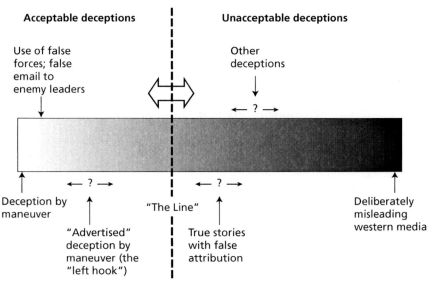

Acceptable deceptions | Unacceptable deceptions

Use of false forces; false email to enemy leaders

Other deceptions

← ? →

Deception by maneuver

"The Line"

Deliberately misleading western media

"Advertised" deception by maneuver (the "left hook")

True stories with false attribution

← ? →   ← ? →

RAND *MG607-4.1*

to have factual (and favorable) stories written by U.S. forces printed in Iraqi newspapers but attributed to Iraqi authors and a marine lieutenant announcing that operations in Fallujah have begun before they actually had done so are in this gray area.[40]

The following are examples of what might influence whether a particular deception is considered to benefit the accomplishment of operational objectives:

- *Target audience:* It is arguably acceptable to use deceptive communications against adversary military forces or decisionmakers. Alternatively, deceptions aimed at noncombatants would likely have a higher threshold. "Planting" true stories might be acceptable in a local newspaper for educational purposes but less advisable in media with an international audience.

---

[40] Mark Mazzetti and Kevin Sack, "The Challenges in Iraq: Planted PR Stories Not News to Military," *Los Angeles Times*, December 18, 2005, p. A1; Mazzetti (2004).

- *Source of a message:* Design and distribution of deceptive PSYOP is likely best left to specialists rather than a unit commander who needs to establish and maintain credibility with local leaders
- *Context:* It is important to consider the possible consequences of employing deception even during major combat. "It's hard to argue against deceiving the enemy in wartime, but it must also be noted that such deceptions are soon covered by the media, which is to say, uncovered."[41] This does not argue against using deception, but rather makes it clear that the shaping consequences of deception—like those of any action by a unit—should be war-gamed.

When an individual draws the line closer to the unacceptable end of the spectrum than U.S. public opinion would and that deception is found out, credibility with domestic audiences may be damaged. Location of the line will vary internationally based on cultural factors; different types of deception will also tend to pose different credibility risks with different foreign audiences. The challenge comes in assessing the implications of a deception that may ultimately become known and that many audiences are likely to perceive with a variety of tolerances. These risks and means of addressing them should all be part of war-gaming a course of action, just as is the case with decisionmaking regarding alternative maneuver options.

U.S. forces should be prepared with contingency plans for avoiding credibility damage or repairing harm already done (e.g., the breaking of news regarding mistreatment of detainees at Abu Ghraib prison). Chapter Three addressed the importance of managing expectations. Failing to meet indigenous expectations can impair U.S. and allied credibility even when those expectations are not borne of direct coalition pronouncements. Fostering transparency is critical. Known falsehoods damage credibility. Alternatively, credibility may be enhanced when authorities take responsibility and admit mistakes. Consider the very first words broadcast over Voice of America (VOA) on February

---

[41] James P. Pinkerton, "Covering the News with Deception," *Long Island Newsday*, December 16, 2004.

25, 1942: "Daily, at this time, we shall speak to you about America and the war. The news may be good or bad. We shall tell you the truth."[42] By sticking to that creed, VOA maintained high credibility for as long as it was on the air. Contemporary U.S. forces need to embrace the same principle.[43]

Organize for Credibility

As addressed in Chapter Two, the credibility of PSYOP and its IO brethren are impaired. This credibility problem has limited the degree to which PA, CA, and interagency partners are willing to coordinate their activities with PSYOP and its IO umbrella. Part of this stems from the correct perception that PSYOP and IO are tools of influence. More substantively, however, although 99 percent of IO and PSYOP effort is truthful, these organizations are known to house deceptive operations. As long as deceptive manipulation is within an organization's auspices, it is going to suffer from a deceitful reputation.

Consequently, it is suitable to discuss potential reorganization for PSYOP and IO. To return to the corporate analogy, when U.S. businesses face serious threats to their credibility and prestige, they sometimes choose the route of rebranding. Rebranding an organization involves changing the people's perceptions of that organization. Negatively perceived structures or practices are eliminated or divested, other operations are changed to suit the new brand identity, and the corporate name and logo are often changed.

Such a route may be necessary for IO and PSYOP. This section opened with Joseph Galloway's quote admonishing us not to mix "the liars and the truth-tellers in one pot." The overarching recommenda-

---

[42] First words broadcast in German over VOA on February 25, 1942, quoted in Sanford J. Ungar, "Pitch Imperfect," *Foreign Affairs*, Vol. 84, No. 3, May–June 2005.

[43] Former Assistant Secretary of Defense for Public Affairs Torie Clarke (2006, p. 78) concurs,

> And getting it right includes flooding the zone with negative information as well as positive news. Once you endorse transparency as a standard, you get the benefit of credibility. You also get the responsibility of airing all your laundry. The first time you withhold a single nugget of information for fear that you'll look bad, you forfeit every bit of credibility you've gained—and probably erode what you had before.

tion is to be truthful while still allowing deception as required. Such an approach may prove particularly valuable for PSYOP and IO. We recommend consideration of dividing both into deceptive and truthful entities. Maintain coordination, but do not mix the two.

Changing organizational names may also be important. An anonymous PA officer observed, "I think we need to change the name, because 'information operations' is tainted. If you ask a general citizen about information operations, they immediately think about half-truths, military deception, propaganda."

Integrate Communication

> If it is the mission of DoD to explain what we are doing and why, then PA and PSYOP have an equal stake in the outcome.
> —*LTC (retired) Charles Krohn, U.S. Army, PA*[44]

> PA, PSYOP, IO . . . let's all get along.
> —*COL Kenneth A. Turner, U.S. Army, 4th PSYOP Group*[45]

Shaping messages and activities need to be coordinated. Contradictory messages are ineffective, damage credibility, and feed other challenges and barriers. Effective message development arranges for unity, coordination, and synchronization of messages across communication entities and across levels.

The prior section recommended that IO and PSYOP be separated into deceitful and truthful components. This separation would facilitate integration, as PA, CA, and U.S. embassies would more amenably coordinate their activities with what is now—in many minds—a tainted influence community. Coordination among these different shaping entities should be improved, whether or not such reorganization takes place.[46] Where PSYOP officers have successfully embedded

---

[44] LTC (retired) Charles Krohn, Office of the Assistant Secretary of Defense for Public Affairs, interview with Christopher Paul, Arlington, Va., December 16, 2005.

[45] Turner (2005).

[46] Rhynedance (2006).

themselves in U.S. embassies, they have, in turn, garnered the trust and respect of ambassadors and DoS employees alike. The cultivation of such working relationships should be continued and fostered through joint and interagency exercises.

The PA/IO relationship should be a special focus of concern. This relationship, according to PA chief LTC Steve Boylan, "should be a cooperative, completely informed, and coordinated working relationship."[47] There is one critical ingredient in this relationship: PA should recognize its influence role. The mantra that PA "informs, but doesn't influence" is naïve; there is no such thing as value-free information and there is no influence-free communication. While PA communication must be truthful in both content and attribution, the pretense that it presents truthful information and does not seek to influence should end.

Messages conveyed to different AOs will vary (e.g., Afghanistan versus Iraq; Shiite neighborhoods and Sunni) depending on differences in ethnic makeup or progress of U.S. pacification efforts. Messages directed to one audience will find their way to others. Conflicting messages must be avoided. These messages have to be synchronized with policies and operations to avoid the contradiction of saying one thing while doing another.

Integration and coordination of messages is required at each juncture in the chain of command. Figure 4.2 represents a notional chain of command from the President of the United States to the company level. The U.S. government and military require information-coordinating bodies at each link to orchestrate shaping initiatives; these bodies should include representatives from all appropriate federal, multinational, nongovernmental, and local organizations. Consider the top two tiers of Figure 4.2, which represent the major figures of the U.S. government: the President of the United States, DoD, DoS, USAID, and others at the top tiers of the federal government. Several different bodies have put forward plans for coordinating and organizing "strategic communication" across the U.S. government. The current

---

[47] Boylan (2006).

Figure 4.2
The Information Chain of Command

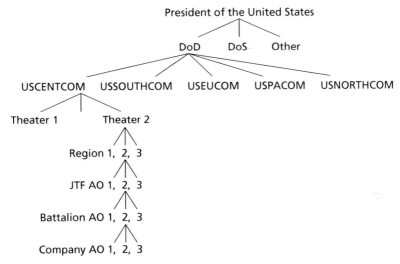

NOTE: USCENTCOM = U.S. Central Command. USSOUTHCOM = U.S. Southern
Command. USEUCOM = U.S. European Command. USPACOM = U.S. Pacific
Command. USNORTHCOM = U.S. Northern Command. JTF = joint task force.

RAND *MG607-4.2*

plan, which gives DoS the lead, is in its initial stages of execution at the
time of this writing.[48]

The objective is to maintain unity of message throughout U.S.
enterprises worldwide. It may be an impossible goal, which in no way
implies that it is not worth striving for and achieving to the greatest
extent possible. For example, via general but clear guidance similar
to a commander's intent, USCENTCOM would provide organizations supporting OIF and OEF with shaping guidelines supportive of
presidential policy, DoD strategic objectives, and the USCENTCOM
commander's intentions to ensure proper synchronization of themes,
messages, and operations throughout that combatant command's area
of responsibility. Theater-level commanders and staffs would similarly
work to provide subordinate units guidance based on that received

---

[48] It is unclear whether the current plan gives DoS sufficient authority to command coordination of strategic communication or if DoS will offer nonbinding "guidance."

from above. Each echelon would be responsible for overseeing shaping activities at the subordinate and its own level, being cautious to provide subordinates the freedom to best address U.S. objectives in light of local conditions.

This coordination of shaping themes therefore extends from the President of the United States to the level of individual soldiers, sailors, marines, and airmen. U.S. forces currently receive "smart cards" that provide ROE guidance. Similar cards, updated frequently with the current messages to receive emphasis, should accompany every soldier who might interact with the civilian population or the enemy. In the words of one soldier, "Everybody needs to have their little smart card, which tells them what they are doing here and why they are doing it."[49]

Improve Communication Resource Allocation, Joint Training, and Processes

> We need folks who are going to do IO as a career if we are going to do this right. Otherwise, we get "talented amateurs."
> —*Anonymous IO officer*

> Nobody knows what the hell it is we do.
> —*Anonymous PSYOP officer*

> Ultimately, part of the equation is educating the leadership on how to use these resources.
> —*LTC (retired) Charles Krohn, U.S. Army Public Affairs*[50]

Christopher Lamb, in a recently released study of PSYOP lessons learned, suggested that an additional $100 million per year would be required to substantially improve theater-level PSYOP capabilities.[51] The 2006 Quadrennial Defense Review has taken important steps in this direction by expanding the force structure of PSYOP and CA by

---

[49] McDonald (2006).

[50] Krohn (2005).

[51] Lamb (2005, p. 3).

3,700 personnel, a 33-percent increase.[52] Whether this increase and any corresponding budget increases are sufficient for successful prosecution of GWOT and ongoing counterinsurgencies in Iraq and Afghanistan will have to be monitored carefully. The adequacy of funding for other communication entities should similarly be monitored. Other resource problems revolve around limitations in grade structure and training.

One size does not fit all. Flag-rank and senior field-grade officers assigned to PA, IO, and PSYOP positions should be thoroughly trained and well experienced in their field. If appropriately qualified officers are unavailable to fill senior positions, retired PAO Pamela Keeton suggests,

> Another radical approach might be for the Secretary of the Army to appoint a civilian PA chief and a military deputy, similar to the organizational construct of the Army's acquisition, logistics, and technology office. The civilian chief should be an experienced communicator who can develop and lead the overall program while the uniformed deputy leads the schools and serves as the branch proponent.[53]

The armed services should better ensure that those assigned to these fields are adequately prepared for their assignments.[54] Some interviewees had concerns that assignments to individuals were, in some ways, unrelated to the officers' previous experience. These concerns included a fear that men and women with little qualification other than a desire to complete a joint tour obtained IO assignments, i.e., the positions were staffed by those "less [concerned] about IO careers than they are about ticket punching."[55]

There is, similarly, a call for improved training at all echelons. Training in field doctrine, message development, and graphic artistry

---

[52] U.S. Department of Defense, *2006 Quadrennial Defense Review Report*, Washington, D.C., February 6, 2006.

[53] Keeton and McCann (2005, p. 86).

[54] Boylan (2006).

[55] Anonymous interview.

was specifically noted as meriting emphasis. Training with civilian and other agencies in the field is an effective complement to military training. One interview was with Army PA officer LTC Jack Amberg, who, at the time, was on a training assignment with Ketchum, a public relations firm.[56] PSYOP and other IO education could be similarly augmented by fellowship tours with top advertising and public relations firms.[57]

There is, unsurprisingly, also a need for cultural and language training for IO and PA personnel. Since it is hard to know which languages and cultures will be critical in the future, incentives should be put in place to learn languages, thereby creating a "cultural reserve" in the active and reserve forces.[58] Currently, civilians assigned to PSYOP positions at the Strategic Studies Detachment do not receive language pay, either to maintain existing language skills or develop new ones.[59] There should be incentives for expanding cultural and language knowledge throughout the force.

Joint and service training exercises would benefit from greater substantive participation by PA, IO, and CA personnel. Current operational tempos and the limited force structure dedicated to these fields pose significant barriers to this participation. Past deficiencies in ensuring such participation have resulted in the unfamiliarity of many field commanders and staff members with these personnel and their organizations' assets, doctrine, and benefits offered. COL Kenneth A. Turner, commander of the 4th PSYOP Group, observes that joint training is "the only way to do it. It gets you in the door with the . . . commander."[60]

---

[56] LTC John Amberg, U.S. Army Public Affairs–Midwest, interview with Todd C. Helmus, Chicago, Ill., February 24, 2006.

[57] LTC (retired) Pamela Keeton, Director of Public Affairs and Communications, United States Institute of Peace, interview conducted as a questionnaire, May 30, 2006.

[58] CDR Ed Burns (2006) suggested that bonuses could be offered for pursuing degrees in specific regional specialties or that DoD could pay for a civilian's degree work with the understanding that, if the government needs him or her, these regional specialists will be available for recall, similar to the existing program for reserve physicians.

[59] Jenks (2005).

[60] Turner (2005).

Training for those at higher military and civilian echelons is likewise called for. One anonymous officer in the field lamented that senior military commanders "think IO is a point-and-shoot weapon. . . . 'Get some IO on this.' IO requires long lead times. You can't just send one message. . . . They expect us to turn it around overnight." Joint training exercises would be part of this education. Complement them with significant exposure at staff and war colleges.

Remove Process Constraints

Shaping efforts face process constraints in addition to resource constraints. PSYOP efforts, specifically, face two important process barriers: the approval process and the law.

The process for approving PSYOP products has been criticized for its lack of timeliness. By the time some products are approved, fast-paced events have too often negated their value. COCOMs control the PSYOP approval process. These headquarters can keep the approval authority or delegate it. Delegation can obviously speed approval, though aforementioned initiatives to maintain unity of message will be in order. PSYOP organizations can, for their part, assist in speeding delivery of their products in the field by preparing and obtaining approval in advance of operations. In his PSYOP lessons-learned report, Christopher Lamb notes, "Prepared and pre-approved products offer a ready solution, since many themes and messages are consistent across the range of military operations and can easily be anticipated."[61] This advance preparation will further permit PSYOP personnel the time to test products with target audiences prior to their application.

Arguing for preapproved products does not mitigate the necessity of providing PSYOP products that are uniquely tailored to the circumstance. Observes Dirk Blum of the Lincoln Group, "Truly effective information content exploits situational context."[62] However, just as modifying an existing order speeds supporting planning and execution, approval of modifications to preapproved PSYOP products would generally be more readily forthcoming than that for initial offerings.

---

[61] Lamb (2005, p. 16).

[62] Blum (2007).

PSYOP is prohibited from targeting U.S. citizens, even second-arily. PA officer LTC Steve Boylan told us that the "laws that prevent PSYOP from targeting American citizens were written before the age of instantaneous global communications. Laws and rules and regulations have to be revamped and brought up to date."[63] While all interview respondents with whom we discussed targeting agreed that PSYOP should not be aimed at U.S. citizens, they felt that it was unreasonable to prohibit employment of products intended for foreign audiences simply because U.S. citizens might see them.[64] This is an extremely sensitive issue that merits thorough study before specific changes are proposed or implemented.

Address Shaping Intelligence Requirements

As noted in Chapter Two, shaping efforts have significant intelligence requirements. Prior RAND work discusses the need to include detailed population analyses when conducting intelligence preparation of the battlefield (IPB) in support of urban operations and shaping efforts.[65] In addition, Chapter Three addressed the importance of coalition forces gaining a deep and thorough understanding of indigenous audiences. This information would include, but not be limited to, cultural intelli-gence, geographic, demographic, psychographic (e.g., social class, life-style, personality), and behavioral characteristics, as well as the media habits of pertinent audience segments. In addition, collection should include information on audience perceptions related to reconstruction priorities and U.S. force actions. Collection of such details will pose new challenges for military intelligence organizations. It will, by defi-nition, demand that they focus efforts on more than just adversaries. Consequently, intelligence doctrine, TTP, and training will require modification.

---

[63] Boylan (2006).

[64] The need to remove or change this prohibition was mentioned by Bloom (2005), Gregory (2005), and M. A. Thomas (2005).

[65] Medby and Glenn (2002).

While it is clear that cultural intelligence and knowledge of population characteristics are required once U.S. forces are committed to a specific theater of operations, it will also be wise to ensure that there is a cultural or population information clearinghouse for venues not yet host to major U.S. military operations. A variety of efforts are under way in this regard.[66] To be maximally effective, such a database requires constant updating by personnel who have traveled abroad.[67] For example, U.S. force personnel who return from anticipatory shaping operations in the horn of Africa should contribute to the database, as should U.S. embassy and USAID personnel. Barriers to database contribution should be minimized to gain this broad-based input. The database should therefore be unclassified.

It would be beneficial to present cultural and indigenous population intelligence in a graphical format. This format would be similar to map overlays that are currently part of IPB. Target-audience analysis is currently presented in prose format, which is not as easily digested by information consumers. Graphical presentation, argues IO officer LTC Michael Williams, shows the relevant information in an intuitive format: "Everyone who has seen a well-thought-out graphical presentation of the information environment has had an epiphany about it."[68]

Reach-back resources are key. Personnel should be able to not only access up-to-date information through databases, but also call or otherwise contact regional experts outside the theater of operations. Other shaping entities, such as PA and CA, would similarly benefit from reach-back resources.[69] Currently, the 4th PSYOP Group provides this type of reach-back, but its program would benefit from expansion.

---

[66] Jenks (2005).

[67] Novosel (2005).

[68] LTC Michael Williams, Chief, Plans Support Branch, Information Operations Division, Deputy Director for Global Operations, and Ted Tzavellas, Senior Information Policy and Strategy Advisor, Lockheed Martin, interview with Christopher Paul, the Pentagon, Arlington, Va., May 26, 2006.

[69] Jenks (2005).

Establish and Maintain the Relationships That Shaping Requires

> Once you're doing the stability thing, it's the continuity. . . . You've got to build the human ties . . . and I think this is more important in the Third World. We are used to dealing with people based on their position. . . . They are used to dealing with people they know.
>
> —*Col. Jim Howcroft, U.S. Marine Corps*[70]

> Face-to-face PSYOP with the host population is critical, and PSYOP forces must use conventional forces to support this objective.
>
> —*Christopher Lamb*[71]

The most effective shaping takes place through actions and utterances in the presence of observers. Chapter Three addressed the important shaping role of U.S.–indigenous population interactions. Personal relationships—in-depth connections made between U.S. service members and their indigenous counterparts—constitute an especially important shaping opportunity. These relationships cultivate trust, permit sustained dialogue, and build friendships.

All personnel who come into contact with noncombatants should be reminded of the power of personal relationships and encouraged to create them, thereby contributing to positive attitudes. This requires more than one-off interactions. Sustained presence reinforced by repeated contact and dialogue magnifies the impact of these relationships. U.S. forces have realized some enormous successes in this regard, especially in Iraq and Afghanistan.[72] Lieutenant Colonel Chris Hickey,

---

[70] Col. Jim Howcroft, 1st Marine Expeditionary Force G-2, interview with Russell W. Glenn, Camp Pendleton, Calif., December 17, 2003.

[71] Lamb (2005, p. 16).

[72] See, for example, the account in Thomas E. Ricks, "The Lessons of Counterinsurgency: U.S. Unit Praised for Tactics Against Iraqi Fighters, Treatment of Detainees," *Washington Post*, February 16, 2006, p. A14.

stationed in Tal Afar, Iraq, lived in close proximity to city residents. Reporter Thomas Ricks describes part of his approach:

> Hickey also has spent months living in the city, perched in the Ottoman-era ramparts that dominate it. He slept at the base only rarely. From his position downtown, he said, "I hear every gunshot in the city." His conclusion: "Living among the people works, if you treat them with respect." When the electricity goes out for Iraqis, he noted, it does for him too, even though he has a generator for military communications.[73]

Rotations

Unfortunately, the exigencies of military troop rotations often sever these personal relationships and end their positive shaping potential. Several interviewees suggested rethinking tour lengths for selected personnel.[74] Incentives may be put in place, for example, that encourage select individuals to remain in the theater.[75] Others have suggested greater efforts to maintain or transfer personal relationships through troop transitions. By having longer periods of overlap during a relief in place (RIP), departing troops would have more opportunities to transition relationships to new arrivals. Other observers suggested greater efforts to keep troops who have left theater involved long distance. This can take the form of a reach-back resource for newly arrived troops in the same operating area. Consider the following idea recommended by John Rendon:

> In Iraq, forces get deployed for a year or half year and then they rotate out. Now it is election day, quarter to 11 at night in Iraq. Somewhere in the Mansur district, a U.S. platoon is on patrol. [An indigenous woman is yelling] at the [patrol]; [the lieutenant leading the patrol] can ask her captain what to do . . . or she

---

[73] Ricks (2006).

[74] Barak Salmoni, Assistant Professor, Naval Postgraduate School, interview with Todd C. Helmus, Naval Postgraduate School, Monterey, Calif., April 4, 2005; Costantini (2005); Anthony H. Cordesman, "Outside View: Spin Loses Wars," United Press International, December 13, 2005.

[75] Blum (2007).

could talk to the lieutenant who patrolled in that district last year via [personal digital assistant], and that lieutenant can tell her that [this indigenous person's second cousin lives down the street and can help quiet her]. We have to find a way to keep people in the fight when they are not in theater. So, that lieutenant needs to be able to talk to the lieutenant who walked the Mansur district before she did. The government should enable [these interactions]. . . . Reserve units, we do not need them for weekends; we need them for one hour every day. That has to be enduring across time for commanders that rotate to different positions.[76]

Technology can assist in maintaining these relationships. There have been a number of examples of rotated-out officers maintaining their indigenous contacts via email. Marine CA officer LtCol. Alan Burghard maintains email contact with Shia tribe members in Hilla.[77]

We recommend that DoD seek to mitigate the negative effects that rotation has on operational objectives by considering extended rotations for selected personnel, increased periods of overlap during RIP, increased opportunities for individuals to voluntarily remain in theater, and the promotion of maintenance of contacts after departure if appropriate.

Better Respond to Mistakes

If we make a mistake, we have to admit it.
—*LTC (retired) Charles Krohn, U.S. Army, PA*[78]

U.S. forces will inevitably be involved in negative shaping events during the course of COIN operations. These might include prisoner abuse, ROE violations, and compromised deception efforts. These events will impair U.S. credibility and further harm indigenous per-

[76] Rendon (2005).

[77] Burghard (2006).

[78] Krohn (2005).

ceptions of the U.S. force. The consequences of failing to deal effectively with mistakes receive detailed treatment in Chapter Two. This section provides recommendations for better mitigating the effects of these actions.

Time and again, interviewees and current literature recommend forthcoming transparency when mistakes are made. For example,

- "The hard facts of reality need to be brought forth. You know in war mistakes are made and accidents happen. We need to come clean."
- "Deliver the bad news yourself, and when you screw up, say so—fast!"
- "In everything I've studied and looked at, we have always fared better with the public and international community when we admit mistakes right away."
- Mistakes or allegations of mistakes need to be answered. "No matter what's being alleged, charges unanswered are charges assumed to be true."[79]

Failure to admit wrongs damages credibility, looks like a cover-up, and makes audiences wonder what has not been revealed. Timely transparency would have served U.S. forces well with regard to allegations about both the Abu Ghraib and Guantanamo Bay detention facilities. In the former case, misconduct had taken place. Admitting this was a first step toward preventing its repetition, addressing the uncharacteristic nature of the perpetrators' actions, and restoring the coalition's reputation. Clear, credible accounts about exactly what has and *has not* taken place can reduce speculation, rumor, and reputation damage.

Second, as part of a commitment to transparency and as a way to build credibility, be the first to expose negative news, if possible. Former Assistant Secretary of Defense for Public Affairs Torie Clarke explains,

---

[79] Bulleted quotes from Boylan (2006), Clarke (2006, p. 1), M. A. Thomas (2005), and Clarke (2006, p. 11), respectively.

At first glance, our strategy may sound counterintuitive. React to questions about the mistakes, sure. Explain the facts, absolutely. But why would the Pentagon go out of its way to *announce* bad news? The reason is simple: in the Information Age, the bad news is going to get out. The only questions are who will tell it first and will they tell it accurately.[80]

As M. A. Thomas of the 4th PSYOP Group observed, "It is better for the public to have a slightly negative view of what you're doing than completely hostile. We're talking long term."[81] Protecting credibility and long-term shaping requirements is more important than the short-term negative consequences of whatever error is committed. The U.S. military should greet shortcomings with transparency, conduct thorough investigations, and hold perpetrators to public account. Wargaming can assist in determining other advisable actions in response to such circumstances.

Similarly, the military should take initiative when dealing with unfortunate events and be prepared for likely problems, such as collateral damage, military vehicle accidents involving civilians, and ROE violations. It is important to conduct worst-case analyses and preparation of mitigation messages in the event that the worst case is realized. For example, plan on collateral damage or an adversary disinformation effort. What can be done to minimize adverse shaping as a result of collateral damage? What can be done to limit the adversary's disinformation effectiveness? Perhaps having medical personnel standing by to treat collateral casualties or having a CA group available to quickly restore critical services should be among the mitigation preparations put in place. Even if worst cases do not come to pass, thinking about them and planning contingencies for them contributes significantly to a shaping campaign.

---

[80] Clarke (2006, p. 29). Emphasis in original.

[81] M. A. Thomas (2005).

Counter Adversaries' Shaping Efforts

> We should not interfere if the new Iraqi government decides to place restrictions on al-Jazeera. . . . If the War on Terror really is a war of ideas, we shouldn't let our enemies win with lies.
> —*Ralph Peters*[82]

> If that [attack] ad runs at five and we see it and press deadline is six, we need to say something quotable and accurate in the hour.
> —*Robert Zeiger, Alticor*[83]

Adversaries often fabricate stories and events that paint the United States and its forces in a negative light. U.S. forces must correct enemy disinformation in a rapid and transparent manner. IO officer LTC Gary Martel observed that violent extremists use crisis and conspiracy to provide an excuse for violence. U.S. efforts can remove the excuse for violence and discredit false information.[84] U.S. kinetic operations often set the stage for adversary misinformation campaigns as adversaries use real or falsified collateral civilian deaths to justify anticoalition attacks. For example, in May 2006, U.S. forces successfully bombed a terrorist way station along Iraq's border with Syria. A disinformation campaign inflamed local opinions by claiming that the target was a wedding party with 40 civilian casualties.[85]

To avoid this, PA or IO personnel should help plan kinetic operations. With their experience in thinking about press fall-out and adverse influence, they can help spot negative shaping opportunities inherent in an operation, generate worst-case scenarios, plan mitigation strategies, and provide communication support. Former IO officer Greg Rowe observed, "Get an info person into the strike-planning loop

---

[82] Ralph Peters, "Killers with Cameras," *New York Post*, June 21, 2004.

[83] Zeiger (2006).

[84] Martel (2006).

[85] Scott Wilson and Sewell Chan, "Dozens Killed in U.S. Attack Near Syria; Target Disputed," *Washington Post*, May 20, 2004, p. A1.

[and] publish information [about the operation] right after the strike."[86] Releasing factual information right after a strike limits the period in which an adversary can spread disinformation. Rowe elaborates,

> Attack planning needs to integrate consideration of the information environment—local, regional and global media outlets—and aggressively and proactively release our results. The first reporting of an event most shapes how it is perceived; therefore, if we proactively announce the results of an attack like Al Qaim or the Mustafa Husseiniya, our factual version undercuts any attempt at disinformation. When we plan an attack—a newsworthy event that we know will happen beforehand—we should also plan to brief the media on the results, as well as plan for potential negative outcomes and deceitful reporting to pre-empt disinformation efforts.[87]

Embedded reporters further increase the accuracy of reports pertaining to U.S. strikes.[88] If an adversary claims a military victory or claims to have inflicted heavy casualties on U.S. forces, an embedded reporter can immediately and credibly report what he or she witnessed, debunking false adversary claims. Likewise, when accounts of an event conflict and enter the realm of "he said/she said" between competing parties (e.g., the Iraqi terrorist way station/wedding party strike mentioned previously), an objective account of a professional journalist present at the scene reduces the likelihood of disinformation success.

Effective countering of adversary shaping will sometimes require strikes against enemy IO capabilities. For example, in March 2006 the Coalition Against Terrorist Media persuaded the U.S. Department of the Treasury to designate Hizballah's Al-Manar satellite television

---

[86] Greg D. Rowe, Senior Information Operations Planner and Certified Information Systems Security Professional, Syracuse Research Corporation, interview with Todd C. Helmus and Christopher Paul, Chantilly, Va., December 16, 2005.

[87] Greg D. Rowe, "Hang Fires in Strategic Communication," email to authors, March 30, 2006.

[88] Yantis (2006); Christopher Paul and James J. Kim, *Reporters on the Battlefield*, Santa Monica, Calif.: RAND Corporation, MG-200-RC, 2004.

outlet a specially designated global terrorist organization.[89] This prohibits commercial transactions between U.S. firms and the station and clears the path for further dissuasive efforts, such as legal action or boycotts.

Direct action against an adversary communication apparatus may be required, as is the case when EW and CNO jam or otherwise disrupt television and radio signals or Internet sites. Risks associated with these actions demand careful consideration, however. First, civilian-owned stations that are temporarily co-opted by adversaries may not be legitimate or desirable targets for military action. Second, employment of IO technologies demonstrates their existence; the trade-off between exposing U.S. technological capabilities in exchange for limited disruption of adversary broadcasts may not be worth the benefit obtained. Third, disrupting adversary IO might be interpreted as restraint on freedom of speech. This may appear to contradict U.S. operational objectives and shaping-campaign themes. Nonetheless, U.S. forces should limit adversaries' shaping capabilities, provided that the approaches employed are prudent with regard to other considerations.

Sometimes, even the best efforts cannot prevent successful enemy disinformation. U.S. and coalition representatives should nevertheless dispel potentially damaging allegations through communication that better informs target audiences. Charles Krauthammmer notes in the *Washington Post* with regard to charges of abuse at the Guantanamo Bay detention facility, "One does not run and hide simply because allegations have been made. If the charges are unverified, as they overwhelmingly are in this case, then they need to be challenged. The United States ought to say what it has and has not done, and not simply surrender to rumor."[90] Transparency can provide protection.

Speed in responding is of the essence in such situations, though accuracy must accompany that speed. News is presented in cycles as newer, more compelling stories replace those that are older. The sooner

---

[89] Clifford D. May, "Turning Off Terrorist Television," Scripps Howard News Service, March 29, 2006.

[90] Charles Krauthammer, "Gitmo Grovel: Enough Already," *Washington Post*, June 3, 2005, p. A23.

the United States responds to an allegation, the sooner the newer story can take over and the less time there is for disinformation to be uncontested. There is, of course, tension between speed and accuracy. This must be dealt with on a case-by-case basis, but it can be addressed, in part, by good training, skilled personnel, and proper procedures. For example, slow PA clearance processes often introduce unnecessary delays. It may be necessary to empower junior PAOs to forgo burdensome clearance delays so that rebuttals of obvious falsehoods can be quickly cleared. Colonel Boylan agrees: "PAOs, or even operations folks, have to be empowered to pass us the information without having to wait . . . for it to be cleared."[91]

The medium in which facts are communicated matters: The United States must, at a minimum, respond in the same medium and over the same area in which the false allegation was initially leveled.[92] PSYOP officer LTC Bradley Bloom related an unfortunate anecdote in which the mainstream media relayed a Taliban claim to have shot down a U.S. helicopter in Afghanistan. When U.S. forces immediately disputed the claim on short-wave radio broadcasts, the broadcasts reached a hinterland Afghan audience that had never heard the original Taliban claim.[93] The denial ended up informing more Afghans of the Taliban claim than may have heard the original message on mainstream media. Such rebuttals will be less effective and may cause more harm than good when the audience for the disinformation and the audience for the denial are different.

Direct refutations of false allegations are not without risk. For example, M. A. Thomas cautions that such denials place U.S. forces in a defensive position and put "a question in the back of peoples' minds of whether you're telling the truth."[94] Instead, he urges, "You should be more innovative in how you send the message. You should do something through [indigenous] civilian or media" contacts who, in turn,

---

[91] Boylan (2006).

[92] Bloom (2005).

[93] Bloom (2005).

[94] M. A. Thomas (2005).

correct the disinformation themselves.[95] Perhaps allies or other coalition and indigenous partners can more persuasively correct enemy propaganda. Perhaps the U.S. military should subtly avail information to indigenous or foreign journalists who then "discover" stories that serve coalition purposes. The U.S. military's handling of comic outtakes from Abu Musab al-Zarqawi's propaganda footage in May 2006, while effective, might have been more so if distributed differently.[96] Fred Kaplan suggests that Iraqis could have better distributed the footage, either via indigenous journalists, Iraqi security forces, or both.[97]

Improve Relations with the News Media

> Include the media. Let *their* cameras capture the images.
> —*LTC Ryan Yantis, U.S. Army, Public Affairs*[98]

Chapter Two introduced the challenges the news media and contemporary journalism pose to U.S. shaping operations. To meet these challenges, the United States should increase media coverage of military operations and cultivate Western-style journalism in areas in which journalistic ethics and standards are lacking.

First, make it easy for reporters to do their jobs. Include them. Talk to them. Give them context and background information so that they do not have to figure it out themselves and risk getting it wrong. Give reporters access to commanders and to operators, not only to PA personnel. Embed reporters within units. Previous RAND research shows that embedding has benefits from the military perspective.[99] Torie Clarke concurs:

---

[95] M. A. Thomas (2005).

[96] Fred Kaplan, "Candid Camera: The Trouble with Releasing Zarqawi's Outtakes," *Slate*, May 5, 2006.

[97] Fred Kaplan (2006).

[98] Yantis (2006).

[99] Paul and Kim (2004).

To a very large extent, embedding did achieve our objectives. A few days into the war, a front-page photo in the *New York Times* showed Iraqi soldiers dressed as civilians, a clear violation of the Geneva Conventions. Showing the photo to Secretary Rumsfeld, I said, "We could have said a thousand times that the Iraqi regime was dressing its soldiers as civilians to ambush coalition forces. Some people would have believed us; others wouldn't." It was a clear win to have the international news media report Saddam's atrocities.[100]

Outreach to indigenous media outlets and journalists is particularly important given their local influence. Interacting with indigenous media may require different resources (e.g., translators). Including them should be part of both plans and operations.[101] PA LTC Ryan Yantis recalls a general officer in Bosnia who specifically made time during his regular press conferences to take questions from local media; he had a translator available and made it clear that he was reaching out to them and wanted to engage.[102] Yantis recalls that this was extremely effective. The friendly force received "better" coverage (in every sense of the word) in local news as a consequence.

A second suggestion is to cultivate Western-style journalism in areas in which U.S. forces operate. Dealing with reporters who adhere (or try to adhere) to Western journalistic standards (such as truthfulness, accuracy, objectivity, impartiality, fairness, and public accountability) has its benefits. Further, a free press and professional journalists are a key part of U.S. efforts to foster democracy worldwide. As Eileen O'Connor and David Hoffman note,

> [B]uilding independent media may take more time than Washington policy-makers would like, especially in places such as the former Soviet Union. But the work spreads a valuable lesson: Free speech matters. When it works, it can change the entire political

---

[100]Clarke (2006, p. 73).

[101]Boylan (2006); Tallman (2006).

[102]Yantis (2006).

landscape, as was seen recently in Lebanon, and before that in Serbia, Indonesia, Georgia, Ukraine and Kyrgyzstan.[103]

Similarly, Georgian President Mikheil Saakashvili has said that the money spent developing independent media in his nation was worth "more than 5,000 marines."[104]

How can DoD contribute to the development of professional indigenous journalists? First, avoid actions that compromise journalistic principles, such as paying to place stories. Anything that creates a "do as I say, not as I do" situation undermines credibility and impairs the message. Second, fund and support programs that seek to develop independent media.[105] Training programs can either provide journalism training in the host nation or arrange for U.S.-based internships, fellowships, or educational grants. Third, as part of stability-and-support operations, create and support local independent press outlets. For example, as a *Wall Street Journal* op-ed writer observed, regarding Iraq in 2004,

> If the Marines can get these moribund [local television] stations back on the air, the coverage area would include Fallujah and Ramadi. The VHF/UHF stations are owned as cooperatives by TV-competent Iraqis already vetted by the Army. Some broadcast Al-Jazeera for lack of other content. In return for the upgrades, the Iraqi operators would be asked two things: Criticism is fine, but do not run anti-coalition propaganda; and let the Marines *buy* air time to broadcast public-service announcements, such as the reopening of schools or clinics—or indeed, pending military operations.[106]

---

[103] Eileen M. O'Connor and David Hoffman, "Media in Iraq: The Fallacy of Psy-Ops," *International Herald Tribune*, December 17, 2005.

[104] Quoted in O'Connor and Hoffman (2005).

[105] Cindy Santos, "USC Teams Up to Create New Fellowship," *Daily Trojan*, January 18, 2006.

[106] Daniel Henninger, "Spirit of America: Here's a Way You Can Help the Cause in Iraq," *Wall Street Journal Opinion Journal*, April 16, 2004. Emphasis in the original.

Summary

This chapter has presented 11 primary recommendations for improving U.S. efforts to shape indigenous audiences. We first recommended that U.S. forces pursue anticipatory shaping activities that influence the attitudes and behaviors of indigenous populations in areas not otherwise subjected to full-scale stability operations. U.S. forces should also better leverage CA/CMO activities by enhancing publicity of good works, balancing short-term projects and demonstrations of good will with long-term support of ultimate end states, and using aid as a carrot for indigenous compliance with operational objectives. Second, they should manage use of force carefully so as to facilitate rather than threaten shaping-campaign objectives to the extent possible. Maintain U.S. force credibility by limiting acts of deception and demonstrating a commitment to the truth. In addition, integrate communication across the operational environment by implementing coordination cells that ensure that messages tailored to diverse audiences are well synchronized. Intelligence resources should focus collection efforts among the indigenous population. We further recommend enhanced resourcing for key shaping entities such as PSYOP and PA organizations. This includes joint training exercises, elimination of process constraints, and removal of legal barriers. We recommended changes to U.S. troop rotation policies to facilitate sustaining relationships between U.S. forces and indigenous personnel. Mistakes should be met with acceptance of responsibility for errors. Counter-disinformation tactics were also addressed. To improve U.S. handling of the media, increase reporter access to the battlefield and cultivate Western-style journalism in areas in which development of journalistic ethics and standards is immature.

CHAPTER FIVE

Summary of Conclusions and Recommendations

COIN and other stability operations are central to the current operational environment and are likely to remain so in the future. These operations demand a unique focus on shaping indigenous audiences. Virtually every action, message, and decision of a force shapes the opinions of an indigenous population. Creating a unified message is key in this regard, as the words and deeds of coalition forces must be synchronized to the greatest extent possible. U.S. force actions help set conditions for establishing credibility and fostering positive attitudes among the indigenous population, which, in turn, enable effective and persuasive communication. We have identified commercial marketing practices that can assist the U.S. military in its COIN shaping endeavors. We have also drawn on the insights of U.S. military personnel and past operational experiences. This chapter reviews the resulting recommendations.

Applying Marketing Principles to Shaping

Our review of commercial marketing practices led to 11 distinct recommendations:

- *Know the target audience through segmentation and targeting.* The U.S. military should adopt the business strategy of segmentation and targeting, wherein the military partitions the indigenous population into groups based on the individuals' levels of anticipated support for coalition presence and operations.[1] This segmentation strategy should be based on data collected from the indigenous population that cover a host of information, including coalition- and end-state–relevant attitudes and geographic, demographic, psychographic, and behavioral variables. Targeting should focus on those segments that offer the most promise for assisting in the accomplishment of U.S. objectives. The potential impact of U.S. policies and operations on identified segments should be considered.

- *Develop meaningful and salient end states.* Positioning is a business tool used to create product identities that are meaningful and salient in the consumer marketplace. The essence of positioning is the promise a brand makes regarding what consumers will achieve by using the brand. Positioning may hold value for U.S. efforts to craft end states for indigenous audiences. Perspectives regarding desirable end states should be sought from the indigenous population and incorporated into U.S. shaping initiatives and the selection of aid projects. A concept that is in line with U.S. operational interests and fits the needs of the indigenous population should be selected for the campaign. This positioning will then serve as a platform from which consistent messages can be launched.

- *Understand key branding concepts.* While the term *brand* often refers to a product name (e.g., Lexus is a brand name), it is more importantly construed as a collection of perceptions in the minds of consumers (e.g., Lexus may mean different things to different people: expensive, luxury, Japanese, and so on). Every interaction influences user perceptions of a product or service. Properly managed brands have a unique identity and are defined by a clear and nonconflicting set of associations. Virtually every organization or entity has a brand identity or reputation. The U.S. military is no different. The perceptions the indigenous population holds

---

[1]   For further information about population segments and how they view opposing sides in an adversarial environment, see the discussion of the spectrum of relative interest in Medby and Glenn (2002).

toward the U.S. force will significantly influence how members of that population align their support. Successful branding will help to influence the character of those perceptions in ways favorable to friendly force desired ends.

- *Update the U.S. military brand to reflect operational realities.* Commercial brand identities rarely last forever, and a given product may require a brand update to fit new competitive environments. The U.S. military should adjust its brand identity to fit operational demands.

- *Synchronize the U.S. operational portfolio.* The business practice of strategically synchronizing brand actions so that they convey a single and clear message to target audiences affords another valuable lesson. If the U.S. military opts for a new brand identity, it should seek to synchronize all its actions and messages around that identity. All actions in a theater of operations should be designed to serve shaping needs. Where U.S. operations appear to conflict with shaping goals, as may be the case during combat operations, efforts should be made to help the indigenous audience better understand U.S. intentions. The United States should also attempt to understand the impact that operations and policies have on the military's brand identity and ensure that the effects are consistent with the brand's long-term goals. The military should similarly assess the impact of U.S. government actions and policies that appear to conflict with key shaping themes.

- *Synchronize the U.S. military workforce.* Indigenous perceptions of U.S. forces are based largely on the population's interactions with U.S. servicemen and -women. Business practices that help align customer service actions with the intended brand identity can benefit the U.S. military. These include creating a brand-driven organization, addressing civilian complaints quickly, establishing "rules of interaction" that follow an audit of all U.S. military–civilian points of interaction, and carefully selecting and training U.S. personnel who conduct negotiations with indigenous counterparts.

- *Achieve civilian satisfaction: Manage and meet expectations. Customer satisfaction* refers to the level of fulfillment consumers experience after using a product or service. Civilians who live in areas where U.S. and coalition forces are conducting stability operations have a choice to make in terms of which side they support (or refuse to support). The degree to which they are satisfied with the various aspects of force presence will be a critical determinant in their decisionmaking. The management of expectations plays a prominent role in achieving customer satisfaction. The promises a business makes to customers create high customer expectations, which, in turn, increase the levels needed to achieve customer satisfaction. Unfulfilled promises create disappointed customers. The U.S. military should be wary of making promises to civilian populations. This warning includes creating the expectation of an improved standard of living. It applies to all levels of war. Popular expectations for U.S. forces should be regularly surveyed and corrected via shaping messages when necessary.

- *Listen to the voice of the civilian: Make informed decisions.* The most successful business endeavors are those that are premised on meeting customer needs and desires. Products that are thought to be superior from a business standpoint but fail to meet customer needs court failure. The U.S. military should seek to tailor CA and reconstruction activities around projects that meet civilian priorities. The coalition can apply a similar approach to understanding indigenous perspectives regarding use of force and tolerance of civilian casualties.

- *Listen to the voice of the civilian: Monitor outcomes.* Businesses frequently conduct surveys to monitor satisfaction levels. Customer advisory boards and complaint lines provide additional avenues for customer feedback. Coalition forces can use these techniques to gauge attitudes toward U.S. force actions and to determine ways to modify efforts to increase popular support. Civilian satisfaction should be monitored from multiple perspectives, including surveys, town hall–style meetings, and civilian advisory boards.

- *Harness the power of influencers.* Businesses strive to harness the power of influencers and word of mouth in their marketing efforts. The U.S. military can apply business-based word-of-mouth approaches to its shaping efforts in several ways. First, it should cultivate relationships with important influencers. The U.S. military should harness the influencing power of indigenous government employees and security forces by having them blog about their views regarding coalition forces and the indigenous government. The military might further consider the benefits of enhancing the Internet access of indigenous populations via distribution of cheap and durable Wi-Fi–capable laptops and by sponsoring Wi-Fi clouds around U.S. operating bases.

- *Apply discipline and focus to communication campaigns.* Social marketing is the application of well-grounded commercial marketing techniques to influence noncommercial behavioral change in a target audience. Social marketing campaigns have previously sought to motivate audiences to quit smoking, reduce littering, give blood, and recycle paper. Social marketing practices provide a well-grounded template for U.S. military efforts to motivate specific behaviors. Key steps include audience segmentation, careful delineation of specific program goals, harnessing the four Ps (product, price, place, and promotion), pretesting message products, and carefully monitoring campaign success in terms of previously identified program goals.

Shaping Solutions Based on Recent Operational Experiences

Our review of recent U.S. COIN and stability-and-support operational experiences led to 11 primary recommendations:

- *Pursue anticipatory shaping.* The United States should continue to conduct anticipatory shaping efforts, including the training of indigenous security forces, conducting CA activities, cultivating relationships with indigenous influencers, and collecting cultural intelligence. The United States should provide humanitarian assistance to nations subjected to natural disasters. It should further capitalize on gains made by fostering enduring relationships with foreign military personnel and by continuing to provide humanitarian and CA assistance, even long after an initial disaster has subsided. The allotment of greater resources to planning for the shaping component of future military contingencies is also an important anticipatory action.

- *Better leverage CA/CMO activities.* U.S. forces should better capitalize on CA/CMO efforts. First, enhance publicity for CA actions through integration with communication shaping assets, such as combat camera, PA, and PSYOP. CA operations should further take advantage of natural word-of-mouth networks. Second, balance CMO efforts between short-term projects and demonstrations of good will and long-term support of ultimate end states. Through CA and strategic spending of CERP funds, implement projects that have immediate impact and high visibility. Finally, CMO should encourage civilian behaviors that are key to counterinsurgency success.

- *Manage use of force for shaping.* In applying firepower, U.S. forces should ensure that the risk of civilian casualties is minimized to the extent feasible while demonstrating commitment to security by vigorously pursuing adversaries. Give preference to the employment of precision weapons when possible, monitor the number of U.S.-inflicted civilian casualties, and correct TTP at vehicle control points and elsewhere to minimize the likelihood of civilian death or injury. The threat or actual use of lethal fire can influence those witnessing the effects, as was the case when the hard-fought second battle of Fallujah may have, at least briefly, persuaded civilians in other areas to be less hospitable to insurgent forces. Precision attacks on symbolic targets further serve shaping purposes.

- *Establish and preserve credibility.* Discovery of deliberate falsehoods impairs the credibility of U.S. forces. Consequently, shaping activities evident to the public should be based wholly on truth. Deceptive shaping should instead be conducted in such a manner such that it not be revealed publicly. The impaired credibility of IO and PSYOP can be addressed by dividing the two into deceptive and truthful components. It will be important to maintain coordination between the two entities, but it must be done without mixing these elements.

- *Integrate communication.* Adopting the previous recommendation suggesting that PSYOP and its IO umbrella be separated into deceptive and truthful efforts will greatly assist the goal of integrated communication, as PA and CA would more amenably coordinate their activities with those of PSYOP and IO. Barriers between PA and PSYOP can be further overcome if PA recognizes its influence role (albeit one constrained to truth). Significant efforts should be undertaken to integrate and coordinate shaping messages across distinct operating environments. At the highest level, DoS may be assigned to coordinate U.S. government strategic communication. The U.S. military should institute information-coordination bodies, possibly comprising PA, IO (including PSYOP), and maneuver commanders, at appropriate echelons. Messages emanating from line troops should be synchronized via distribution of frequently updated smart cards that remind them of shaping themes and current message emphasis.

- *Improve communication-resource allocation, joint training, and processes.* Shaping would benefit from the commitment of greater resources and improved emphasis on the importance of shaping during all phases of an operation. This includes granting the topic increased emphasis during service and joint training, regardless of echelon or branch. Laws regarding military shaping activities should be modified to account for today's mission demands and advances in communication technologies.

- *Address shaping intelligence requirements.* U.S. military intelligence units should focus their efforts on gaining a deep and thorough understanding of indigenous audiences. This information would generally include—but would not be limited to—geographic, demographic, psychographic (e.g., social class, lifestyle, personality), and behavioral characteristics and media habits. This focus will demand modifications to intelligence doctrine, TTP, and training. It is important to collect cultural intelligence in locales where U.S. forces are presently operating, as well as in those of future interest. Reach-back resources should be developed so that troops in the field can contact regional experts outside the theater of operations.

- *Establish and maintain the relationships that shaping requires.* All personnel who come into contact with noncombatants must be reminded of the power of personal relationships. DoD should recognize the damage that troop rotations do to these personal relationships and address the problem through extended rotations for critical shaping personnel, increased periods of overlap during unit handovers, and extending opportunities for troops from previous rotations to stay in the fight by maintaining post-redeployment communication with their replacements and indigenous noncombatants.

- *Respond better to mistakes.* When U.S. operating forces make mistakes in the form of misconduct, ROE violations, or inadvertent infliction of noncombatant casualties, the United States should be the first to admit the errors. Clear and credible accounts about exactly what has and *has not* taken place can limit speculation, rumor, and reputation damage. Those responsible should be held accountable. Systematically developing procedures and courses of action will facilitate response to frequent or likely events, such as collateral damage or individual misconduct. Conduct of worst-case scenario analyses for kinetic operations and development of mitigation strategies will also improve response efforts.

- *Better counter adversaries' shaping efforts.* Adversaries often attempt to fabricate stories and events that paint the United States and its forces in a negative light. Making false accusations of U.S.-inflicted noncombatant casualties is one adversary approach to disinformation. Consequently, PA and IO personnel should be part of kinetic operational planning and execution so that they can identify positive and negative shaping opportunities and develop mitigation strategies as needed. Embedding reporters with strike forces facilitates accurate and credible accounts of operations. The United States should attack enemy IO capabilities, and false allegations should be challenged with transparency and a speedy rendering of facts. This may be achieved by making information available to indigenous or foreign journalists.

- *Improve relations with news media.* Recommendations include providing reporters background information to assist in report development, enhancing reporter access to field commanders, increasing media embedding, and conducting more extensive outreach to indigenous media representatives. The United States should also cultivate Western-style journalism in areas in which journalistic ethics and standards are lacking. Actions that compromise journalistic principles, such as paying to place stories, should be avoided, and training programs that develop independent media should be adequately funded.

These recommendations address the multifaceted and interconnected range of U.S. force actions that serve shaping requirements. While adopting these recommendations will not completely eliminate the challenges to shaping identified in Chapter Two, it will serve to noticeably improve the effectiveness of future U.S. shaping efforts.

A Synthesis of Marketing and Military Approaches

The research methods used in this study demand that marketing approaches and military lessons learned receive separate analytical treatments. This does not imply that their implementation requires dual consideration. Success demands an interwoven approach. The following narrative integrates the general recommendations and themes addressed in this monograph. Key synthesis themes include knowing the target audience and aligning operations accordingly, managing coalition force actions and messages critical to shaping, synchronizing words and deeds to convey clear and nonconflicting messages, and effectively employing influencers.

The central premise of commercial marketing ventures is the notion that a business must identify and know its customer base and orient its products to those customers' needs and wants. This principle applies equally to the U.S. military's efforts to influence civilian populations. U.S. forces must gain a deep and thorough understanding of indigenous populations and use that understanding to identify and target audiences. Given this understanding, U.S. and coalition forces should begin the process of tailoring policies and operations to best address those identified target audiences. Such tailoring will impact the definition of desired end states, the conduct of CA activities, and the extent to which the use of force is employed among other aspects of operations. Accomplishing these ends demands a new emphasis on civilian populations by the military and interagency intelligence apparatus.

U.S. force actions invariably speak louder than words in terms of laying the groundwork for indigenous public support. This monograph addresses numerous activities that are critical to successful shaping. These include the careful management of military force; reconstruction, economic revitalization, and employment programs run by CA and maneuver units; soldier-civilian interactions that are polite, professional, and culturally attuned; and in-depth personal relationships forged between U.S. personnel and members of the civilian population. Measuring the shaping success of these activities is a critical endeavor. U.S. forces should consequently monitor civilian satisfaction with different aspects of U.S. force presence and recalibrate U.S. efforts as necessary.

Words matter, too. The communication architecture of the U.S. military conveys U.S. intentions, seeks to build support for operational objectives, and attempts to motivate specific behavior changes key to operational success. The success of these communication campaigns rests, to a great degree, on the trust U.S. forces earn with their actions. This monograph identifies several recommendations geared toward improving the U.S. military's communication architecture. All members of the U.S. force, but particularly those involved in the communication disciplines of PA and IO and its PSYOP subsidiary should maintain their credibility to the fullest extent possible. These entities would further benefit from enhanced funding and greater emphasis on service and joint training. Successful execution of communication campaigns requires the direct application of a social marketing framework similar to that commonly used to reduce cigarette smoking and other social ills. Communication will also be important in managing popular expectations prior to and during the conduct of U.S. operations. When U.S. forces make mistakes or are confronted with false adversary claims, they should respectively admit their errors or challenge untrue accusations.

The panoply of U.S. force words and deeds will achieve shaping success only when these words and deeds are coordinated and synchronized to the greatest extent possible. Building a U.S. force brand identity that is attuned to shaping requirements and that serves as a guiding light for all corporate actions and messages is a fundamental first step in this process. Actions of the U.S. force that appear to contradict shaping goals (e.g., the use of force) should be thoroughly explained. Internal training and educational programs should seek to build a brand-driven organization, and all U.S. military–civilian points of interaction should be surveyed and realigned around "rules of interaction" that serve shaping interests. The creation of military and interagency coordinating bodies at appropriate command echelons will help to ensure synchronization throughout the U.S. government and theater of operations. Smart cards containing shaping themes would go far in ensuring synchronized communication among individual line troops. PA, CA, and PSYOP and its IO umbrella organization should work to overcome any cultural or operational differences that impede full coordination.

Operational success demands that civilians residing in a theater of operations help spread positive word of mouth about U.S. force intentions and activities. This constitutes the most credible form of communication available. Building and fostering relationships with social nodes and empowering everyday citizens through Internet access and blogging tools are two vital approaches. CA success can be further harnessed through the facilitation of selected natural word-of-mouth networks. The media will also play a critical role in this regard. Embedded media would facilitate accurate reporting on the success and accuracy of U.S. operations. Cultivation of Western-style media through journalistic training programs may improve the accuracy of local coverage, as would enhanced local media access to U.S. commanders.

Looking Ahead: Future Avenues for Research

This review of challenges to shaping and recommendations based on commercial marketing practices and recent operational experiences provides a broad overview for improving U.S. efforts to instill popular trust in U.S. forces and enhance the quality of related communication. While U.S. force actions and messaging with regard to civilian inhabitants are key to COIN success, they are only part of the equation. The actions and policies of the indigenous government will also play a shaping role. U.S. shaping efforts will ultimately prove futile if the population does not back its new government. Consequently, indigenous shaping efforts should be coordinated across efforts to develop indigenous governance, security-force professionalization, and other aspects of developing and sustaining national capabilities.

Shaping is critically important to success, not only as it is conducted during U.S. military operations, but also when performed before operations ensue and after their conclusion. The successful conduct of anticipatory shaping should preclude the need for U.S. military intervention or pave the way for subsequent victory. Likewise, postconflict shaping efforts should dramatically increase the likelihood of long-term operational and strategic success. Both anticipatory and postconflict shaping merit further analytical attention.

Because of the breadth of this study, finer-grained analysis is required of many of the topics covered here. For example, CMO currently lack a strategic framework for integrating projects and operations across a theater. The appropriate mechanisms for orchestrating communication between operating theaters also require further attention. This monograph recommends that military intelligence capabilities be expanded to assist in better understanding indigenous audiences, a recommendation with significant force design and training implications. Finally, the preceding pages provide an introduction to commercial marketing approaches and how they might favorably influence military shaping activities. The details of how best to integrate marketing concepts throughout the U.S. armed forces and interagency operations—and thereafter to design and conduct operations and campaigns with shaping adequately orchestrated throughout—promises to be a considerable challenge, yet one with tremendous potential for enhancing U.S. success during international undertakings.

Linking Shaping Challenges with Recommendations

Chapter Two addressed the extensive challenges faced by the U.S. military in its efforts to shape the attitudes and behaviors of civilian populations residing in military theaters of operation. Chapters Three and Four provided recommendations to address these challenges and improve U.S. military relationships with foreign audiences. This appendix is intended to facilitate understanding of how shaping challenges are connected to recommendations. The primary items are derived from challenges addressed in Chapter Two. The secondary items (derived from Chapters Three and Four) propose solutions relevant to the identified challenges.

- Anti-American sentiment:
  - Apply business positioning strategies to the development of meaningful and salient end states.
  - Harness the power of influencers.
  - Pursue anticipatory shaping.
  - Better leverage CA/CMO activities.
  - Establish and preserve credibility.
- Adversary shaping efforts:
  - Counter adversaries' shaping efforts.
- News and news media issues:
  - Improve relations with the media.
- Context, culture, and technology:
  - Know your target audience through segmentation and targeting.

- Apply business positioning strategies to the development of meaningful and salient end states.
- Apply discipline and focus to communication campaigns.
- The traditional kinetic focus of military operations:
  - Update the U.S. military brand to reflect operational realities.
  - Strategically synchronize the U.S. military brand.
  - Manage use of force for shaping.
- Interactions between U.S. forces and indigenous personnel:
  - Understand key branding concepts.
  - Update the U.S. military brand to reflect operational realities.
  - Strategically synchronize the U.S. military brand.
  - Synchronize the U.S. military brand workforce.
  - Establish and maintain the relationships that shaping requires.
- Information fratricide:
  - Understand key branding concepts.
  - Update the U.S. military brand to reflect operational realities.
  - Apply discipline and focus to communication campaigns.
  - Better leverage CA/CMO activities.
  - Integrate communication.
  - Improve communication-resource allocation, grade structure, joint training, and processes.
- Perceptions of PSYOP and IO:
  - Harness the power of influencers.
  - Establish and preserve credibility.
- Lack of shaping resources:
  - Harness the power of influencers.
  - Better leverage CA/CMO activities.
  - Improve communication-resource allocation, grade structure, joint training, and processes.
- Legal barriers to shaping:
  - Improve communication-resource allocation, grade structure, joint training, and processes.
- Matching message, medium, and audience:
  - Know the target audience through segmentation and targeting.

- Apply business positioning strategies to the development of meaningful and salient end states.
- The difficulty of measuring shaping effectiveness:
  - Listen to the voice of the civilian: Monitor outcomes.
  - Apply discipline and focus to communication campaigns.
- Intelligence requirements for shaping:
  - Know your target audience through segmentation and targeting.
  - Listen to the voice of the civilian: Make informed decisions.
  - Apply discipline and focus to communication campaigns.
  - Pursue anticipatory shaping.
  - Address shaping-intelligence requirements.
- Dealing with mistakes:
  - Synchronize the U.S. military brand workforce.
  - Establish and preserve credibility.
  - Respond better to mistakes.
- Fallout and second-order consequences of expedient choices:
  - Understand key branding concepts.
  - Update the U.S. military brand to reflect operational realities.
  - Synchronize the U.S. military brand workforce.
- "Damned if you do, damned if you don't" situations:
  - Strategically synchronize the U.S. military brand.
- Command use of shaping assets:
  - Improve communication-resource allocation, grade structure, joint training, and processes.
- Balancing short-, medium-, and long-term goals:
  - Manage and meet expectations.

Bibliography

Adams, Darrell, "WP: Enemy Body Counts Revived," email to Russell W. Glenn, October 24, 2005.

"Afghan: U.S. Bomb Hits Wedding Party," *CNN.com*, July 1, 2002. As of October 10, 2006:
http://archives.cnn.com/2002/WORLD/asiapcf/central/07/01/afghanistan.bombing/

Ajzen, Icek, and Martin Fishbein, "The Influence of Attitudes on Behavior," in Dolores Albarracin, Blair T. Johnson, and Mark P. Zanna, eds., *The Handbook of Attitudes*, Mahwah, N.J.: Lawrence Erlbaum Associates, 2005, pp. 173–221.

Albarracin, Dolores, Blair T. Johnson, and Mark P. Zanna, eds., *The Handbook of Attitudes*, Mahwah, N.J.: Lawrence Erlbaum Associates, 2005.

Ali, Sarmad, "Technology (A Special Report); Videogame Publishers Set Their Sights on Your Cellphone," *Wall Street Journal*, December 19, 2005, p. R7.

"Al-Jazeera a 'Terror Channel,'" Agence France-Presse, November 24, 2004.

Allard, Tom, "Film Rolls as Troops Burn Dead," *Sydney Morning Herald*, October 19, 2005. As of January 11, 2006:
http://www.smh.com.au/news/world/film-rolls-as-troops-burn-dead/2005/10/18/1129401256154.html

Allison, Kevin, "Who's Afraid of the Big, Bad Blog?" *Financial Times*, November 4, 2005, p. 12.

Al-Marashi, Ibrahim, "Iraq's Hostage Crisis: Kidnappings, Mass Media and the Iraqi Insurgency," *Middle East Review of International Affairs*, Vol. 8, No. 4, December 2004, pp. 1–11. As of March 13, 2007:
http://meria.idc.ac.il/journal/2004/issue4/jv8no4a1.html

Al-Qaisi, Salih, and Oliver Poole, "Sadr Shows How to Win Hearts and Minds," *Daily Telegraph* (London), August 29, 2005, p. 12.

Amberg, LTC John, U.S. Army Public Affairs–Midwest, interview with Todd C. Helmus, Chicago, Ill., February 24, 2006.

Anis, SSgt Jason, Joint Information Operations Center, interview with Christopher Paul and Todd C. Helmus, Lackland AFB, Tex., February 16, 2006.

Archer, Ron, Intelligence Analyst, 4th Psychological Operations Group, interview with Todd C. Helmus and Christopher Paul, Ft. Bragg, N.C., December 14, 2005.

Argenti, Paul, "Measuring the Value of Communications," New York: Communications Consulting Worldwide with the Tuck School of Business, Dartmouth University, November 2005. As of March 21, 2007: http://www.ccworldwide.com/reading/WhitePaper.pdf

Associated Press, "New Figures Put Quake Toll at More Than 79,000," *MSNBC*, October 19, 2005. As of May 8, 2007: http://www.msnbc.msn.com/id/9626146/

Aylwin-Foster, Nigel, "Changing the Army for Counterinsurgency Operations," *Military Review*, November–December 2005, pp. 2–15. As of March 14, 2007: http://usacac.army.mil/CAC/milreview/download/English/NovDec05/aylwin.pdf

Bailey, Major General Jonathan, British Army, interview with Russell W. Glenn and Todd C. Helmus, Upavon, UK, December 3, 2003.

Baker, COL Robert, U.S. Army, Commanding Officer, 2nd Brigade, 1st Armored Division, interview with Russell W. Glenn and Todd C. Helmus, Baghdad, Iraq, February 21, 2004.

Ballen, Kenneth, "War on Terror Needs More Humanitarian Efforts," *Christian Science Monitor*, March 2, 2006. As of March 15, 2006: http://www.csmonitor.com/2006/0302/p09s01-coop.html

Barber, Lionel, "America's Soft Power Needs Hard Work," *Financial Times*, July 22, 2005, p. 19.

Barnes, Julian E., "When Banter Beats Bullets: In Afghanistan and Iraq, Soldiers Try New Ways to Gain Support," *U.S. News and World Report*, Vol. 138, No. 8, March 7, 2005, p. 21. As of June 26, 2006: http://www.usnews.com/usnews/news/articles/050307/7afghan.htm

Barnett, Thomas P. M., *The Pentagon's New Map: War and Peace in the Twenty-First Century*, New York: G. P. Putnam's Sons, 2004.

Barry, Tom, "U.S. Isn't 'Stingy,' It's Strategic," International Relations Center, January 10, 2005. As of March 21, 2007: http://ggn.irc-online.org/neighbor/7

Bedingfield, CAPT (retired) Robert, Chaplain, U.S. Navy, interview with Todd C. Helmus, Grand Rapids, Mich., June 7, 2006.

Bloom, LTC Bradley, U.S. Army, Commanding Officer, 3rd Psychological Operations Battalion, 4th Psychological Operations Group, interview with Todd C. Helmus and Christopher Paul, Ft. Bragg, N.C., December 15, 2005.

Blum, Dirk, Lincoln Group, written comments provided to the authors, February 1, 2007.

Boase, Jeffrey, and Barry Wellman, "A Plague of Viruses: Biological, Computer and Marketing," *Current Sociology*, Vol. 49, No. 6, November 2001, pp. 39–55.

Boltz, COL Steven, U.S. Army, G-2, V Corps, interview with Russell W. Glenn and Todd C. Helmus, Heidelberg, Germany, February 26, 2004.

Boris, Bill, interview with Todd C. Helmus, Seattle, Wash., March 28, 2006.

Boylan, LTC Steve, U.S. Army, Public Affairs Chief, Strategic Communication, Combined Arms Center, telephone interview with Christopher Paul, May 24, 2006.

Braig, Bridgette M., and Alice M. Tybout, "Brand Extensions," in Alice M. Tybout and Tim Calkins, eds., *Kellogg on Branding*, Hoboken, N.J.: John Wiley and Sons, 2005, pp. 91–103.

BrainyQuote, "Mohammad Saeed al-Sahaf Quotes," undated. As of July 17, 2006: http://www.brainyquote.com/quotes/authors/m/mohammed_saeed_alsahaf.html

"Brand Rehab: How Companies Can Restore a Tarnished Image," *Knowledge@Wharton*, Wharton School of the University of Pennsylvania, September 21, 2005. As of November 29, 2005: http://knowledge.wharton.upenn.edu/article/1279.cfm

Brandon, James, "To Fight Al Qaeda, US Troops in Africa Build Schools Instead," *Christian Science Monitor*, January 9, 2006. As of March 21, 2007: http://www.csmonitor.com/2006/0109/p01s04-woaf.html

Brennan, John, "We've Lost Sight of His Vision," *Washington Post*, February 26, 2006, p. B4.

Brown, MAJ George, Joint Psychological Operations Planner, Joint Information Operations Center, and LTC George McDonald, Joint Information Operations Center, interview with Christopher Paul and Todd C. Helmus, Lackland AFB, Tex., February 17, 2006.

Burghard, LtCol. Alan G., U.S. Marine Corps, Civil Affairs Officer during OIF, interview with Todd C. Helmus, Santa Monica, Calif., March 23, 2006.

Burns, CDR Ed, U.S. Navy, Joint Information Operations Center, interview with Christopher Paul and Todd C. Helmus, Lackland AFB, Tex., February 16, 2006.

"Bush: Arabic TV Gives False Impression of US," Reuters, January 5, 2006.

"Bush Salute a Satanic Sign? Norwegians Think So," Associated Press, January 21, 2005. As of March 13, 2007: http://www.msnbc.msn.com/id/6852171/

Calder, Bobby, Professor of Marketing, Northwestern University, interview with Todd C. Helmus, Evanston, Ill., February 21, 2006.

Calkins, Tim, "Brand Portfolio Strategy," in Alice M. Tybout and Tim Calkins, eds., *Kellogg on Branding*, Hoboken, N.J.: John Wiley and Sons, 2005a, pp. 104–128.

———, "The Challenge of Branding," in Alice M. Tybout and Tim Calkins, eds., *Kellogg on Branding*, Hoboken, N.J.: John Wiley and Sons, 2005b, pp. 1–8.

———, Clinical Associate Professor of Marketing, Northwestern University, interview with Todd C. Helmus, Evanston, Ill., February 21, 2006.

Caples, John, *Tested Advertisting Methods*, 5th ed., Paramus, N.J.: Prentice Hall, 1997.

Carroll, Wallace, *Persuade or Perish*, Cambridge, Mass.: Riverside Press, 1948.

Caruso, Robert C., Voice of the Consumer Leader, J. D. Power and Associates, interview with Todd C. Helmus, Westlake Village, Calif., June 5, 2006.

Caywood, Clark L., Professor, Northwestern University, interview with Todd C. Helmus, Evanston, Ill., February 21, 2006.

Champagne, Dave, Head of Strategic Studies Directorate, 4th Psychological Operations Group, interview with Todd C. Helmus and Christopher Paul, Ft. Bragg, N.C., December 14, 2005.

Chapman, Steven, and Hibist Astatke, "Appendix to Annex 5: The Social Marketing Evidence Base," *Review of DFID Approach to Social Marketing, Annex 5: Effectiveness, Efficiency and Equity of Social Marketing*, London: DFID Health Systems Resource Centre, April 2003. As of April 11, 2007: http://www.dfidhealthrc.org/publications/srh/SM_Annex5.pdf

Charan, Ram, "10 Tools of Profitable Revenue Growth," from *Profitable Growth is Everyone's Business*, book excerpt, *Business Week*, February 13, 2004. As of March 31, 2006: http://www.businessweek.com/smallbiz/content/feb2004/sb20040213_4917_sb011.htm

Charney, Craig, and Nicole Yakatan, *A New Beginning: Strategies for a More Fruitful Dialogue with the Muslim World*, Washington, D.C.: Council on Foreign Relations, May 2005.

Cialdini, Robert B., *Influence: The Psychology of Persuasion*, New York: William Morrow, 1984.

———, *Influence: The Psychology of Persuasion*, revised ed., New York: Quill, 1993.

Clancy, Kevin, "Marketing Strategy Overview," American Marketing Association, 2001.

Clark, Don, "Ad Measurement Is Going High Tech; Explosion of Media Offerings Complicates Finding Whether Message Is Getting Through," *Wall Street Journal*, April 6, 2006, p. B4.

Clarke, Torie, *Lipstick on a Pig: Winning in the No-Spin Era by Someone Who Knows the Game*, New York: Free Press, 2006.

Clausen, Ned, President, Business Marketing Association, interview with Russell W. Glenn and Todd C. Helmus, New York, February 6, 2006.

Cohen, Jared, "Public Diplomacy in an Age of Terror: A Strategy for Winning the Hearts and Minds of Middle Eastern Youth," briefing, RAND Corporation, Santa Monica, Calif., December 14, 2005.

Cohen, Michael A., and Maria Figueroa Küpçü, "Privatizing Foreign Policy," *World Policy Journal*, Vol. 22, No. 3, Fall 2005, pp. 34–52. As of March 21, 2007: http://www.worldpolicy.org/journal/articles/wpj05-3/cohen.html

Coleman, COL John C., Chief of Staff, First Marine Expeditionary Force during OIF, interview with Russell W. Glenn, Camp Pendleton, Calif., December 17, 2003.

Collins, COL (retired) Glenn, U.S. Army, "WP: Enemy Body Counts Revived," email to Russell W. Glenn, October 25, 2005.

Combelles Siegel, Pascale, "Perception Management: IO's Stepchild?" *Low Intensity Conflict and Law Enforcement*, Vol. 13, No. 2, Autumn 2005, pp. 117–134.

Committee to Protect Journalists, "Attacks on the Press 2004: Documented Cases from Middle East and North Africa: Iraq," undated Web page. As of May 26, 2006: http://www.cpj.org/attacks04/mideast04/iraq.html

Cordesman, Anthony H., *The "Instant Lessons" of the Iraq War: Main Report*, third working draft, Washington, D.C.: Center for Strategic and International Studies, April 14, 2003.

———, "Outside View: Spin Loses Wars," United Press International, December 13, 2005. As of May 8, 2007: http://www.upi.com/Security_Terrorism/Analysis/2005/12/13/outside_view_spin_loses_wars/9021/

Coronna, David, Senior Counselor, Burson-Marsteller, interview with Todd C. Helmus, Chicago, Ill., February 24, 2006.

Costantini, LtCol. William R., U.S. Marine Corps, Commanding Officer, 1st Light Armored Reconnaissance Battalion, 1st Marine Regiment, Operation Iraqi Freedom (February–October 2004), interview with Todd C. Helmus, Naval Postgraduate School, Monterey, Calif., April 4, 2005.

Cragin, Kim, and Scott Gerwehr, *Dissuading Terror: Strategic Influence and the Struggle Against Terrorism*, Santa Monica, Calif.: RAND Corporation, MG-184-RC, 2005. As of March 21, 2007: http://www.rand.org/pubs/monographs/MG184/

Damp, MAJ Kevin, J-35 in support of U.S. Northern Command and U.S. Southern Command, Joint Urban Operations Center, interview with Christopher Paul and Todd C. Helmus, Lackland AFB, Tex., February 17, 2006.

Darley, William M., "Why Public Affairs Is Not Information Operations," *Army Magazine*, Vol. 55, No.1, January 2005. As of May 24, 2006: http://www.ausa.org/webpub/DeptArmyMagazine.nsf/byid/CCRN-6CCSFT

Davis, COL John, U.S. Army, Special Operations Command, interview with Todd C. Helmus, Tampa, Fla., January 19, 2006.

Davis, Scott, "Building a Brand-Driven Organization," in Alice M. Tybout and Tim Calkins, eds., *Kellogg on Branding*, Hoboken, N.J.: John Wiley and Sons, 2005, pp. 226–245.

Dempsey, BG Martin, U.S. Army, Commanding General, 1st Armored Division, interview with Russell W. Glenn and Todd C. Helmus, Baghdad, Iraq, February 19, 2004.

Denove, Chris, Vice President and Executive Director, J. D. Power and Associates, interview with Todd C. Helmus, Westlake Village, Calif., June 5, 2006.

Denove, Chris, and James D. Power IV, *Satisfaction: How Every Great Company Listens to the Voice of the Customer*, New York: Penguin, 2006.

DePaulo, Bella, written comments to Scott Gerwehr, RAND Corporation, January 12, 2004.

Devlin, Brigadier General Peter J., Canadian Army, interview with Russell W. Glenn, Carlisle, Pa., June 2, 2005.

Diamond, Darrough, entrepreneur, interview with Todd C. Helmus, Tampa, Fla., January 20, 2006.

DiMarco, LTC Louis, briefing, U.S. Army Command and General Staff College, Combat Studies Institute, Ft. Leavenworth, Kan., undated.

Douglas, Jack, Jr., "Mixed Signals: Bush's Use of UT Hand Sign Causes Confusion Overseas," *Ft. Worth Star-Telegram*, January 22, 2005, p. 1.

Douglas, Susan, Professor of Marketing, New York University, interview with Russell W. Glenn and Todd C. Helmus, New York, February 7, 2006.

Drake, O. Burtch, President, American Association of Advertising Agencies, interview with Russell W. Glenn and Todd C. Helmus, New York, February 6, 2006.

Duffy, LTC Robert, U.S. Army, Civil Affairs Officer and Provincial Reconstruction Team Commander during Operation Enduring Freedom, interview with Russell W. Glenn and Todd C. Helmus, Bagram, Afghanistan, February 14, 2004.

Dunn, LT Robert, U.S. Navy, Joint Information Operations Center, interview with Christopher Paul, Lackland AFB, Tex., February 16, 2006.

Edelman, *2006 Edelman Trust Barometer*, New York, 2006. As of March 23, 2007: http://www.edelman.com/trust/2007/prior/2006/FullSupplement_final.pdf

Emery, Norman, Jason Werchan, and Donald G. Mowles, Jr., "Fighting Terrorism and Insurgency: Shaping the Information Environment," *Military Review*, January–February 2005, pp. 32–38. As of March 13, 2007: http://usacac.leavenworth.army.mil/cac/milreview/download/english/JanFeb05/Beme.pdf

Edwards, Tom, President, Englobe, telephone interview with Todd C. Helmus, March 31, 2006.

Eggspueler, Cari, Business for Diplomatic Action, interview with Todd C. Helmus, San Francisco, Calif., March 22, 2006.

Eisenhower, Dwight D., campaign speech, San Francisco, October 8, 1952, Eisenhower Presidential Archives, records of C. D. Jackson, box 2.

Etherington, Mark, *Revolt on the Tigris: The Al-Sadr Uprising and the Governing of Iraq*, Ithaca, N.Y.: Cornell University Press, 2005.

Eubanks, LTC Dallas, U.S. Army, G-3 Operations Officer, 2nd Brigade, 4th Infantry Division during OIF (July to April 2004), interview with Russell W. Glenn, Ft. Leavenworth, Kan., April 27, 2005.

Fair, C. Christine, and Bryan Shepherd, "Who Supports Terrorism? Evidence from Fourteen Muslim Countries," *Studies in Conflict and Terrorism*, Vol. 29, No. 1, January 2006, pp. 51–74.

Fakhreddine, Jihad N., "Public Diplomacy 101: A Required Course for Karen Hughes," *Transnational Broadcasting Studies Journal*, 2005. As of March 17, 2006: http://www.tbsjournal.com/Fakhreddine.html

Ford, Peter, "Europe Cringes at Bush 'Crusade' Against Terrorists," *Christian Science Monitor*, September 19, 2001, p. 12. As of September 29, 2006: http://www.csmonitor.com/2001/0919/p12s2-woeu.html

Forney, Matthew, "How Nike Figured Out China," *Time*, October 17, 2004. As of December 11, 2004: http://www.time.com/time/globalbusiness/article/0,9171,1101041025-725113,00.html

Fowler, Geoffrey A., "China Bans Nike's LeBron Ad as Offensive to Nation's Dignity," *Wall Street Journal*, December 7, 2004, p. B4.

Friedman, Herbert A., "Operation Iraqi Freedom," undated. As of August 18, 2006:
http://www.psywarrior.com/OpnIraqiFreedom.html

Galloway, Joseph L., "Lies Are a Part of War Strategy," *Miami Herald*, December 10, 2004.

Galvin, SGT Matthew, U.S. Army, Psychological Operations, interview with Todd C. Helmus and Christopher Paul, Ft. Bragg, N.C., December 15, 2005.

Gass, Robert H., and John S. Seiter, *Persuasion, Social Influence, and Compliance Gaining*, Boston, Mass.: Pearson Education, 2003.

Gautschi, Thomas, "History Effects in Social Dilemma Situations," *Rationality and Society*, Vol. 12, No. 2, May 2000, pp. 131–162.

Geehan, Sean, "Your Customers Can Be Your Most Powerful Advisors," American Marketing Association, 2004.

Gerth, Jeff, "Military's Information War Is Vast and Often Secretive," *New York Times*, December 11, 2005, p. 1.

Gerwehr, Scott, and Russell W. Glenn, *The Art of Darkness: Deception and Urban Operations*, Santa Monica, Calif.: RAND Corporation, MR-1132-A, 2000. As of March 21, 2007:
http://www.rand.org/pubs/monograph_reports/MR1132/

—————, *Unweaving the Web: Deception and Adaptation in Future Urban Operations*, Santa Monica, Calif.: RAND Corporation, MR-1495-A, 2002. As of March 21, 2007:
http://www.rand.org/pubs/monograph_reports/MR1495/

Giesler, Bob, Director, Information Operations and Strategic Studies, Office of the Deputy Under Secretary of Defense, Intelligence and Warfighting Support, interview with Christopher Paul, the Pentagon, Arlington, Va., April 26, 2006.

Gilmore, Allison B., *You Can't Fight Tanks with Bayonets: Psychological Warfare Against the Japanese Army in the Southwest Pacific*, Lincoln, Neb.: University of Nebraska Press, 1998.

Gladwell, Malcolm, *The Tipping Point: How Little Things Can Make a Big Difference*, New York: Back Bay Books/Little, Brown and Company, 2002.

Glenn, Russell W., *Counterinsurgency in a Test Tube: Analyzing the Success of the Regional Assistance Mission to Solomon Islands (RAMSI)*, Santa Monica, Calif.: RAND Corporation, MG-551-JFCOM, 2007. As of May 2, 2007:
http://www.rand.org/pubs/monographs/MG551/

Glenn, Russell W., Christopher Paul, Todd C. Helmus, and Paul Steinberg, *"People Make the City," Executive Summary: Joint Urban Operations Observations and Insights from Afghanistan and Iraq,* Santa Monica, Calif.: RAND Corporation, MG-428/2-JFCOM, 2007. As of May 15, 2007: http://www.rand.org/pubs/monographs/MG428.2/

Goetz, Thomas, Deputy Editor, *Wired,* interview with Todd C. Helmus, San Francisco, Calif., March 22, 2006.

Goldfarb, Michael, *Ahmad's War, Ahmad's Peace,* New York: Carroll and Graf, 2005.

Gouillart, Francis J., and Frederick D. Sturdivant, "Spend a Day in the Life of Your Customers," *Harvard Business Review,* Vol. 72, No. 1, January–February 1994, p. 116.

Greenberg, Martin, Professor of Psychology, University of Pittsburgh, interview with Todd C. Helmus, Pittsburgh, Pa., January 13, 2006.

Gregory, Bruce, Director, Public Diplomacy Institute, George Washington University, interview with Todd C. Helmus, Washington, D.C., December 26, 2005.

Guerin, Bill, "The Not So Ugly Americans," *Asia Times Online,* January 11, 2005. As of November 29, 2005: http://www.atimes.com/atimes/Southeast_Asia/GA11Ae02.html

Gurganis, Col. Charles M. (Mark), U.S. Marine Corps, Commanding Officer, Regimental Combat Team 8, interview with Russell W. Glenn, Fallujah, Iraq, July 13, 2005.

"Hamas Launches TV Station in Gaza," Associated Press, January 10, 2006.

Harding, Thomas, "British Brigadier Attacks America's John Wayne Generals," *Daily Telegraph* (London), April 19, 2006, p. 1.

Headquarters, U.S. Department of the Army, *Information Operations: Doctrine, Tactics, Techniques, and Procedures,* Washington, D.C., Army Field Manual 3-13, November 28, 2003a.

———, *Psychological Operations Tactics, Techniques, and Procedures,* Washington, D.C., December 31, 2003b.

———, *Psychological Operations,* Washington, D.C., Field Manual 3-05.30, April 15, 2005.

Heinz, "Heinz Top-Down Ketchup™," *Heinz World,* undated Web page. As of May 24, 2006: http://www.heinz.com/World.aspx#htd

Henninger, Daniel, "Spirit of America: Here's a Way You Can Help the Cause in Iraq," *Wall Street Journal Opinion Journal,* April 16, 2004. As of July 8, 2004: http://www.opinionjournal.com/columnists/dhenninger/?id=110004958

Hess, Pamela, "Officer Commands Respect from Locals: 'Sledgehammer' Strategy Working," *Washington Times*, September 26, 2005. As of November 16, 2005: http://washingtontimes.com/world/20050925-104444-7855r.htm

Hill, MAJ John, J-24 Intelligence Support to Special Operations Team Leader, and LTC Jayson Spade, J-31 Team Chief, Combatant Command Support Team for U.S. Pacific Command, interview with Christopher Paul and Todd C. Helmus, Joint Information Operations Center, Lackland AFB, Tex., February 16, 2006.

Hillen, John, "Our Best and Bravest," *National Review Online*, February 28, 2005. As of July 17, 2006: http://www.nationalreview.com/comment/hillen200502280847.asp

Hoffman, Adonis, Senior Vice President and Counsel, American Association of Advertising Agencies, interview with Todd C. Helmus and Christopher Paul, Washington, D.C., December 15, 2005.

Hosmer, Stephen T., *Psychological Effects of U.S. Air Operations in Four Wars 1941–1991: Lessons for U.S. Commanders*, Santa Monica, Calif.: RAND Corporation, MR-576-AF, 1996. As of March 21, 2007: http://www.rand.org/pubs/monograph_reports/MR576/

Howcroft, Col. Jim, 1st Marine Expeditionary Force G-2, interview with Russell W. Glenn, Camp Pendleton, Calif., December 17, 2003.

Howes, Lieutenant Colonel F. H. R., Commander, 42nd Commando Royal Marines during Operation Telic, interview with Russell W. Glenn and Todd C. Helmus, Upavon, UK, December 12, 2003.

Huntington, Samuel P., "The Clash of Civilizations?" *Foreign Affairs*, Vol. 72, No. 3, Summer 1993, pp. 22–49. As of March 21, 2007: http://www.foreignaffairs.org/19930601faessay5188/samuel-p-huntington/the-clash-of-civilizations.html

"Iraq: Al-Sadr Accuses Al-Qaeda and U.S. of Sunday's Carnage," Adnkronosinternational, March 13, 2006.

Jaffe, Greg, "Widening Gulf: For U.S. Military, a Key Iraq Mission Is Averting Civil War; a Small Victory in Tal Afar, as Sunnis, Shiites Form Reconciliation Committee; Col. Hickey's Ramadan Feast," *Wall Street Journal*, October 14, 2005, p. A1.

Jalal, Faraydoon, "Iraqi Journalists Risking Their Lives," *Kurdish Media*, June 16, 2005.

Jamestown Foundation, "New Magazine for al-Qaeda in Iraq," *Terrorism Focus*, Vol. 2, No. 5, March 3, 2005, p. 3.

Jenks, Robert, Deputy Commanding Officer for Research, Analysis, and Civilian Affairs, 4th Psychological Operations Group, interview with Todd C. Helmus and Christopher Paul, Ft. Bragg, N.C., December 15, 2005.

Johnson, Lynn, Rendon Group, interview with Todd C. Helmus and Christopher Paul, Washington, D.C., December 15, 2005.

Joint Chiefs of Staff, *Doctrine for Joint Urban Operations*, Joint Publication 3-06, September 16, 2002. As of March 13, 2007:
http://www.dtic.mil/doctrine/jel/new_pubs/jp3_06.pdf

—————, *Doctrine for Joint Psychological Operations*, Joint Publication 3-53, September 5, 2003. As of March 21, 2007:
http://www.dtic.mil/doctrine/jel/new_pubs/jp3_53.pdf

—————, *Doctrine for Public Affairs in Joint Operations*, Joint Publication 3-61, May 9, 2005. As of March 16, 2007:
http://www.dtic.mil/doctrine/jel/new_pubs/jp3_61.pdf

—————, *Joint Doctrine for Information Operations*, Joint Publication 3-13, February 13, 2006. As of March 15, 2007:
http://www.dtic.mil/doctrine/jel/new_pubs/jp3_13.pdf

Jones, Jeffrey B., "Strategic Communication: A Mandate for the United States," *Joint Force Quarterly*, No. 39, October 2005, pp. 108–114. As of May 31, 2006:
http://www.dtic.mil/doctrine/jel/jfq_pubs/1839.pdf

Kaplan, Fred, "Candid Camera: The Trouble with Releasing Zarqawi's Outtakes," *Slate*, May 5, 2006. As of May 30, 2006:
http://www.slate.com/id/2141087/

Kaplan, Robert D., "The Real Story of Fallujah," *Wall Street Journal*, May 27, 2004, p. A20.

Kassab, Mike, "Optimizing Your Brand Focus," *NOP World Perspectives*, Vol. 2, No. 1, Spring 2005, pp. 24–27.

Keeton, LTC (retired) Pamela, Director of Public Affairs and Communications, United States Institute of Peace, interview conducted as a questionnaire, May 30, 2006.

Keeton, Pamela, and Mark McCann, "Information Operations, STRATCOM, and Public Affairs," *Military Review*, November–December 2005, pp. 83–86. As of March 16, 2007:
http://usacac.army.mil/CAC/milreview/download/English/NovDec05/keeton.pdf

Kennett, Brigadier Andrew C. P., British Army, interview with Russell W. Glenn, Warminster, UK, December 15, 2004.

Knickmeyer, Ellen, "Text Messaging Allows Iraqis to Tip Off Authorities to Attacks," *Pittsburgh Post-Gazette*, June 22, 2005, p. H3.

Knights, Michael, "'Iraqi Freedom' Displays the Transformation of US Air Power," *Jane's Intelligence Review*, May 2003, p. 18.

Kotler, Philip, and Gary Armstrong, *Principles of Marketing*, 11th ed., Upper Saddle River, N.J.: Pearson Education, 2006.

Kotler, Philip, Ned Roberto, and Nancy Lee, *Social Marketing: Improving the Quality of Life*, 2nd ed., Thousand Oaks, Calif.: Sage Publications, 2002.

Krauthammer, Charles, "Gitmo Grovel: Enough Already," *Washington Post*, June 3, 2005, p. A23. As of March 20, 2007:
http://www.washingtonpost.com/wp-dyn/content/article/2005/06/02/AR2005060201750.html

Krohn, Charles, LTC (retired), Office of the Assistant Secretary of Defense for Public Affairs, interview with Christopher Paul, Arlington, Va., December 16, 2005.

Krulak, Charles C., "The Strategic Corporal: Leadership in the Three Block War," *Marines Magazine*, Vol. 28, No. 1, January 1999, pp. 26–33. As of July 24, 2006:
http://www.au.af.mil/au/awc/awcgate/usmc/strategic_corporal.htm

Kucera, Joshua, "Military and the Media—Weaponising the Truth?" *Jane's Defence Weekly*, June 8, 2005a.

———, "Djibouti: US Foothold in Africa—African Foothold," *Jane's Defence Weekly*, October 26, 2005b.

Kurilla, LTC Michael E., U.S. Army, interview with Russell W. Glenn, Mosul, Iraq, July 9, 2005.

Lake, James, Chair, U.S. Public Affairs Practice, Burson-Marsteller, interview with Todd C. Helmus, Chicago, Ill., February 24, 2006.

Lamb, Christopher, *Review of Psychological Operations Lessons Learned from Recent Operational Experience*, Washington, D.C.: National Defense University Press, September 2005. As of March 15, 2007:
http://www.ndu.edu/inss/Occassional_Papers/Lamb_OP_092005_Psyops.pdf

Lambert, MG (retired) Geoffrey, Booz Allen Hamilton, Retired Special Operations Forces Mentor, Joint Forces Command, J9, interview with Todd C. Helmus, Tampa, Fla., January 20, 2006.

Larson, Eric V., Richard E. Darilek, Daniel Gibran, Brian Nichiporak, Amy Richardson, Lowell H. Schwartz, and Cathryn Quantic Thurston, *Foundations of Effective Influence Operations*, unpublished RAND research, April 2006.

Lee, Angela, Professor of Marketing, Northwestern University, interview with Todd C. Helmus, Evanston, Ill., February 21, 2006.

Lee, Louise, "Dell: In the Bloghouse," *Business Week Online*, August 25, 2005. As of January 25, 2007:
http://www.businessweek.com/technology/content/aug2005/tc20050825_2021.htm

Lehning, Maj. Amber, U.S. Marine Corps, Civil Affairs Officer during OIF, interview with Todd C. Helmus, Santa Monica, Calif., March 23, 2006.

Leslie, John (Jack) W., Chair, Weber Shandwick Worldwide, interview with Todd C. Helmus and Russell W. Glenn, New York, February 6, 2006.

Leung, Shirley, "Arch Support: McDonald's CEO Talks About the Moves That Are Turning His Chain Around," *Wall Street Journal*, classroom ed., April 2004. As of May 26, 2006:
http://wsjclassroom.com/archive/04apr/bigb_mcdonalds.htm

Levine, Robert, *The Power of Persuasion: How We're Bought and Sold*, Hoboken, N.J.: John Wiley and Sons, 2003.

Lopez, Col. Matthew, U.S. Marine Corps, Commander, 3rd Battalion, 7th Marine Regiment during OIF, interview with Todd C. Helmus, Suffolk, Va., March 28, 2007.

Losman, Don, "Hate's Inevitable Harvest: Sources of and Solutions for Middle East Hatred," *Indonesia Watch*, February 2006. As of April 11, 2007:
http://www.indonesiawatch.org/eng_under.php?news_id=195

"Lucius Cornelius Sulla," *Encyclopaedia Britannica*, 2007. As of March 16, 2007:
http://www.britannica.com/eb/article-9070258/Sulla

Lumm, Andrew, Burson-Marsteller, interview with Todd C. Helmus, Chicago, Ill., February 24, 2006.

Martel, LTC Gary, Joint Information Operations Center, interview with Christopher Paul, Lackland AFB, San Antonio, Tex., February 16, 2006.

Mattis, James N., and Frank G. Hoffman, "Future Warfare and the Rise of Hybrid Wars," *Proceedings* (U.S. Naval Institute), Vol. 132, No. 11, November 2005, pp. 18–19.

Maurer, Kevin, "Fort Bragg Troops Are on a Goodwill Mission in Africa," *Fayetteville* (N.C.) *Observer*, August 6, 2006.

Maxwell, Mark David, "The Law of War and Civilians on the Battlefield: Are We Undermining Civilian Protections?" *Military Review*, September–October 2004, pp. 17–25. As of March 21, 2007:
http://usacac.army.mil/cac/milreview/download/English/SepOct04/maxm.pdf

May, Clifford D., "Turning Off Terrorist Television," Scripps Howard News Service, March 29, 2006.

Mayhew, Leon H., *The New Public: Professional Communication and the Means of Social Influence*, Cambridge, UK: University Press, 1997.

Mazzetti, Mark, "PR Meets Psy-Ops in War on Terror: The Use of Misleading Information as a Military Tool Sparks Debate in the Pentagon; Critics Say the Practice Puts Credibility at Stake," *Los Angeles Times*, December 1, 2004, p. A1.

———, "Planted Articles May Be Violation: A 2003 Pentagon Directive Appears to Bar a Military Program That Pays Iraqi Media to Print Favorable Stories," *Los Angeles Times*, January 27, 2006, p. A3.

Mazzetti, Mark, and Kevin Sack, "The Challenges in Iraq: Planted PR Stories Not News to Military," *Los Angeles Times*, December 18, 2005, p. A1.

McDonald, LTC George, Joint Information Operations Center, and MAJ George Brown, Joint PSYOP Planner, Joint Information Operations Center, interview with Christopher Paul and Todd C. Helmus, Lackland AFB, Tex., February 17, 2006.

Medby, Jamison Jo, and Russell W. Glenn, *Street Smart: Intelligence Preparation of the Battlefield for Urban Operations*, Santa Monica, Calif.: RAND Corporation, MR-1287-A, 2002. As of March 16, 2007:
http://www.rand.org/pubs/monograph_reports/MR1287/

Medcalf, Graham, "What's the Buzz? Is Advertising as We Know It Dying and If So What's the New Paradigm?" *New Zealand Marketing Magazine*, Vol. 22, No. 10, November 1, 2003, pp. 18–19.

Medhurst-Cocksworth, Captain Christopher R., British Army, Intelligence Officer, Grade 3, G2 (Intelligence) Brigade during OIF, interview with Russell W. Glenn and Todd C. Helmus, Bergen, Germany, December 10, 2003.

Mendenhall, Bill, President, Mendenhall and Associates, interview with Todd C. Helmus, Holland, Mich., November 28, 2006.

Middle East Online, "US Suspends Publication of Arab Youth Magazine," last updated December 23, 2005. As of March 12, 2007:
http://www.middle-east-online.com/english/culture/?id=15306

Milburn, Maj. A. R., "Preliminary Report on USMC Civil Military Operations (CMO) in Iraq," report to Director, Security Assistance and Education Training Center from its representative to the Marine Corps Center for Lessons Learned, November 28, 2004.

Mockenhaupt, Brian, "I Miss Iraq. I Miss My Gun. I Miss My War," *Esquire*, March 2007, pp. 120–123. As of March 15, 2007:
http://www.esquire.com/features/essay/ESQ0307ESSAY

Morgan, Daniel, "Going to Fight in Iraq? Lessons from an Infantry Company Commander," *After Action Report, Infantry Company in Iraq*, January 23, 2004, p. 6.

MountainRunner, "DoD as Our Public Diplomat in Pakistan," blog entry, *MountainRunner*, January 13, 2006. As of March 19, 2007:
http://www.mountainrunner.us/2006/01/us_scratch_the_.html

Munson, CDR Thurman, U.S. Navy, Joint Information Operations Center Support Team Chief, U.S. European Command, interview with Christopher Paul and Todd C. Helmus, Lackland AFB, Tex., February 17, 2006.

Myers, David G., *Social Psychology*, 8th ed., New York: McGraw-Hill, 2005.

Norwitz, Jeffrey H., "Defining Success at Guantanamo: By What Measure?" *Military Review*, July–August 2005, pp. 79–83. As of March 21, 2007:
http://usacac.army.mil/CAC/milreview/download/English/JulAug05/norwitz.pdf

Novosel, Nicholas, Balkan Area Analyst, U.S. European Command, Strategic Studies Detachment, 4th Psychological Operations Group, interview with Todd C. Helmus and Christopher Paul, Ft. Bragg, N.C., December 14, 2005.

O'Connor, Eileen M., and David Hoffman, "Media in Iraq: The Fallacy of Psy-Ops," *International Herald Tribune*, December 17, 2005, p. 9.

Office of the Surgeon, Multi-National Force–Iraq, and Office of the Surgeon General, U.S. Army Medical Command, *Mental Health Advisory Team (MHAT) IV: Operation Iraqi Freedom 05-07*, November 17, 2006. As of May 8, 2007:
http://www.armymedicine.army.mil/news/mhat/mhat_iv/mhat-iv.cfm

Olson, David, "Principles of Measuring Advertising Effectiveness," American Marketing Association, 2001.

One Laptop per Child, undated homepage. As of March 19, 2007:
http://www.laptop.org/

Orban, LTC Jerry, U.S. Army, Special Operations Command, Concept Developer, Army Futures Center, interview with Todd C. Helmus and Christopher Paul, Ft. Bragg, N.C., December 14, 2005.

Ostrum, Amy L., Dawn Iacobucci, and Felicia N. Morgan, "Services Branding," in Alice M. Tybout and Tim Calkins, eds., *Kellogg on Branding*, Hoboken, N.J.: John Wiley and Sons, 2005, pp. 186–200.

Overdorf, Jason, "The $100 Un-PC," *Newsweek*, international ed., February 12, 2007. As of April 6, 2007:
http://www.msnbc.msn.com/id/16959219/site/newsweek/

Paletz, David L., *The Media in American Politics: Contents and Consequences*, New York: Longman, 2002.

Patton, Gary S., "Public Affairs and Information Operations: Integral or Incompatible?" Carlisle, Pa.: U.S. Army War College, April 10, 2000.

Patton, BG Steve, interview with Russell W. Glenn, the Pentagon, Arlington, Va., November 7, 2003.

Paul, Christopher, and James J. Kim, *Reporters on the Battlefield*, Santa Monica, Calif.: RAND Corporation, MG-200-RC, 2004. As of March 20, 2007:
http://www.rand.org/pubs/monographs/MG200/

Pearce, MAJ Edward L., "Trip Report—Fast Train VI," memorandum to Director, Combined Arms and Tactics Directorate, U.S. Army Infantry School, September 13, 2004.

Perloff, Richard M., *The Dynamics of Persuasion Communication and Attitudes in the 21st Century*, 2nd ed., Mahwah, N.J.: Lawrence Erlbaum Associates, 2003.

Peters, Ralph, "Killers with Cameras," *New York Post*, June 21, 2004.

Pethokoukis, James M., "Spreading the Word: Corporate Evangelists Recruit Customers Who Love to Create Buzz About a Product," *U.S. News and World Report*, Vol. 139, No. 21, December 5, 2005. As of February 28, 2006: http://www.usnews.com/usnews/biztech/articles/051205/5eeevangelist.htm

Pew Global Attitudes Project, *America's Image Slips, but Allies Share U.S. Concerns Over Iran, Hamas; No Global Warming Alarm in the U.S., China*, Washington, D.C.: Pew Research Center, June 13, 2006. As of June 28, 2006: http://pewglobal.org/reports/display.php?ReportID=252

Pincus, Phil, Executive Director, J. D. Power and Associates, interview with Todd C. Helmus, Westlake Village, Calif., June 5, 2006.

Pingitore, Gina, Chief Research Officer, J. D. Power and Associates, interview with Todd C. Helmus, Westlake Village, Calif., June 5, 2006.

Pinkerton, James P., "Covering the News with Deception," *Long Island Newsday*, December 16, 2004.

"Podcasting: Fiddly No Longer," *Economist*, July 9, 2005, p. 56.

"Political Islam, Forty Shades of Green," *Economist*, February 4, 2006, p. 23.

Power, J. D. III, Founder, J. D. Power and Associates, interview with Todd C. Helmus, Westlake Village, Calif., June 5, 2006.

Power, James D. IV, Executive Vice President, J. D. Power and Associates, telephone interview with Todd C. Helmus, June 26, 2006.

"The Product Life Cycle," *QuickMBA.com*, undated. As of May 25, 2006: http://www.quickmba.com/marketing/product/lifecycle/

Program on International Policy Attitudes, *What the Iraqi Public Wants: A WorldPublicOpinion.org Poll*, January 31, 2006. As of February 27, 2006: http://www.pipa.org/OnlineReports/Iraq/Iraq_Jan06_rpt.pdf

Quigley, Samantha L., "Funding, Public Opinion Pose Challenges in War on Terrorism," American Forces Press Service, Washington, March 14, 2006.

Rainey, James, "Aiming for a More Subtle Fighting Force," *Los Angeles Times*, May 9, 2006, p. A1.

Rand, Paul M., "Identifying and Reaching Influencers," American Marketing Association, 2004.

———, "Understanding and Managing Negative Word of Mouth," transcript of speech presented at Word of Mouth Marketing Association conference, September 28, 2005.

———, Director of Global Technology Practice, Ketchum, interview with Todd C. Helmus, Chicago, Ill., February 24, 2006.

Rasmussen, MAJ David C., U.S. Army, Battalion Executive Officer, 2-87th Infantry Battalion, 10th Mountain Division, interview with Russell W. Glenn and Todd C. Helmus, Bagram, Afghanistan, February 14, 2004.

Rayment, Sean, "US Tactics Condemned by British Officers," *Sunday Telegraph* (London), April 11, 2004, p. 6. As of March 14, 2007:
http://www.telegraph.co.uk/news/main.jhtml?xml=/news/2004/04/11/wtact11.xml&sSheet=/news/2004/04/11/ixnewstop.html

———, "Trigger-Happy US Troops 'Will Keep Us in Iraq for Years,'" *Sunday Telegraph* (London), May 15, 2005. As of December 13, 2005:
http://www.telegraph.co.uk/news/main.jhtml?xml=/news/2005/05/15/wirq15.xml&sSheet=/news/2005/05/15/ixworld.html

Reinhard, Keith, Chairman, DDB Advertising, interview with Todd C. Helmus, New York, February 28, 2006.

Rendon, John, Rendon Group, interview with Todd C. Helmus and Christopher Paul, Washington, D.C., December 15, 2005.

Rhynedance, COL George, Director, Army Public Affairs Center, telephone interview with Christopher Paul, May 23, 2006.

Ricks, Thomas E., "The Lessons of Counterinsurgency: U.S. Unit Praised for Tactics Against Iraqi Fighters, Treatment of Detainees," *Washington Post*, February 16, 2006, p. A14.

Rincon, Paul, "US Troops Taught Iraqi Gestures," *BBC News*, February 19, 2006. As of May 25, 2006:
http://news.bbc.co.uk/1/hi/technology/4729262.stm

Ritz-Carlton, "Gold Standards," undated Web page. As of March 17, 2007:
http://corporate.ritzcarlton.com/en/About/GoldStandards.htm

Ritzer, George, *The McDonaldization of Society*, revised ed., Thousand Oaks, Calif.: Pine Forge Press, 2004.

Robinson, Glenn E., and Kalev Sepp, "Current Insurgency in Iraq in the Context of Historical Islam," presentation at Conference on Understanding Terrorist Networks and Organizations, Naval Postgraduate School, Monterey, Calif., April 7, 2005.

Rosen, Emannuel, author, telephone interview with Todd C. Helmus, February 3, 2006.

Rosenbach, Marcel, "The Global News War," *Spiegel Online*, May 1, 2006. As of March 21, 2007:
http://www.spiegel.de/international/0,1518,413423,00.html

Rowe, Greg D., Senior Information Operations Planner and Certified Information Systems Security Professional, Syracuse Research Corporation, interview with Todd C. Helmus and Christopher Paul, Chantilly, Va., December 16, 2005.

————, "Hang Fires in Strategic Communication," email to authors, March 30, 2006.

Ryan, Tim, "Media's Coverage Has Distorted World's View of Iraqi Reality," *WorldTribune.com*, January 18, 2005. As of May 30, 2006:
http://www.worldtribune.com/worldtribune/05/breaking2453389.0680555557.html

Salmoni, Barak, Assistant Professor, Naval Postgraduate School, interview with Todd C. Helmus, Naval Postgraduate School, Monterey, Calif., April 4, 2005.

Santos, Cindy, "USC Teams Up to Create New Fellowship," *Daily Trojan*, January 18, 2006. As of January 23, 2006:
http://www.dailytrojan.com/media/paper679/news/2006/01/18/News/Usc-Teams.Up.To.Create.New.Fellowship-1434819.shtml

Schleifer, Ron, "Psychological Operations: A New Variation on an Age Old Art: Hezbollah Versus Israel," *Studies in Conflict and Terrorism*, Vol. 29, No. 1, January 2006, pp. 1–19.

Schrager, Stanley N., Public Diplomacy Advisor, Special Operations Command, interview with Todd C. Helmus, Tampa, Fla., January 19, 2006.

Schudson, Michael, *The Power of News*, Cambridge, Mass.: Harvard University Press, 1995.

————, *The Sociology of News*, New York: W. W. Norton, 2003.

Schwartz, Lowell, "War, Propaganda and Public Opinion," *Baltimore Sun*, December 18, 2005. As of February 8, 2006:
http://www.rand.org/commentary/121805BS.html

Semple, Kirk, "U.S. Backs Hot Line in Iraq to Solicit Tips About Trouble," *New York Times*, November 5, 2006, p. 14.

Smart, Barry, ed., *Resisting McDonaldization*, London: Sage Publications, 1999.

Smith, Dorrance, "The Enemy on Our Airwaves," *Wall Street Journal*, April 25, 2005, p. A14.

Smith, Rupert, Nigel Howard, and Andrew Tait, "Confrontations in War and Peace," Brighton, UK: dramatec, undated. As of March 21, 2007:
http://www.dramatec.com/pdf/warandpeace.pdf

Sosin, Jennifer, President, KRC Research, telephone interview with Todd C. Helmus, March 28, 2006.

Spade, LTC Jayson, J-31 Team Chief, Combatant Command Support Team for U.S. Pacific Command, and MAJ John Hill, J-24 Intelligence Support to Special Operations Team Leader, interview with Christopher Paul and Todd C. Helmus, Joint Information Operations Center, Lackland AFB, Tex., February 16, 2006.

Speulda, Nicole, "Documenting the Phenomenon of Anti-Americanism," The Princeton Project on National Security, posted November 7, 2005. As of September 1, 2006:
http://www.wws.princeton.edu/ppns/papers/speulda.pdf

Spira, CDR Alan M., U.S. Navy, Civil Affairs Officer, interview with Todd C. Helmus, Santa Monica, Calif., March 23, 2006.

Steele, Robert David, "Information Operations: Putting the 'I' Back into Dime," Carlisle, Pa.: Strategic Studies Institute, U.S. Army War College, February 2006. As of May 31, 2006:
http://www.strategicstudiesinstitute.army.mil/pdffiles/PUB642.pdf

Steinberg, Brian, "House Training: Now, Employees Get Brand Boost," *Wall Street Journal*, January 18, 2005a, p. B1.

———, "Speaking Up Through Bespoke Ads," *Wall Street Journal*, February 11, 2005b, p. B5.

———, "Madison Avenue Is Getting the Beat," *Wall Street Journal*, March 23, 2005c, p. B3.

———, "How Old Media Can Survive in a New World," *Wall Street Journal*, May 23, 2005d, p. B1.

———, "Advertisers Attempt to Say a Lot Using Very Little Words," *Wall Street Journal*, November 29, 2005e, p. B1.

Steinberg, Brian, and Suzanne Vranica, "Careerbuilder Plans Super Bowl Ads," *Wall Street Journal*, January 17, 2005, p. B3.

Steinmetz, George, "Introduction: Culture and the State," in George Steinmetz, ed., *State/Culture State-Formation After the Cultural Turn*, Ithaca, N.Y.: Cornell University Press, 1999, pp. 1–49.

Sternthal, Brian, and Angela Y. Lee, "Building Brands Through Effective Advertising," in Alice M. Tybout and Tim Calkins, eds., *Kellogg on Branding*, Hoboken, N.J.: John Wiley and Sons, 2005, pp. 129–149.

Stewart, Rory, *The Prince of the Marshes and Other Occupational Hazards of a Year in Iraq*, Orlando, Fla.: Harcourt, 2006.

Stockman, Farah, "US Image a Tough Sell in Mideast," *Boston Globe*, October 24, 2005, p. A5.

Stringer, Kortney, "In Ad Blitz, Wal-Mart Counters Public Image as Harsh Employer," *Wall Street Journal*, January 14, 2005, p. B3.

Strycula, MAJ John J., U.S. Army, "Intelligence Support to Information Operations," unpublished briefing, Santa Monica, Calif.: RAND Corporation, undated.

———, RAND Army Fellow, interview with Todd C. Helmus, Santa Monica, Calif., March 17, 2005.

Summe, COL Jack, J-39, Psychological Operations Division Chief, interview with Todd C. Helmus, MacDill AFB, Fla., January 19, 2006.

Tallman, LTC Gary, U.S. Army, Public Affairs Officer, interview with Christopher Paul, the Pentagon, Arlington, Va., April 24, 2006.

Technorati, "About Technorati," undated Web page. As of March 14, 2006: http://www.technorati.com/about/

Terror Free Tomorrow, "Poll: Dramatic Change of Public Opinion in the Muslim World," 2005. As of August 30, 2006: http://www.terrorfreetomorrow.org/articlenav.php?id=71

Tessier, MAJ Lawrence, Assistant Operations Officer, 6th Psychological Operations Battalion, Psychological Operations Support Element in Nigeria, in Kuwait in support of OIF, interview with Todd C. Helmus and Christopher Paul, Ft. Bragg, N.C., December 14, 2005.

Thomas, David C., and Kerr Inkson, *Cultural Intelligence: People Skills for Global Business*, San Francisco, Calif.: Berrett-Koehler Publishers, 2004.

Thomas, M. A., Area Analyst, 4th Psychological Operations Group, interview with Todd C. Helmus and Christopher Paul, Ft. Bragg, N.C., December 14, 2005.

Tootal, Major Stuart, Second-in-Command, 1st Parachute Battlalion during Operation Telic, interview with Russell W. Glenn and Todd C. Helmus, Codford, UK, December 12 2003.

Treadwell, COL, interview with Todd C. Helmus, Joint Psychological Operations Support Element, Special Operations Command, MacDill AFB, Fla., January 19, 2006.

Turner, COL Kenneth A., U.S. Army, Commanding Officer, 4th Psychological Operations Group, interview with Todd C. Helmus and Christopher Paul, Ft. Bragg, N.C., December 14, 2005.

Tybout, Alice, Professor of Marketing, Northwestern University, interview with Todd C. Helmus, Evanston, IL, February 21, 2006.

Tybout, Alice M., and Tim Calkins, eds., *Kellogg on Branding*, Hoboken, N.J.: John Wiley and Sons, 2005.

Tybout, Alice M., and Brian Sternthal, "Brand Positioning," in Alice M. Tybout and Tim Calkins, eds., *Kellogg on Branding*, Hoboken, N.J.: John Wiley and Sons, 2005, pp. 11–26.

Tzavellas, Ted, "Strategic Communication . . . a Perspective," Joint Chiefs of Staff, briefing to Christopher Paul, the Pentagon, Arlington, Va., April 26, 2006.

———, Senior Information Policy and Strategy Advisor, Lockheed Martin, and LTC Michael Williams, Chief, Plans Support Branch, Information Operations Division, Deputy Director for Global Operations, interview with Christopher Paul, the Pentagon, Arlington, Va., May 26, 2006.

Tzu, Sun, *The Art of War*, New York: Oxford University Press, 1963.

Ungar, Sanford J., "Pitch Imperfect," *Foreign Affairs*, Vol. 84, No. 3, May–June 2005, pp. 7–13. As of March 20, 2007:
http://www.foreignaffairs.org/20050501facomment84302/sanford-j-ungar/pitch-imperfect.html

UK Ministry of Defence, *Operations in Iraq: Lessons for the Future*, London: Directorate General Corporate Communication, December 2003. As of March 20, 2007:
http://www.mod.uk/NR/rdonlyres/
734920BA-6ADE-461F-A809-7E5A754990D7/0/opsiniraq_lessons_dec03.pdf

Unidentified Marine Expeditionary Force Planner, U.S. Marine Corps, "Perspectives on HA/CMO in Iraq," briefing, Security Cooperation Education and Training Center, undated.

UN Office of the Special Envoy for Tsunami Recovery, "The Human Toll," undated. As of March 20, 2007:
http://www.tsunamispecialenvoy.org/country/humantoll.asp

U.S. Code, Title 22, Foreign Relations and Intercourse, Section 1461-1a, Ban on Domestic Activities by the United States Information Agency (Smith-Mundt Act).

U.S. Department of Defense, Office of the Under Secretary of Defense for Acquisition, Technology, and Logistics, *Report of the Defense Science Board Task Force on Strategic Communication*, Washington, D.C., September 2004. As of March 12, 2007:
http://www.acq.osd.mil/dsb/reports/2004-09-Strategic_Communication.pdf

U.S. Department of Defense, *2006 Quadrennial Defense Review Report*, Washington, D.C., February 6, 2006. As of August 30, 2006:
http://www.defenselink.mil/qdr/report/Report20060203.pdf

U.S. Department of State, *Cultural Diplomacy: The Linchpin of Public Diplomacy*, report of the Advisory Committee on Cultural Diplomacy, September 2005.

———, "Promote Strategic Communications—Developments," Bureau of Near Eastern Affairs, Iraq Weekly Status Report, October 5, 2005, p. 28.

U.S. Government Accountability Office, *U.S. Public Diplomacy: Interagency Coordination Efforts Hampered by the Lack of a National Communication Strategy*, Washington, D.C., GAO-05-323, April 2005. As of March 15, 2007:
http://www.gao.gov/new.items/d05323.pdf

U.S. Marine Corps, "Perspectives on HA/CMO in Iraq," *Security Cooperation Education and Training Center*, undated.

U.S. Marine Corps Security Cooperation Education and Training Center, "Perspectives on HA/CMO in Iraq," briefing notes, undated.

U.S. Marine Corps, and U.S. Joint Forces Command, *Joint Urban Warrior 2004 (JUW 04) Executive Report*, war game conducted March 21–26, 2004, Lansdowne, Va., pp. 8–9.

Vest, Jason, "Willful Ignorance: How the Pentagon Sent the Army to Iraq Without Counterinsurgency Doctrine," *Bulletin of the Atomic Scientists*, Vol. 61, No. 4, July–August 2005, pp. 40–48. As of March 14, 2007:
http://thebulletin.metapress.com/content/d22w34270172045l/fulltext.pdf

Vick, Karl, "Iraqi Security Forces: Hunters and Hunted," *Washington Post*, January 11, 2005, p. A1. As of March 20, 2007:
http://www.washingtonpost.com/ac2/wp-dyn/A64244-2005Jan10

Wade, LTC Norm, U.S. Army Public Affairs, telephone interview with Christopher Paul and Todd C. Helmus, March 15, 2006.

Waller, J. Michael, "Ridicule as a Weapon," Washington, D.C.: Institute of World Politics, Public Diplomacy White Paper No. 7, January 24, 2006a. As of May 31, 2006:
http://www.iwp.edu/news/newsID.258/news_detail.asp

———, "Making Jihad Work for America," *Journal of International Security Affairs*, No. 10, Spring 2006b. As of March 21, 2007:
http://www.securityaffairs.org/issues/2006/10/waller.php

WarRug.com, undated homepage. As of March 13, 2007:
http://www.warrug.com/

Wells, William, Sandra Moriarty, and John Burnett, eds., *Advertising: Principles and Practice*, 7th ed., Upper Saddle River, N.J.: Prentice Hall, 2006.

West, Alan, *Marketing Overseas*, Philadelphia, Pa.: Trans-Atlantic Publications, 1987.

West, Bing, *No True Glory: A Frontline Account of the Battle for Fallujah*, New York: Bantam Books, 2005.

Wilford, Lieutenant Colonel J. G., "OP TELIC—COIN Lessons Identified," briefing, notes for slide, "OP TELIC—COIN Lessons Identified—Firepower," undated.

Williams, LTC Michael, Chief, Plans Support Branch, Information Operations Division, Deputy Director for Global Operations, and Ted Tzavellas, Senior Information Policy and Strategy Advisor, Lockheed Martin, interview with Christopher Paul, the Pentagon, Arlington, Va., May 26, 2006.

Williams, Brigadier General Peter B., British Army, Chief, J3 Operations Support, and Senior Military Advisor to the Regional Coordinator, Coalition Provisional Authority–South, interview with Russell W. Glenn and Todd C. Helmus, Al Basrah, Iraq, February 22, 2004.

Wilson, Scott, and Sewell Chan, "Dozens Killed in U.S. Attack Near Syria; Target Disputed," *Washington Post*, May 20, 2004, p. A1. As of September 27, 2006: http://www.washingtonpost.com/wp-dyn/articles/A40848-2004May19.html

Wipperfürth, Alex, *Brand Hijack: Marketing Without Marketing*, New York: Portfolio, 2005.

———, Plan B, interview with Todd C. Helmus, San Francisco, Calif., March 23, 2006.

Wong, Edward, and Zaineb Obeid, "In Anger, Ordinary Iraqis Are Joining the Insurgency," *New York Times*, June 28, 2004, p. A9.

Wreford, Lieutenant Colonel Peter R., British Army, Deputy Chief, Command and Control, V Corps during Operation Telic, interview with Russell W. Glenn, Baghdad, Iraq, July 12, 2005.

Yantis, LTC Ryan, Director, U.S. Army Public Affairs—Midwest, telephone interview with Christopher Paul and Todd C. Helmus, May 15, 2006.

Youssef, Nancy A., "U.S. Army Detained Suspects' Daughters, Wives as Leverage," *Seattle Times*, January 28, 2006, p. A1.

Zedong, Mao, "The Military Principles of Mao Tse-tung," in Stuart R. Schram, ed., *The Political Thought of Mao Tse Tung*, New York: Praeger, 1970.

Zeiger, Robert, Chief of Corporate Communications, Alticor, interview with Todd C. Helmus, Grand Rapids, Mich., April 17, 2006.

Zogby International, *Impressions of America 2004: How Arabs View America, How Arabs Learn About America*, a six-nation survey commissioned by the Arab American Institute, 2004.